# The UK Big-3

The French and German Intelligence Reforms, Intelligence Diversity and Foreign Espionage

# The UK Big-3

The French and German Intelligence
Reforms, Intelligence Diversity and
Foreign Espionage

## Musa Khan Jalalzai

Vij Books India Pvt Ltd

New Delhi (India)

*Published by*

**Vij Books India Pvt Ltd**
(Publishers, Distributors & Importers)
2/19, Ansari Road
Delhi – 110 002
Phones: 91-11-43596460, 91-11-47340674
Mobile: 98110 94883
e-mail: contact@vijpublishing.com
www.vijbooks.in

Copyright © 2022, *Musa Khan Jalalzai*

ISBN: 978-93-93499-76-9 (Hardback)
ISBN: 978-93-93499-77-6 (Paperback)
ISBN: 978-93-93499-78-3 (ebook)

# Contents

Introduction        1

Executive Summary        10

Chapter 1    Challenges of European Union's Intelligence
Cooperation, Institutional Reforms, Management
of Law and Order, Foreign Espionage and Intelligence
Failure        20

Chapter 2    Intelligence Failure, the Achilles heel of Interoperability,
Foreign Espionage, and Security Sector Reforms within
European Union and the United Kingdom        36

Chapter 3    The UK Big-3: Challenges of Foreign Espionage,
and Intelligence Cooperation with European Union        59

Chapter 4    Terrorist Attacks, Radicalization and Security Sector
Reforms in the UK and European Union        73

Chapter 5    Surveillance Blankets, in Estonia, Bulgaria and Sweden,
Challenges of Intelligence Cooperation and Human
Rights        87

Chapter 6    The Crisis of Danish Intelligence, Iran and China's
Espionage Networks in Denmark, The PET Report,
State Surveillance and Human Rights        100

Chapter 7    The Home Office Web-Spying Powers, the French
and German Intelligence Reforms, Intelligence Diversity
and Foreign Intelligence Networks in the
United Kingdom        112

Chapter 8    Dematerialization of Civilian Intelligence in Romania:
War of Strength between Democratic and Communist
Intelligence Stakeholders        123

Chapter 9     The Key to Intelligence Reform in Germany:
              Strengthening the G10- Commission's Role to
              Authorise Strategic Surveillance                      132

              *Dr. Thorsten Wetzling*

Chapter 10    Caught in the Act? An analysis of Germany's
              new SIGINT reform                                     155

              *Kilian Vieth-Ditlmann and Thorsten Wetzling*

Noted to Chapters                                                  211

*Index*                                                            241

# Introduction

Relationship between policy makers and intelligence analysis after the Iraq, Syria and Afghan wars evolved in multitudinous shapes. In Europe, the United States and Asia, intelligence operations, analysis and infrastructure became politicised. Political and bureaucratic stakeholders, together with their private partners have been using intelligence agencies to stabilize their position, and influence since 2001. The French Parliament designed legal strategies by overhauling the legal framework for intelligence surveillance mechanism after the Paris terrorist attacks in 2015. France maintains a professional and competent intelligence infrastructure that experienced and lived through different phases of world war-I and II, and the extensive Cold War period. Its share with different EU intelligence agencies on law enforcement level is considered indispensable and critical. French intelligence remained a very secretive world from the public view in yesteryears, but after the cold war and emergence of radicalized and terrorist infrastructure in the country, and the development of modern intelligence and cyber technology that challenged its operational mechanism, French intelligence emerged as a well-organized and a competent infrastructure in a divided Europe. In 2008, the process of reorganization and reinvention of intelligence and policing to fit law enforcement and the police to the fight against radicalization and home-grown extremism was the uttermost need of that times security approach. These reforms were discussed in parliament and different legal forums to prepare a better panacea for the ongoing destabilization conspiracies. The establishment of the National Commission (CNCTR) for the control of intelligence techniques in 2015 was the doorstep to the introduction of all around and wide-ranging security sector reform in France. Expert and analyst Anne Lise Michelot has reviewed the French oversight efforts (Reforms of the French Intelligence Oversight system. The Security Distillery-30 November 2018):

"The creation of the CNCTR in 2015 to oversee the usage of intelligence techniques has attempted to bring France up to high democratic standards in terms of intelligence oversight. However, the commission's limited means hinder its ability to perform its duties fully. And let's not forget that its recommendations are not binding. These considerations require particular attention now that France has entered the age of mass data collection, with the first IMSI catchers set up in November 2017 and no additional workforce for the CNCTR insight. In 2021, the French government passed a major reform of the legislative framework for intelligence surveillance. But on several key issues, such as international data sharing, open-source surveillance or the right to information, French law still lags behind international standards in intelligence oversight. This is all the more worrying given that the staff and resources of major French agencies have vastly expanded over the past few years. Alas, during the latest reform, almost all proposals to strengthen oversight measures have gone unheeded, whether they came from the Parliamentary Delegation on Intelligence (the DPR, composed of members of the National Assembly and senators), the data protection authority (CNIL, which is supposed to control intelligence databases), or the National Commission for the Control of Intelligence Techniques (the CNCTR, which issues opinions on surveillance measures requested by the services)."

The legal framework for the French intelligence received less attention from Parliamentarians and successive governments, but surveillance measures are in place to help the police in managing law and order. Adopted by the Parliament in June 2015, the new surveillance law was corroborated by the President on July 24, 2015 and published in an Official Journal in July 2015. On 06 August 2015, Director of the Law and Digital Technology Studies Winston Maxwell wrote in Chronicle of Data Protection that new surveillance law was presented by the French government after the 2015 terrorist attacks to create a single legal framework for intelligence gathering activities. Global Britain in a Competitive Age, the Integrated Review of Security, Defence, Development and Foreign Policy, presented to Parliament by the Prime Minister by Command of Her Majesty-March 2021, highlights the government's vision for the UK's role in the world over the next decade. Prime Minister Boris Johnson in his front matter note elucidated: "My vision for the UK in 2030 sets high ambitions for what this country can achieve. The Union between England, Scotland, Wales and Northern Ireland has proved its worth time and again, including in this pandemic. It is our greatest source of strength at home and abroad. Our country overflows with creativity in the arts and sciences: the wellsprings of unique soft power that spans the globe. Few nations are better placed to navigate the challenges ahead, but we must be willing to change our approach and adapt to the new world emerging around us. Open and democratic societies like the UK must demonstrate they are match-fit for a more competitive world". Prime Minister Johnson's inventiveness and perception for Global Britain was not a news pandemonium for the European Union. The Brexit wounded Britain deeply and immeasurably when the country lost free and digital markets, and now fights with the European Union to justify its political existence.

The UK government's vision for Global Britain means to restore the British colonial power but Prime Minister Boris Johnson's government has been implicated in the Brexit trawl. Analysts and experts, Jeremy Shapiro and Nick Witney in their paper (Beyond Global Britain: A realistic foreign policy for the UK. The European Council on Foreign Relations (ECFR). Policy Brief-15 December 2021) viewed Global Britain in a different frame of reference: "On 3 February 2020, Prime Minister Boris Johnson, fresh from the triumphant conclusion of Britain's withdrawal from the European Union and a crushing general election victory, chose the historic setting of the Old Royal Naval College at Greenwich to set out his vision of the country's new role in the world. New, but also old: Johnson exulted in the Painted Hall's baroque celebration of the United Kingdom's past maritime greatness, as he coloured the glorious future awaiting Britain as a global champion of free trade. Johnson's vision for Global Britain had little role in it for the EU. Having executed at long last the geopolitical miracle of Brexit and unwound the UK from the thick tangle of its EU obligations, it only made sense for the UK to stride out into the world in a similarly independent fashion."

In the aftermath of the terrorist attacks in London, Manchester, Paris and Germany, the EU and UK intelligence agencies became subject to a hot-blooded assessment. Taking the case of EU and UK intelligence failure, I am going to stress the need of reforms to fit intelligence to the fight against terrorism and foreign espionage. The British, French and German intelligence agencies suffered from lack of check and balance in the past. In Germany, France and the UK, intelligence oversight is working on internal, executive and parliamentary level to make sure intelligence is transparently purveyed to policy makers and law enforcement agencies. The problem technically lies with the approach toward intelligence failure. However, the UK and EU intelligence agencies never revealed stories about their failures and successes. The UK Big 3, the EU-27 and Eyes-Five are responsible to secure the state and play a major role in producing intelligence relating to counterterrorism, but they are failing on different fronts due to the use of outdated technology and unreformed infrastructures, lack of efficient online surveillance, lack of severe shortages in terms of trained manpower.

The intelligence relationship between the US and UK has spread over 75 years. Notwithstanding decades of intelligence sharing and cooperation, the two states advocating their own national interests, and there is a significant misalignment. The United States intelligence was politicised, ethnicised and polarised during the Trump and Obama era, while the State Department started instructing Middle Eastern states to provide more funds to ISIS in Iraq and Syria, and Pentagon, FBI and CIA established political associations. During the last election, officers of the FBI, CIA and other intelligence agencies were openly supporting candidates of their own choice, and openly discussing politics in their offices. The UK intelligence remains committed to its professional demonstration on domestic and on international fronts. Experts and analysts, Riley McCabe and Jake Harrington in their paper (The Case for Cooperation: The Future of the U.S.-UK Intelligence Alliance, Centre for Strategic and International Studies. CSIS Briefs. March 15, 2022) have deeply highlighted the intelligence relationship between the two states:

"International intelligence collaboration is ultimately about expanding a service's access to collection, analysis, technology, tradecraft, or training at lower costs than if they unilaterally attempted to replicate these activities....This transactional approach to intelligence liaison enables both sides of the partnership to leverage their comparative strengths, such as geographical, political, and technological advantages, to the mutual benefit of both parties. Inefficiencies in how allies share intelligence information, including between the United States and the United Kingdom, have long been factored as a cost of doing business. All agencies and disciplines grapple with this issue, and still, these barriers have not undercut the willingness of individual leaders or officers to develop joint operations or conduct bilateral analysis. In short, the problem is not the willpower of people. While navigating technical, legal, and regulatory obstacles, individuals' aspirations often collide with reality. Information and technology sharing between intelligence allies is guided by a combination of interconnected frameworks, policies, and protocols. These are intended to balance commitments across a complex array of often overlapping frameworks, including legal; counterintelligence; personnel, physical, and information security; and privacy and civil liberties considerations. Intelligence is expensive and perishable, with the lives of human sources and costly technical access often in the balance."

The amendment of the legal framework for German intelligence by Parliament in March 2021 was a better change to bring intelligence under democratic control. According to Kilian Vieth-Ditlmann and Thorsten Wetzling, (25 November 2021): "Recent European jurisprudence such as the Schrems II ruling by the European Court of Justice and the Big Brother Watch and Centrum för Rättvisa decisions by the European Court of Human Rights brought additional momentum to the international quest for better standards in legislation and oversight practice." However, a doctoral candidate at the Vrije Universiteit Brussel (VUB) and the University of Luxembourg, Juraj Sajfert, in his paper (The Big Brother Watch and Centrum för Rättvisa judgments of the Grand Chamber of the European Court of Human Rights – the Altamont of privacy? 08 June 2021) documented efforts of human rights organizations against the UK and Sweden surveillance mechanism:

"In the case of the UK, the violation of Article 8 ECHR results from three shortcomings out of eight criteria: 'the absence of independent authorisation, the failure to include the categories of selectors in the application for a warrant, and the failure to subject selectors linked to an individual to prior internal authorisation' (paragraph 425). In the Swedish case, the Court again finds three shortcomings: 'the absence of a clear rule on destroying intercepted material which does not contain personal data, the absence of a requirement in the Signals Intelligence Act or other relevant legislation that, when making a decision to transmit intelligence material to foreign partners, consideration is given to the privacy interests of individuals; and the absence of an effective ex post facto review' (paragraph 369). Hence, violations of Article 8 ECHR found by the Grand Chamber are of a technical nature and constitute 'easy fixes' for the UK's, the Swedish or any other national mass surveillance regime. After the Grand Chamber judgments came out, Privacy International declared it 'an important win for privacy and freedom for everyone in the UK and beyond'. Admittedly, the Grand Chamber found Article 8 of the European Convention on Human Rights (ECHR; the right to private life) violations in both cases, thereby overturning the Chamber outcome of Centrum för Rättvisa. The Grand Chamber also took the opportunity to develop the Court's case-law further, specifically regarding bulk interception regimes. It did not content itself with a mere application of the somewhat outdated Weber and Saravia criteria. The optimism of privacy activists is, therefore, understandable at the outset".

Experts and Analysts Danny Pronk, and Claire Korteweg (Sharing the Burden, Sharing the Secrets: The future of European intelligence cooperation. Clingendael Report. September 2021) in their research paper highlighted intelligence cooperation, hybrid conflict and early warning method: "Over the past two decades, the EU has put considerable effort into protecting external security and has been actively engaged in regions far from its borders. The next decades of the 21st century, however, ask for additional and different types of action much closer to home and within our borders. One of the most pressing security issues of our time is the emergence of hybrid conflict, also known as grey zone operations. In this section, the need for a clear definition and common understanding of the term 'hybrid' is discussed, as well as the importance of sense-making in this field and the potential contribution of both EU and NATO collaborative frameworks. Furthermore, the possibility of applying early warning methods to these new kind of threats is assessed. When working with complex issues such as hybrid threats, it is perhaps helpful to consider the existing concept of sense-making in crisis applied to so-called 'wicked problems'. Wicked problems are gaining importance because of their transnational character, "in a world where nation-states are no longer the principal actors".

There are multitude perceptions about the work, popular and communal relationships, and the course of action of British intelligence agencies (The Big-3), the policing and their private partners in research papers, newspapers, journals and books that spotlight their course of action and weaknesses in domestic and international fronts. There are countless books available in markets and libraries that discuss professionalization and controversies-elucidating operational mechanism of The Big-3 and the whole body of other horses who sometimes run in unknown directions. From Iraq to Afghanistan, Syria and Ukraine, experts and scholars raised different questions in the realm of strategic and technological intelligence operations, and its relevance to parliament and policy makers. The reason that the UK Big-3 have often been reluctant to engage directly with the public due to concerns surrounding their secrecy. They are being represented by print and electronic media to convince communities and policymakers that everything is going in the right direction.

The facia near to the UK Big-3 demonstrates different approaches to openness and secrecy, with Britain seemingly favouring the latter when compared to her American counterpart. Now they are more open in the media in their professional and sometimes political statements. We read political statements of the Big-3 leadership in newspapers and electronic media every day. The Big-3 are in full cooperation with domestic and international security actors, sharing intelligence and receiving reciprocity to ensure security of the United Kingdom. Small and private actors are doing their entrusted job to help the Big-3 against complex and globalised threats. The Police is dancing not very well but shares its role with the Big-3. In world wars, the Big-3 were playing an excellent role, in the cold war they played against the communist bloc magnificently, but after the cold war, their way of operation and perceptions of war on terrorism in Iraq, Libya and Afghanistan changed.

Intelligence tactics of British intelligence in Iraq to find weapons of mass destruction caused distress and anxiety. There were chain of debates in the UK parliament to discuss the catastrophe inflicted on Iraqi Muslims. The three pillars of the UK intelligence machinery are Big-3 with important work carried out by Defence Intelligence and the Joint Terrorism Analysis Centre. Since 2016, the word global Britain has been appearing in British and international media that Britain wanted to have an independent voice, but things evolved differently while it faced a different political and economic crisis. Altercation with the European Union over the border of Northern Ireland further caused mistrust. Experts and analysts, Anisa Heritage and Pak K. Lee, (Global Britain': The UK in the Indo-Pacific: While its involvement is broadly welcomed in the region, the U.K. must first clarify what its Indo-Pacific presence will entail. The Diplomat-- January 08, 2021) in their paper have highlighted challenges faced by the UK after the announcement of Brexit referendum:

"Since 2016, the phrase "Global Britain" has been used to signal the ambition and intent of the United Kingdom to seek "an independent voice" in international diplomacy outside and beyond the European Union. But to date, the phrase remains deliberately vague. The current Integrated Review of Security, Defence, and Development Policy, the most comprehensive review of its kind undertaken in the U.K., was heralded by Prime Minister Boris Johnson as a much-needed overhaul that would consider "the totality of global opportunities and challenges the U.K. faces and determining how the whole of government can be structured, equipped and mobilized to meet them." The first House of Commons report on the integrated review in August 2020 acknowledged that Brexit and a more isolationist U.S. have challenged the U.K.'s position as the bridge between the EU and the United States. The report also recognized the vulnerabilities of a middle power navigating an increasingly competitive and tense international environment. Although the U.K.'s foreign policy strategy will be officially revealed later in 2021, evidence already points to a substantial orientation of its security, development, and trade policies toward the Indo-Pacific – a tilt welcomed by many U.K. partners in the region. Prior to the U.K.'s official exit from the EU, the Johnson government started pursuing partnerships and initiatives beyond EU-27 collective positions. It issued a joint statement on Hong Kong in coordination with other Five Eyes partners in May 2020, before the EU released its own statement in July. Johnson is also leading an initiative to build a "D10" alliance of democracies–the G-7 plus Australia, South Korea, and India–to create alternative suppliers of 5G equipment and other technology to reduce China's domination of global digital infrastructure. It is as yet unclear how the proposed D10 arrangements might synchronize with U.S. President-elect Joe Biden's plans to convene a Summit for Democracy".

Intelligence cooperation between the EU and Britain has never been fair-minded since the announcement of the Brexit referendum in 2016 by the former British Prime Minister Theresa May. That announcement caused distrust and wariness. Research reports, books and newspapers articles have often spotlighted enfeebled and misunderstood approaches of intelligence leadership to national security challenges. No state wanted to share its national secrets with another state on terrorism and extremism in yesteryears. In 2016, debate on Brexit generated further misunderstanding that Britain no longer wanted the EU instruction and dictations on its foreign and domestic policy. The failure of EU intelligence agencies to intercept or identify terrorists before the carried out attacks against civilians in Germany, France and the UK, the counterterrorism approach of Brussels, Germany and French remained in question. There were so many hindrances due to which the EU member states couldn't move ahead with a single voice.

The speculation that the security assurance of all member states within the EU was mere hyperbole as complaints of some Eastern European allies about the Brussels attitude raised several questions. The Netherlands, Denmark, Moldova and Baltic states felt threatened. Their complaints against the weak intelligence-sharing mechanism were a matter of great concern. European intelligence agencies lack the confidence of political parties on their mass surveillance system. In Germany, intelligence law does not allow the Federal Intelligence Service (BND) to support police or involve itself in policing business, while in Estonia and Latvia, intelligence plays an important role in policing communities. Targeted surveillance in all EU states is being conducted on different lines. Intelligence agencies of the member states use surveillance but also give importance to human intelligence. In Brussels, Denmark, Finland, France and Italy targeted surveillance of groups and individuals has strong roots in society.

Musa Khan Jalalzai

Expert of Telepathic Intelligence

Geospatial Intelligence

London, May 2022

# Executive Summary

Recent discussions on British intelligence diversity, interoperability and rendezvous with its EU friendly agencies have received considerable attention from policymakers and bureaucratic stakeholders in and outside the country that this way of engagement and inclusiveness can make intelligence agencies competent across the border to fight terrorism and radicalisation by adopting professional strategies. The matter in question of inaccessibility, ostracism, banishment and marginalisation of minority communities is considerably wider than policymakers think. Recent intelligence reform and a colourful package of diversity in the UK have received pleasant reception that now MI5, MI6 and GCHQ will be represented by all communities and will be serving Britain with a strong voice. These reforms have been greatly appreciated by the leadership of the intelligence community, and politicians. Policymakers and intelligence experts and named this evolution as a welcome development. Intelligence reforms in France and Germany have also received a cordial welcome. The French and German governments have introduced a series of intelligence and security sector reforms to bring intelligence agencies under democratic control and make law enforcement cooperative and resilient. The French and German governments have also introduced surveillance oversight reforms to bring their intelligence agencies in a long hard lock and confine them to the legal bodywork.

Now, the strongest intelligence infrastructure of these three states will cohere to the culture of interoperability to understand each other and their EU associates in the domain intelligence sharing palatinate. As a result of these friendly interoperability perceptions, a new working environment will emerge. Incorporation of ethnic minorities in the infrastructure of security agencies is a positive development in the UK, France and Germany. Expert Kendall Francis has noted the importance of development in her research paper: "In recent years there have been many attempts by organisations and individuals to expand diversity within the workplace to create more inclusive cultures. An inclusive culture is one where the various identities that makeup individuals are all acknowledged and embraced, and differences are utilised for the benefit of everyone. Developing cultures of inclusivity is fundamental for bringing equitable ideas and unique understandings to organisations, and fostering new attitudes and behaviours, creating profitable outcomes and abandoning outdated ideology".

We still need to fix broken windows of inequality, racism and discrimination. Commission on Race and Ethnic Disparities Report (March 2021) noted: "Yes, there are still some 'snowy white peaks' at the very top of the private and public sectors, and not all of that can be accounted for by the fact that members of the ethnic minorities have not, by definition, been embedded in the country's human networks and institutions for as long as the White majority. The word mistrust was repeated often as some witnesses from the police service, mental health, education and health services felt that the system was not on their side. Once we interrogated the data we did find some evidence of biases, but often it was a perception that the wider society could not be trusted. For some groups historic experience of racism still haunts the present and there was a reluctance to acknowledge that the UK had become open and fairer.... The evidence shows that geography, family influence, socio-economic background, culture and religion have more significant impact on life chances than the existence of racism. That said, we take the reality of racism seriously and we do not deny that it is a real force in the UK".[1]

Multitude reviews of culture, racism and ethnic disparity were commissioned by successive governments in yesteryears, but all those reviews and other inquiries relating to diversity remained on papers. No single window was fixed, there are still clefts and cracks in the system. Successive governments never concentrated on challenges of ethnic minorities and viewed them with scorn and derision. The road to inclusiveness and diversity was diverted to nowhere. "Racism has become one of the most potent taboos in the UK, which was not the case 50 years ago. Some argue this has just driven it underground where it operates as powerfully as ever to deny equality to ethnic minorities. That assumption is at odds with the stories of success that this report has found, together with survey evidence of dwindling White prejudice. It is certainly true that the concept of racism has become much more fluid, extending from overt hostility and exclusion to unconscious bias and micro-aggressions". Commission on Race and Ethnic Disparities Report (March 2021) noted.[2] At the minute, credit goes to Richard Moore, the Chief of MI6-the UK Secret Intelligence Service who realised the threat of social and political alienation and detachment on national and institutional level. Expert of intelligence and security Professor Daniel W. B. Lomas (ForgetJamesBond: diversity, inclusion and the UK's intelligence agencies, 02 Jul 2021) noted the Times news story about the relaxation of rules by the Secret Intelligence Service (SIS or MI6) to allow application of dual UK nationals:

"In February 2021, The Times reported that Britain's foreign intelligence agency, the Secret Intelligence Service (SIS or MI6), was relaxing rules to allow applicants with dual UK nationality, or with one parent being a UK national or having 'substantial ties to the UK', to apply. Sources told the paper it was just the latest move to access a 'larger talent pool', adding: 'We want a diversification of thought, a diverse workforce, not people who all think in similar ways'.1 Later, marking LGBT History Month 2021, SIS's Chief ('C') Richard Moore followed other agency heads in apologising for the historical treatment of LGBT (Lesbian, gay, bisexual and transgender) officials and the bar to gay men and women serving in SIS. In a video shared on his Twitter feed, Moore said the ban deprived SIS of 'some of the best talent Britain could offer' and was 'wrong, unjust and discriminatory.... Such statements show a clear determination by the UK's agencies to promote diversity and inclusivity, an issue that has received limited attention from academics". Professor Daniel W. B. Lomas noted.[3]

In 2018, the Intelligence and Security Committee of Parliament in its report identified the gap and outlined a comprehensive report to ensure implementation of the inclusion of diversity plan institutionally and socially. However, the government responded to the Intelligence and Security Committee of Parliament Report on Diversity and Inclusion in the Intelligence Community-Presented to Parliament by the Prime Minister by Command of Her Majesty-September 2018: "As outlined in the Prime Minister's response on 18 July, the heads of all of the organisations covered by the report (GCHQ, MI5, the Secret Intelligence Service, Office for Security and Counter-Terrorism in the Home Office, National Security Secretariat in the Cabinet Office, Defence Intelligence and Joint Intelligence Organisation (collectively referred to in this report as the 'Intelligence Community) consider the issue of diversity to be of crucial importance to the success of their organisation. The National Security Adviser, Sir Mark Sedwill explains it as follows: "The current national security environment is more complex than ever before. We face multifaceted threats from many corners of the world, facilitated by rapidly evolving technologies. To meet these challenges, we need a national security workforce of different backgrounds, perspectives and ways of thinking. Diversity and inclusion are Mission Critical."[4]

Today, GCHQ has designed a professional strategy to help ensure the agency as an inclusive workplace for the LGBT community. However, Deputy Director of GCHQ, Nikesh Mehta in response to the Intelligence and Security Committee report (GCHQ website) on inclusiveness said: "As one of the few senior officials from a Black, Asian or Minority Ethnic (BAME) background in the intelligence services, I read the report with a heavy heart. I was disappointed because the report could not, for understandable reasons, explain in detail the underlying reasons for the statistics. And didn't highlight the progress made over the last few years to recruit and develop staff from BAME backgrounds. I was also disappointed because, despite some of the challenges we face, we are making progress. Even if that progress isn't always visible externally....This is not a new mission–we have had this task for over 100 years. We have known from the outset that we need talented, diverse individuals with a broad range of skills to combat the complex threats we face. This was true in the Second World War when people like Alan Turing were successful by thinking differently and challenging assumptions – and it is true now. We recognise that valuing diversity is not just a moral obligation. It is business critical. Our Director, Robert Hannigan, eloquently set this out at April's Stonewall Workplace Conference: 'To do our job, which is solving some of the hardest technology problems the world faces for security reasons, we need all talents and we need people who dare to think differently and be different... Dull uniformity would completely destroy us". Deputy Director of GCHQ, Nikesh Mehta noted.[5]

Intelligence is a complex business that evolves in different shapes in a complex environment. Intelligence assesses national security threats and domestic governance and purveys intelligence information to policy makers. Intelligence and security services take the complexity of an intelligence problem into account when determining the aims of their investigation. Recent development in the UK was a criminal conduct by the covert human intelligence agent law passed by parliament that received voluminous criticism in the international press. The Covert human intelligence sources: criminal conduct, (30 September, 2021) was passed by parliament to authorise covert intelligence sources to take part in criminal activity. In international press and journal papers, this way of addressing issues of domestic governance was deeply criticised. The Regulation of Investigatory Powers law (Criminal Conduct Authorisations-Amendment-

Order 2021) makes consequential changes to various pieces of secondary legislation to reflect some of the amendments made by the act. However, Baroness D'Souza in her parliamentary comment on Regulation of Investigatory Powers (Criminal Conduct Authorisations-Amendment) Order 2021 (SI 2021/601) said: "That this House regrets that the Regulation of Investigatory Powers (Criminal Conduct Authorisations) (Amendment) Order 2021 (SI 2021/601) does not provide adequate safeguards on the actions of covert agents, as the Covert Human Intelligence Sources (Criminal Conduct) Act 2021 failed to include express limits on the crimes covert agents can commit; and calls on Her Majesty's Government to amend the Act to provide proper limits on, and oversight of, crimes committed by covert agents" .[6] Moreover, in her parliamentary debate, Baroness D'Souza argued: "My Lords, I am very grateful that some noble Lords are still here. That is very nice. I make no apologies for returning to the Covert Human Intelligence Sources (Criminal Conduct) Act 2021, which was so thoroughly debated and amended in this House earlier this year. As I said while the Bill was passing through this House, I am truly happy that a previously secret process has been put on a statutory footing. That said, I also wish to have it on record that there remain serious gaps which would allow authorised agents to commit serious crimes with impunity. These gaps have not been adequately addressed in this regulation of investigatory powers statutory instrument and for this reason I have tabled this Motion. The statutory instrument concerns requirements on the level of seniority for MI5 officers and those of other bodies who are authorised to sanction CHIS participation in crime and to record the criminal conduct authorised. The SI includes the crucial phrase; "including any parameters of the conduct authorised." I understand that these parameters will reflect only the conduct being authorised and will not include substantive limits on the crimes which may be committed. This, theoretically at least, enables involvement in serious abuses such as murder and/or torture". Baroness D'Souza Noted.

The Covert Human Intelligence Sources (Criminal Conduct) Bill 2019–21 was introduced in the House of Commons on 24 September 2020. During the bill's second reading debate in the House of Commons, the Labour party stated that it would not oppose its passage. Instead, it would seek to "improve" the bill. House of Lord Library at its web page recorded official opposition about: The conduct that could be authorised under a CCA. Labour said it would need reassurance from the Government that the "most heinous of crimes" would not be carried out by a CHIS. It would push for safeguards on crimes such as murder, rape, and sexual violence.

The oversight powers of the IPCO. It said the bill, as introduced, allowed "self-authorisation", and that Labour would seek prior judicial oversight. The rights for people to seek redress. The Investigatory Powers Tribunal had the jurisdiction to determine complaints against public authorities' use of investigatory powers, which Labour said was "not the same" as a civil claim. If we look at the history of the policing intelligence and secret agents' illegal relationship with innocent women and their criminal attitude, we can find more case of their criminal behaviour.[8]

In 2011, number of secret police officers entered into sexual relationship with different women activists. Different legal actions followed, including eight women who took action filed cases against the Metropolitan Police and the Association of Chief Police Officers (ACPO), stating they were deceived into long-term intimate relationships by five officers. In November 2015, the Metropolitan Police force apologised to seven women "tricked into relationships" over a period of 25 years by officers in the Special Demonstration Squad (SDS) and the National Public Order Intelligence Unit (NPOIU). The disclosures also led to the closing of the units concerned, and a public inquiry, the Undercover Policing Inquiry, concerning the conduct of police in undercover operations. In January 2016, further cases continued to come to light. However, BBC (BBC-20 April 2021) reported: Senior police officers "encouraged or tolerated" undercover officers having sexual relationships with activists they were sent to spy on, a tribunal has heard. Metropolitan Police is being sued by an environmental campaigner who had a long-term relationship with an officer she believed was a fellow activist. They had met while working together at a community hub in Nottingham. Kate Wilson, 41, said the deception had breached her human rights. The Investigatory Powers Tribunal at the Royal Courts of Justice was told by Ms Wilson's solicitor that Mark Kennedy had been sent to infiltrate the Sumac Centre in Nottingham in 2003. Charlotte Kilroy QC said the Met's National Public Order Intelligence Unit believed the centre was used by people "involved in extremism relating to animal rights, environmentalism, anarchy, anti-weapons and war issues and anti-globalisation". "In truth, it was a community space with a vegan cafe used by a wide range of people and groups," she said. BBC noted.[9]

In light of terrorist attacks in several European states, major intelligence and security sector reforms were introduced to make intelligence competent. France introduced intelligence and security sector reforms and surveillance oversight to keep intelligence and law enforcement agencies under democratic umbrella. Germany and Denmark also framed laws to counter foreign espionage networks. The European interoperability to understand each other and their operational strategies in countering foreign spy networks and terrorism can help professionalise their security infrastructures. Interoperability is the ability of information systems to exchange data and enable sharing of information. This system improves the effectiveness of intelligence information sharing tools. Management of data needs to be effective in full respect of fundamental rights in order to professionally secure the EU external borders. After the terrorist attacks in Belgium, the country has strengthened its counterintelligence capabilities by introducing security sector reforms. War between Russia and Ukraine has threatened the internal security of all EU member states. In March 2022, in EU parliament, the establishment of a special committee about countering foreign intelligence was approved and asked Belgium authorities to boost counterintelligence operations, to prevent infiltrations within the EU institutions. Intelligence and diplomatic war between Moscow and the European Union resulted in expelling diplomats from EU capitals.

The Intel Today (10 April 2022) in its analysis of recent development has noted that Belgium's intelligence oversight committee reviewed it two secret services: "The fight against hostile foreign actors on Belgian territory is an everlasting security threat, and policymakers have every reason to consider it as such, as Belgium's privileged role in hosting multilateral institutions inherently obliges it to ensure their secured workings. In terms of intelligence activities, Belgium finds itself at the centre stage in between the big boys, whether it likes it or not, and efficient and effective counterintelligence is therefore an essential instrument to provide security. Of course, none of this is actually new. I have argued these points for years. But it is nevertheless interesting that the Royal Institute is openly making the point that Belgium needs to urgently strengthen its counterintelligence capabilities". The Intel Today noted.[10]

Expert researcher at Egmont Institute, Tom Van Rentergem (07 April 2022) in his article has stressed the need of strengthening Belgium intelligence and counterintelligence networks: "The Belgian intelligence community has recently kick-started a much-needed growth spurt, but it is improbable that this rate of expansion will suffice for an effective counterintelligence apparatus. Below, three important challenges of the expansion are discussed. The time has come for Belgium to significantly strengthen its counterintelligence capabilities, as the Russian war against Ukraine will challenge European security in several ways. As host of the European institutions and NATO, Brussels comprises the second largest pool of diplomatic representatives in the world, just after New York. This reality makes the international city attractive and prosperous, but also turns it into a playground for foreign intelligence services, especially since the Russian invasion of Ukraine on 24 February 2022. Russia, but also other states, including allies, are likely to step up their intelligence efforts on Belgian soil, since the country remains at the centre of Western multilateral decision making in times of crisis".[11]

After intelligence and oversight reforms in Belgium, the country's civilian state security services (VSSE) and military intelligence services (SGRS) recruited more people to reach every corner of the country, and immediately find what developments occurred and how foreign intelligence and where operates. In yesteryears, Belgium intelligence agencies were acknowledging that everything was running on right direction, but after the terrorist attacks, their networks were expanded to all cities and remote areas. Expert researcher at Egmont Institute, Tom Van Rentergem (07 April 2022), has supported these developments and intelligence reforms: "As aforementioned, building capacity and effective intelligence officers does not happen overnight, and should be considered a medium-to-long-term strategy. For example, spotting, assessing, developing, recruiting and ultimately handling human sources, as needed for effective Human Intelligence (HUMINT), takes months and years of time. The whole process of intelligence collection and analysis should be compared to a marathon, not a sprint, and while the explosiveness of the latter might be more direct, it implies a bigger margin of failure, whereas the endurance of the former provides consistent and strong results. Secondly, when intelligence is collected and analysed, VSSE uses the classic prevent–advise–disrupt strategy to counter espionage, interference or terrorist activities on Belgian soil. A whole of society approach is needed for this tripod to work effectively though, through cooperation with the relevant government institutions on the one hand, and by informing (possible) human targets of foreign recruitment on the other hand".[12]

Belgium intelligence lived through difficult experiences during the violent wave of terrorism in yesteryears when the ISIS attempted to attack nuclear plants. After security sector reforms, the Belgium intelligence agencies became professional and competent to counter-terrorism and foreign espionage. Networks of terrorist and extremist organisations have stretched to remote areas of the country, while thousands of members of ISIS, Taliban, Lashkar-e-Taiba and Central Asian based groups safely arrived in Belgium, completed nationality process, became national, and began their subversive activities. Networks of money-laundering, narco smuggling and recruitment of local residents further expanded to collect money and sponsor their allies in Pakistan, Afghanistan and Central Asian states. Director of the Analysis Department at the Belgian State Security Service VSSE, Peter Lanssens in his lecture (The Belgian civil intelligence service VSSE - general overview and current trends and threats, by Peter LANSSENS, director of the analysis department) explained the function of intelligence and its operational mechanism:

"First of all, we have the good old HUMINT or human intelligence. Even in the 21st century this remains the core of intelligence work. Human intelligence means working with human sources that evolve in circles that we are interested in. Members of my service cannot infiltrate themselves in criminal, extremist or terrorist circles, but they can interrogate their "sources" that are actively involved or at least know of these activities. Thus, you have to see this not as something linear but as a kind of a treadmill where we go round and round. Fortunately, we effectively leave this treadmill from time to time to deliver crucial information that can lead to administrative measures or political decisions. Our operational colleagues are thus the ones who collect the necessary information for us. For doing this, they can use different kinds of methods or specialities, that are commonly known as the -INTS. First of all, we have the good old HUMINT or human intelligence. Even in the 21st century, this remains the core of intelligence work. Human intelligence means working with human sources that evolve in circles that we are interested in. Members of my service cannot infiltrate themselves in criminal, extremist or terrorist circles, but they can interrogate their "sources" that are actively involved or at least know of these activities. OTHER -INTS THAT WE USE ARE: OSINT or open sources intelligence and SOCMINT or social media intelligence: information that is collected from open sources (what you can find on the internet, but also information from all kinds of official databases) and from what people post on social media...... Our aim to prevent illicit activities by foreign powers in Belgium will first of all be reached through strengthening the resilience of their targets, to create awareness of the dangers of hostile espionage and interference and to provide them with the guidelines to protect their own and the nation's security. Who are these targets I am talking about? That can be politicians on all kinds of levels, police officers, intelligence agents, scientists, but in fact everybody who can be in possession of a certain knowledge that is interesting for foreign service. Most of these services have long-term aims and can be very patient" .[13]

Director of the Analysis Department at the Belgian State Security Service VSSE, Peter Lanssens has elucidated the real function of his intelligence organisations, partners and government policies. No doubt establishing a strong oversight body is an important part of intelligence accountability in Europe, but it is important to note that oversight must reflect the power of a secret agency. European Union Agency for Fundamental Rights, (2017) in its research report (Surveillance by intelligence services: fundamental rights safeguards and remedies in the EU Volume II: field perspectives and legal update) on matters related to the respect for private and family life (Article 7), the protection of personal data (Article 8) and the right to an effective remedy and a fair trial (Article 47) falling under Titles II 'Freedoms' and VI 'Justice' of the Charter of Fundamental Rights of the European Union has argued:

"European Court of Human Rights case law provides that oversight bodies should be independent and have adequate powers and competences. FRA's research findings show that all EU Member States have at least one independent body in their oversight framework. However, the findings also identified limits to full independence, with some oversight bodies remaining strongly dependent on the executive: the law does not grant those binding decision-making powers, they have limited staff and budget, or their offices are located in government buildings. The European Court of Human Rights has held that an effective remedy is characterised by investigative and decisional powers granted to judicial and non-judicial bodies. In particular, the remedial body should have access to the premises of intelligence services and the data collected; be given the power to issue binding decisions; and inform complainants on the outcome of its investigations. The individual should be able to appeal the body's decision. FRA's data show that 22 EU Member States have at least one non-judicial body with remedial powers. In six Member States, though, these bodies lack the powers to issue binding decisions and access classified data".[14]

Chapter 1

# Challenges of European Union's Intelligence Cooperation, Institutional Reforms, Management of Law and Order, Foreign Espionage and Intelligence Failure

The last few decades have experienced an increasing all-round and resourceful intelligence sharing on law enforcement level among the EU member states to make sure security, and fight against terrorism. Cross border mobility of people, joint interoperability of law enforcement agencies, and intelligence operation has now become extremely important in epoch of intelligence war, military conflicts in Ukraine, Afghanistan, Syria and Iraq, and innovation and development of military and artificial intelligence technologies. Scientific collaboration and interoperability between European police and intelligence agencies, management of border altercations can bring all EU member states to a close. Collaboration among Sweden, Finland, Estonia, Lithuania, and Latvia to manage flow of strategic and technological intelligence and information on law enforcement level to fight crimes and foreign intelligence infiltration. Intelligence and operational police and border forces collaboration in the Baltic Sea, and on the borders, as well as transnational collaboration associated with a rhetorical construction of fighters to defend their national interests is a furthermost demand. The EU and UK intelligence agencies have fought different wars against terrorists and home-grown extremist organizations in and outside the continent. War in Iraq, Syria and Afghanistan became a nursery for terrorist and jihadist groups to send their fighter for military training to the camps of terrorist Islamic State (ISIS). In Syria and Pakistan.

The UK government's vision for Global Britain means to restore the British colonial power but Prime Minister Boris Johnson's government has been implicated in Brexit trawl. Analysts and experts, Jeremy Shapiro and Nick Witney in their paper (Beyond Global Britain: A realistic foreign policy for the UK. The European Council on Foreign Relations (ECFR). Policy Brief-15 December 2021) viewed Global Britain in different frame of reference: "On 3 February 2020, Prime Minister Boris Johnson, fresh from the triumphant conclusion of Britain's withdrawal from the European Union and a crushing general election victory, chose the historic setting of the Old Royal Naval College at Greenwich to set out his vision of the country's new role in the world. New, but also old: Johnson exulted in the Painted Hall's baroque celebration of the United Kingdom's past maritime greatness, as he coloured the glorious future awaiting Britain as a global champion of free trade. Johnson's vision for Global Britain had little role in it for the EU. Having executed at long last the geopolitical miracle of Brexit and unwound the UK from the thick tangle of its EU obligations, it only made sense for the UK to stride out into the world in a similarly independent fashion".[1]

The European Union has been facing the threat of terrorism, radicalization and intelligence war since 2001. The predominant responsibility to counter radicalization lies with each state that they must share intelligence on law enforcement level, maintain trust and share information with member states. They need unplumbed intelligence and technological interoperability and advanced security approaches. Unfortunately, except France and Germany, there is lack of security and intelligence sector reforms in all EU member states as they face internal resistance from the former Soviet policing and intelligence infrastructures. This lack of professional approach to security and law and order management, and lack of public confidence strengthened networks of radicalization and foreign espionage across the continent. Security Sector Reforms in Romania and Poland have been facing challenges due to the existence of former communist intelligence and security stakeholders. Experts and researchers, Thomas Henökl & Tor Georg Jakobsen (Thomas Henökl & Tor Georg Jakobsen (The rising fear of terrorism and the emergence of a European security governance space: citizen perceptions and EU counterterrorism cooperation, Journal of Contemporary European Studies) in their research paper argued that urgent operational coordination between the EU member states is a must:

"There are recent tendencies of enhanced collective securitization and more integration of a European terror-prevention policy framework that is more tightly coordinated at the EU-level. Already in 2004, in reaction to the Madrid train attacks, EU leaders had agreed to establish a Counterterrorism Coordinator. The dreadful attacks in France, 2015, arguably prompted the EU Passenger Names Record (PNR) directive of 2016.

And, in the same year, Europol created the European Counter Terrorism Centre as a response to the EU's urgent operational coordination needs. By discussing the key factors and the drivers of the policy-making process, we study the influence of the perceived threat of terrorist attacks between 2013 and 2018. More precisely, we look at the extent to which the political and societal repercussions of this perceived security crisis have affected policy making in the EU. We argue that the perception of terrorist threats and subsequently the politicization of terrorism in Europe creates pressure for the creation of EU-level initiatives on the issue of terrorism. The hypothesis is, thus, that the occurrence of terrorist attacks positively impacts the threat perception of citizens, which in turn is directly correlated with politicization of terrorism, i.e. attention paid to the issue by political elites at the European level."[2]

Brexit was a serious challenge to all European states after 2021, but not the EU states alone, Britain faced serious challenges, including exacerbation of terrorism and extremism. The UK intelligence agencies suffered deeply due to the bereavement of advanced intelligence information, collaboration and interoperability with the European intelligence agencies. As a leading defence and technological power to dominate force projection capability, intelligence sharing between the EU and UK suffered huge dissipation. Secretary-General of the Council of Europe, Marija Pejčinović Burić warned that convergence between nanotechnology, biotechnology, information technology and cognitive sciences and the speed at which the applications of new technologies have consequences for human rights: "The convergence between nanotechnology, biotechnology, information technology and cognitive sciences and the speed at which the applications of new technologies are put on the market have consequences not only for human rights and the way they can be exercised, but also for the fundamental concept of what characterises a human being".[3] However, security and intelligence expert, Christine Andreeva (Border security became priority for member states in the aftermath of the migrant crisis) has argued that Border security became priority for member states in the aftermath of the migrant crisis:

"Border security became priority for member states in the aftermath of the migrant crisis, whereas that concern has been compounded with anxieties over internal security (criminality and terrorism). Throughout the management of the migration crisis, MS became aware of the added value of Frontex, as front-line officers had access to data useful for intelligence services (Interview n.40). The upgraded Frontex, renamed the European

Border and Coast Guard (EBCG), was launched on 6 October 2016, while its new mandate (adopted in November 2019) authorizes more than double the budget and staff, and provides for more extensive information-sharing with Europol and national authorities (Council of the EU, 2019; European Commission, 2018a; Europol, 2018). Most importantly, EBCG became an executive agency, empowered to deploy a Rapid Reaction Force, and recruiting a standing corps of 10,000 officers, who will be authorized to participate in operations and use force (Interview n.40; European Council on Refugees and Exiles, 2019). The most significant mandate given to an EU agency to date, it demonstrated the thinly-veiled lingering concern of national authorities over irregular migration, despite the counter-narrative of most MS governments".[4]

Global Britain in a Competitive Age, the Integrated Review of Security, Defence, Development and Foreign Policy, presented to Parliament by the Prime Minister by Command of Her Majesty-March 2021 discusses the government's vision for the UK's role in the world over the next decade. Prime Minister Boris Johnson in his front matter note elucidated: "My vision for the UK in 2030 sets high ambitions for what this country can achieve. The Union between England, Scotland, Wales and Northern Ireland has proved its worth time and again, including in this pandemic. It is our greatest source of strength at home and abroad. Our country overflows with creativity in the arts and sciences: the wellsprings of unique soft power that spans the globe. Few nations are better placed to navigate the challenges ahead, but we must be willing to change our approach and adapt to the new world emerging around us. Open and democratic societies like the UK must demonstrate they are match-fit for a more competitive world".[5]Prime Minister Johnson's inventiveness and perception for Global Britain was not a news pandemonium for the European Union. The Brexit wounded Britain deeply and immeasurably when the country lost free and digital markets, and now fights with the European Union to justify its political existence. Analysts and experts, Jeremy Shapiro and Nick Witney in their paper (Beyond Global Britain: A realistic foreign policy for the UK. The European Council on Foreign Relations (ECFR).Policy Brief-15 December 2021) view Global Britain in different perspectives:

"Global Britain is a delusion rooted in a misremembered imperial past. But the UK need not shut itself off from the world or accept a permanent position of subordination in global affairs. The UK, working with the EU, has the capacity and the political will to find a better path – but only if its leaders have the wisdom to seize the opportunity.......The Integrated

Review is not blind to these new realities. It identifies an increasingly contested world, in which "the nature and distribution of global power is changing", and states have diversified and enhanced their approaches to rivalry with one another. As the review puts it: "adversaries and competitors are already acting in a more integrated way – fusing military and civilian technology and increasingly blurring the boundaries between war and peace, prosperity and security, trade and development, and domestic and foreign policy".[6] The UK is operating in a confused world that cannot be understood easily. The European Union is still united by its cultural and political roots. Boris Johnson was adamant to say that no sooner had his country's withdrawal from the European Union, then there would be more cracks in the project, but things evolved differently, and Boris Johnson faced multitude social, political and financial crises. Analysts and experts, Jeremy Shapiro and Nick Witney in their paper (Beyond Global Britain: A realistic foreign policy for the UK. The European Council on Foreign Relations (ECFR).Policy Brief-15 December 2021) have noted Britain's resolve of becoming a greater power:

"Britain is heading into turbulent global waters in the wrong kind of ship and with no reliable forecast to hand. The key uncertainties are whether American hegemony will endure in the face of China's rise –and, for everyone else, how to triangulate between these rival titans. But there are plenty of subordinate dilemmas, too: how to learn from the successes of China's model of state capitalism; how to mitigate vulnerabilities while maintaining a generally open economy; how to balance democratic freedoms with the new demands of internal security; and, while accepting the reality of ever more varied and pervasive state competition, how to foster global cooperation where problems such as climate change and pandemics admit no other solution…..The Integrated Review is not a modest document. Its authors draw particular satisfaction from Britain's status as a "soft power superpower", with the report citing "our model of democratic governance, legal systems and Common Law heritage, the Monarchy, our world-class education, science and research institutions and standards-setting bodies, creative and cultural industries, tourism sector, sports sector, large and diverse diaspora communities, and contribution to international development".[7]

The past decades experienced different types of terrorism, radicalization and extremism that challenged power and authority of intelligence agencies and the police. Terror attack in Britain, and EU ultimately changed operational mechanism of intelligence agencies, while the 07 July 2005

London attacks, were a series of four coordinated suicide attacks carried out by Islamist terrorists in London that targeted commuters travelling on the city's public transport system during the morning rush hour. The terrorists were identified as Mohammad Sidique Khan, Shehzad Tanweer, Germaine Lindsay, and Hasib. On 13 August, The Independent reported that the bombers had acted independently, and on 01 September, the UK intelligence warned that al-Qaeda officially claimed responsibility for the attacks. On 22, May 2017, a suicide bomber used an improvised device in Manchester attacks. These attacks were noted by experts as an intelligence failure.

Armed governance as a mood of rule, violent competition, and control has characterized the modern history of Arab world. Majority of actors participating in determining such a process of governance are militias supported by neighbouring states. The dynamics of Taliban legitimacy, and their disputed leadership, however, is not out of the way from other powerful terrorist groups, suchlike the ISIS, Lashkar-e-Taiba and Central Asian groups. These external actors may also influence the relationship between Taliban and Afghan civilians. Taliban's way of governance has taken place under the conditions of civil war. They have adopted culture of violence, torture and jihad against education of Afghan girls. They haven't relinquished the culture of terrorising civilians. How the Taliban seized power in Kabul is a major question. Contexts of civil war and state weakness are often characterized by situations of governance by terror actors. The failure of Taliban intelligence to provide reliable information about the IS's military strength has raised serious questions about the credibility of their misgovernment. While one of the important functions of an intelligence agency is to provide timely warnings of hostile military action in the battlefield. The Kerslake Report: An independent review into the preparedness for, and emergency response to, the Manchester Arena attack on 22 May 2017, has noted some important aspects of suicide attacks in Manchester:

"The attack at the Manchester Arena on 22 May 2017 took the lives of twenty-two people and left hundreds more with both psychological and physical injuries. Whilst all the emergency services are trained to respond to disasters, the events on 22nd May were ones none had encountered previously. This was a brutal real-world test of plans and assumptions on a scale that was unprecedented in Greater Manchester. There was much to be proud of in the response, and there were many heroes that night. There is learning to share from both this and from the elements that could have gone better. The Review has tried to think through what might apply in the future in another attack, recognising that any lessons learnt will apply not just to Manchester, but nationally and internationally......The attack at the Manchester Arena impacted on the lives of thousands of people. Those most severely affected were in the foyer and its immediate vicinity: the twenty-two people who lost their lives and their family and friends; the gravely injured; those who witnessed the immediate aftermath of the explosion whether as concert goers or waiting relatives and friends, and those who gave assistance, putting their own safety aside. Communities spread throughout the north of England and beyond mourned the loss of their friends, colleagues and neighbours."[8]

The next target of terrorist groups was Paris and Germany. The BBC (09 December 2015) reported former President Francois Hollande's statement that he called the Paris attacks an "act of war" organised by the Islamic State (IS) militant group. Shootings and bomb blasts left 130 people dead and hundreds wounded, with more than 100 in critical condition. "Three coordinated teams" were believed to have been behind the attacks, according to Paris Chief Prosecutor Francois Molins. The first of three explosions occurred outside the Stade de France stadium on the northern fringe of Paris where France were playing Germany in an international football friendly. BBC noted. In Germany, terrorists targeted Christmas Market-killing 12 people. On 24 December 2016, BBC reported a lorry smashing into a crowded Christmas market in central Berlin on 19 December, killing 12 people and injuring 49, leaving 18 in a critical condition. Identified attacker Anis Amri, a Tunisian, was shot dead by Italian police on 23 December in the city of Milan after a Europe-wide manhunt. So-called Islamic State (IS) said one of its "soldiers" carried out the attack on the Breitscheidplatz Christmas market. BBC noted. On July 01,2020, authorities in Italy confiscated the largest-ever shipment of amphetamines, which they believed to had been manufactured by ISIS terrorist network. A non-partisan, and international policy organization, Counter Extremism Project in its comprehensive extremism report (Italy: Extremism and Terrorism) has documented important details about extremist organizations, Lone-wolves and terrorist attack:

"Jihadist networks have operated within Italy since the 1980s. In the 1990s, jihadists began using the country as a transit point enroute to conflicts in the Balkans and North Africa. Up until the early 2000s, jihadists reportedly refrained from directly targeting Italy in order to avoid a crackdown by authorities. That changed following Italy's participation in the U.S.-led interventions in Afghanistan (2001) and Iraq (2003). During the 2000s, Italy experienced a number of lone-wolf terrorist plots perpetrated by Islamic extremists. More recently, since the start of the Syrian civil war and the rise of ISIS, Italian authorities have worked to combat the growing threat from ISIS- and al-Qaeda-linked cells inside Italy and internationally. Nevertheless, Italy has not experienced a jihadist-related attack comparable in size to al-Qaeda's 2003 Madrid attacks or 2007 London bombings, nor ISIS's November 2015 Paris attacks or March 2016 Brussels bombings. (Sources: Combating Terrorism Centre, Jamestown Foundation) However, in the run-up to the Christmas holidays in November and December 2017, the pro-ISIS group Wafa Media Foundation released propaganda posters threatening attacks on the Vatican City, the papal enclave within Rome, as well as Pope Francis himself, the head of the Catholic Church."[9]

These terrorist attacks in France, Germany and the UK have been documented in this chapter to identify weaknesses and failures of intelligence and law enforcement agencies. France and Germany immediately introduced major security sector reforms and reorganization of intelligence infrastructures, but in several Eastern European states, intelligence reforms are still facing trouble. Terrorist attacks in the UK authenticated my perception that intelligence without reforms cannot fight terrorism and extremism. The UK government after a long time introduced law enforcement reforms and admitted that many things were not going in the right direction. The UK police has failed to effectively maintain law and order and fight criminal networks across the country. Reforms under the previous Government emphasised localism and replaced national targets with a "single mission" to cut crime. Government also changed the operational mechanism of the police. The UK Parliament in its website comment (Police reform in England and Wales) has identified changes and reforms in the police department and quoted Liberal Democrats and the Green Party's pledge to reform stop and search in the country:

"The Home Affairs Committee, reviewing the Government's changes to the policing landscape in February 2015, recommended that it was "now time to allow these pieces of the policing puzzle to settle into the new landscape, so that they might achieve the aim of making policing more effective." It seems unlikely that the service will escape further reform. Even if the basic architecture remains unchanged, other reforms are likely. For example, Liberal Democrats and the Green Party have pledged to reform stop and search, and the Tories would also legislate for this if the police failed to make changes. The Conservatives want to develop the role of Police and

Crime Commissioners (PCCs). They accuse Labour of "micromanaging" the police when they were in Government. In Opposition, Labour commissioned an Independent Commission on Policing. The report called PCCs a "failed experiment", not least because of the average 15% turnout at the first election in 2012".[10]

Recent events in Ukraine and Afghanistan prompted new debates and disquietude about the sharing of intelligence on counterterrorism and law enforcement level within the European Union states. After consecutive terrorist attacks in 2015-2016 in Germany, France, Italy and Britain, the question of counterterrorism and intelligence approach again became at the centre of EU domestic and foreign policy agenda. After the Paris attacks, there were perceptions that the French intelligence had failed to intercept terrorist's attacks, but the case was different-the French intelligence never failed in its counterterrorism operations, in reality, French law enforcement had failed due to the lack of coordination and public cooperation. The French authorities opted for a hard response, ordering massive police controls on Mosques and Muslim non-profit organisations. Analysts and experts, Silvia D'Amato and Andrea Terlizzi in their paper (Strategic European counterterrorism? An empirical analysis-01 February 2022) highlighted the EU counter radicalization and counterterrorism approach when on 13 November 2020, the European Union (EU) home affairs Ministers released a joint statement to reinforce surveillance of religious worshiping places and online interactions and released a counterterrorism document:

"On 13 November 2020, the European Union (EU) Home Affairs Ministers released a Joint statement to reinforce surveillance of religious worship places and online interactions. Shortly after, on 9 December 2020, the EU has published a document titled A Counter-Terrorism Agenda for the EU: Anticipate, Prevent, Protect, Respond, the first official agenda to be released after the 2005 Counterterrorism Strategy. The new agenda confirms the attempt by the EU to build internal and international credibility as a "security provider", in line with long-term efforts dedicated to developing an EU strategic vision. Indeed, the fight against terrorism seems to subscribe to the declared intention by European Commission President Ursula von der Leyen to make geopolitics the leitmotiv of the EU, currently involved in the development of the so-called Strategic Compass for security and defence expected for spring 2022. The announcement arrived as a response to mounting challenges facing the EU in recent years, summarised by Emmanuel Macron's remark on the EU finding itself at "the edge of a precipice" surrounded by a "hostile world" (Economist 2019). Yet, despite its clear policy relevance and the efforts made in this direction (Bossong and Rhinard 2018), the specialised literature on counterterrorism still lacks a systematic account of the novel propositions and strategic formula elaborated by the EU in relation to this policy field and in light of this new security scenario".[11]

The European Union struggled to reform institutions on state level, manage military crises and institutional innovation, but some states initiated security sector reforms, which was, later on opposed by their old communist intelligence and law enforcement agencies. The real issue that is still to be addressed was networks of foreign espionage within Europe, but without security sector reforms how can they counter foreign espionage? Secondly, in yesteryears, EU member states spied on each other's institutions, intelligence agencies and politicians that resulted in mistrust and a new intelligence war between Britain and Germany. The three states that countered foreign espionage in a professional way were France, Germany and the Netherlands. These states intercepted foreign intelligence operatives who had planned to retrieve economic and military data and spy on the civilian population. Expert and analyst, Wim Klinkert in his paper (Intelligence and Espionage the Netherlands) noted military power in war and peace:

"Also, based on the legislation that gave the military extra powers in wartime, telegraph and telephone messages were monitored. Censorship gave the military the power to open mail and telegrams, but only when a reason for suspicion already existed and only in areas under military control. Nevertheless, postal censors were used systematically to forward information on belligerent countries and armies that they read in the mail to Army Headquarters in The Hague".[12] Now the EU is facing violent conflicts close to its borders. They are engaged in a kind of intelligence war. The 2015 terrorist attacks tested their resolve and raised important questions including the low quality intelligence sharing. Analyst and scholars, Matthias Deneckere, Ashley Neat and Volker Hauck in their paper (The future of EU security sector assistance: learning from experience-May 2020) highlighted the EU security crisis:

"As the EU is facing the consequences of growing violent conflict close to its external borders and is struggling to adapt to geopolitical shifts, EU decision-makers have been seeking new tools to better deal with conflict and instability. This trend has been further corroborated by the EU's growing aspirations to become a credible global actor in the security domain. A number of developments can be highlighted in this context. First, 2018 saw the launch of a new 'Capacity-Building for Security and Development' (CBSD) initiative to support military activities that contribute to sustainable development. Second, in the past years EU development aid and EU Trust Funds have increasingly been used for projects with a clear security dimension. Third, member states are discussing a proposal for the creation of a European Peace Facility (EPF) to finance a range of assistance measures for foreign military actors in the form of training, advice, infrastructure or equipment. Such developments have triggered a debate on how security sector assistance can and should fit with broader EU external action. Historically, this has relied on development cooperation and trade as its main instruments. During the last two decades, the EU has built its capacities and instruments for security cooperation. This has included the introduction and development of the EU's Common Security and Defence Policy (CSDP) to deploy crisis management operations and security capacity-building missions in third countries, as well as the creation of the Instrument contributing to Stability and Peace (IcSP), to fund a range of activities on the nexus between security and development. Simultaneously, EU policymakers have invested much energy in designing more holistic approaches to violent conflict. Various policy statements have proposed a 'security-development nexus' approach, a 'comprehensive approach' or, more recently, an 'integrated approach' to violent conflict".[13]

The troubled and challenging European Union's intelligence cooperation with the United Kingdom has been discussed in books and journals by different perspectives since 2001. Notwithstanding the UK intelligence leadership's determination to establish an advanced and professional intelligence sharing mechanism with the EU intelligence agencies on law enforcement and counter terrorism levels, the EU intelligence infrastructure's confusion about the sincerity of MI6, MI5 and GCHQ remained in place. Intelligence sharing on an emergency level was already in operation but not wholeheartedly as both sides wanted to engage in all sectors of security and counter radicalization. The European Union as a security and intelligence actor from the perspective of counter-terrorism and counter radicalization needed Britain's intelligence cooperation. The EU intelligence has experienced myriad crisis during the last ten years while terrorist organizations and home grown radicalised elements challenged authority of the state. Analysts and intelligence experts, Javier Argomaniz, Oldrich Bures and Christian Kaunert (A Decade of EU Counter-Terrorism and Intelligence: A Critical Assessment-23 Dec 2014) in their research paper have critically assessed the EU counterterrorism intelligence:

"The Treaty on the European Union (EU) stipulates that one of the key objectives of the Union is to provide citizens with a high level of safety within an Area of Freedom, Security and Justice (AFSJ). Given that the fight against terrorism is a prominent aspect of this general objective, it is remarkable that, in spite of its political relevance and decade-long history, it has only relatively recently received due attention in the academic community. Although 'counterterrorism' is not yet a clearly defined area in its broadest and fullest sense, it already spans across a number of other policy areas across all of the EU's former three pillars. Thus, right from the start, the consensus was to adopt a broadly sectoral approach for this interim evaluation, independently examining policy outputs from some of the main components of the European Union's multifaceted fight against terrorism. These include the exchange of information between police and intelligence agencies, the protection of critical infrastructure, the development of external action, the production of counter-terrorism legislation, the control of European borders and the fight against terrorist recruitment and financing".[14]

Relationship between policy makers and intelligence analysis after the Iraq, Syria and Afghan wars has evolved in multitudinous shapes. In Europe, the United States and Asia, intelligence operations, analysis and its infrastructure has become politicised. Political and bureaucratic stakeholders together with private partners have been using intelligence agencies to stabilize their position, influence and governments since 2001. Intelligence is classified and authenticated information-analysed to assess its relevance. Strategic intelligence is material that informs state intelligence agencies and policy makers. Tactical intelligence inculcates policy makers and intelligence agencies about emerging threats. However, politicization of intelligence has been presented to identify various types of politicisation processes. Politicised intelligence information, its analysis and process creates misunderstandings between policy makers and stakeholders. Expert of intelligence, Glenn Hastedt (The Politics of Intelligence and the Politicization of Intelligence: The American Experience, Intelligence and National Security) in his paper documented the basic function of intelligence and its three distinct focal points that are routinely used for organizing discussion of intelligence analysis:

"Intelligence Estimating Three distinct focal points are routinely used for organizing discussions of intelligence analysis. The first is the concept of an intelligence cycle. In it intelligence analysis is broken down into a series of functional stages (requirement setting, information collection, evaluation, and reporting) each leading logically to the next. The second is the debate over whether intelligence analysis is a craft or science. Is it a skill honed through an apprenticeship and life-long study or a body of knowledge or universal truths arrived at through a structured investigation under controlled circumstances? The third framing device used to organize discussions of intelligence analysis is the long-standing debate over the proper relationship between analysts who produce intelligence and consumers who request it and use it. One position holds that the two must be kept separate so that analysis does not become corrupted by the intrusion of viewpoints and considerations that do not bear directly on the task of understanding and assessing a situation or problem. The opposing position holds that rather than promote objectivity an arm's length relationship between analyst and consumer only encourages irrelevance. Analysts must know the concerns, priorities and blind spots of consumers if they are to produce intelligence that is germane to the decisions being made and courses of action contemplated. Individually or as a group these approaches do The arm's length perspective is in many respects similar to the first two approaches in that it seeks to wall off intelligence analysis from the broader political system. The co-mingling of the two spheres results in the politicization of intelligence which undermines the analytic process. While this may be the result it need not be. As a strategy for bringing about change politicization is value neutral and may be used by reformers as well as obstructionists."[15]

In my perspective as noticeable and evident from the fact, the role of private intelligence agencies within the EU and UK is of great importance, the reason that they are partners of state intelligence agencies and the police and share important intelligence information on law enforcement levels. Private intelligence stakeholders have been playing an important role in managing conflicts, tackling law and order situations, policing and counterterrorism operations both in the UK and European Union for decades. As we have seen in yesteryears, private policing and intelligence agencies as partners in the EU continent have played a major role in surveillance and intelligence information collection. Expert and analyst, and Program Coordinator at the Intelligence Project at the Harvard Kennedy School's Belfer Centre, Maria A. Robson Morrow (Private sector intelligence: on the long path of professionalization-20 Mar 2022) in her paper highlighted the role of private intelligence and its important role in countering terrorism and radicalization, and also noted a robust transnational community of private sector intelligence practitioners that emerged, with representatives from airlines, financial institutions, technology companies, universities, major league sports, non-profits, and many other sectors:

"In response to an uncertain global operating environment, firms are increasingly investing in intelligence teams, and there is a growing transnational private sector intelligence community. The nascent literature on 'private sector intelligence' or 'private sector risk intelligence' is not about private military contractors, espionage, or 'guns, guards, and gates'. Rather, it is about private sector intelligence practitioners legally and transparently employing open-source collection to assess a variety of geopolitical, physical security, and sometimes cyber security risks. Private sector intelligence teams can also support strategic decision-making. For example, if an energy company is exploring new market entries in Nigeria, executives might be concerned about corruption, kidnapping, pipeline tapping, piracy, and Boko Haram. The intelligence assessment would examine what threats would translate into real risks for the company, considering the company's prospective vulnerabilities and the likely impact. Boko Haram would pose a credible threat to operations planned in Borno state, but not the Niger Delta, where more pressing concerns would be pipeline tapping, kidnapping, and piracy. New market entry support can also identify political instability and reputational concerns prior to investment. While some intelligence teams focus on strategic opportunity intelligence, most activity in the private sector intelligence field continues to be concentrated on risk and security. The best term for this field is a matter of debate. Possibilities include: 'private sector intelligence', 'private sector risk intelligence', 'private sector security intelligence', 'private sector security risk intelligence', and 'protective intelligence'. Differences are due both to disagreement on scope, and variation across countries. These discrepancies do not necessarily indicate an absence of professional identity. Just as medicine has anaesthesiology, surgery, and many other specialities, private sector intelligence could develop as an umbrella profession with sub-disciplines. This article uses *private sector intelligence*, encompassing the subfields of risk intelligence, security intelligence, and protective intelligence, and possibly the forward-looking subfield of opportunity intelligence".[16]

The Netherlands, Norway, Sweden, and Brussels and French intelligence agencies have lived through different phases of experiments, experiences and participation in US and NATO war on terrorism in Afghanistan, built professional infrastructures that protected national security of their states. The General Intelligence and Security Service of the Netherlands is the intelligence and security agency of the country, tasked with domestic, foreign and signals intelligence to protect national security. There were some second thoughts in yesteryears when a Dutch businessman Frans van Anraat, was convicted of complicity in war crimes for selling raw materials for the production of chemical weapons to Iraq, allowing Pakistani nuclear scientist, Abdul Kadeer Khan to make an atom bomb on information retrieved from Netherlands, not focussing on extremist groups activities, not focussing on political violence or environmental groups, followed the murder of Pim Fortuyn by an environmental radical and delivering hand grenades to members of the Hofstadgroep through alleged informer Saleh Bouali, the AIVD received deep criticism from different political and social circle. The AIVD has now improved its civilian and military approach and is operating in the right direction. Its relationship with policy makers and the oversight committee has been friendly for years. Review report about the use of cable interception by the AIVD and the MIVD- CTIVD, No. 75. Of Review Committee on the Intelligence and Security Services 15, March 2022 has reviewed investigatory power of cable interception of the intelligence service:

"The new investigatory power of cable interception was a much-discussed topic during the political and social debate on the ISS Act 2017. The term 'dragnet' was frequently used in that context because there was and still is a fear that communication is collected routinely in bulk about people who are not the subject of investigation by the services. During and after the introduction of the ISS Act 2017, the social and political debate focused on how cable interception as a means could be as targeted as possible and on the fact that this investigatory power is linked to investigation assignments, in the attempt to dispel the impression of a dragnet. The services were presented as being able to identify in advance the exact channels through which the relevant information is transported. In addition, the minister of the Interior and Kingdom Relations and the minister of Defence made several pledges, one of which was that there is virtually no prospect of cable interception being used in the coming years for investigation into communication that originates and terminates within the Netherlands (except for cyber defence purposes). Another was that traffic which is known in advance not to be relevant, such as streaming service and bit-torrent traffic, would be filtered out. A further pledge was that cable interception would be conducted 'as targeted as possible'. Since the ISS Act 2017 entered into force on 01 May 2018, the Oversight Department of the CTIVD has concentrated its oversight activities on the implementation and functioning of that new legislation, in particular on those themes that commanded the most attention in the political and social debate. As a consequence, during the debate on the Act, both the House of Representatives and the Senate requested the CTIVD to speed up or intensify its oversight activities. The government also asked the CTIVD to rigorously review proper compliance with the legislation in actual practice. Those requests largely correspond with the key points put forward by the CTIVD itself during and after the parliamentary debate on the Act in 2017 and the referendum on the Act on 21 March 2018".[17]

## Chapter 2

# Intelligence Failure, the Achilles heel of Interoperability, Foreign Espionage, and Security Sector Reforms within European Union and the United Kingdom

Why intelligence failure transpires in Britain and the European Union repeatedly, and why they have been ineffectual to address issues of mistrust, presentation and intelligence sharing. The question is, they lack adequate intelligence information, lack of trained manpower, flow of low-quality intelligence information purveyed by untrained, illiterate and ill-educated agents, failure to understand modern technology, lack of proper intelligence sharing with policy makers, and lack of actionable intelligence. In the aftermath of the terrorist attacks in London, Manchester, Paris and Germany, the EU and UK intelligence agencies became subject to hot-blooded assessment. Taking the case of EU and UK intelligence failure, this chapter stresses the need for reforms to fit intelligence to the fight against terrorism and foreign espionage. The British, French and German intelligence agencies suffered from lack of check and balance and influence of government and private stakeholders. In Germany, France and the UK, intelligence oversight must work on the internal level, executive and parliamentary levels to make sure intelligence is transparently purveyed to policymakers and law enforcement agencies. The problem technically lies with the approach toward intelligence failure. However, the UK and EU intelligence agencies never revealed stories about their failures and successes. The UK Big 3, the EU-27 and Eyes-Five are responsible to secure the state and play a major role in producing intelligence relating to counterterrorism. They are failing on different fronts due to outdated technology and unreformed infrastructures, lack of efficient online surveillance, lack of severe shortages in terms of trained manpower. Politicians of ruling parties have often faced the brunt of most failures of counterterrorism than anybody else in the EU continents, because they control the operation of intelligence agencies.

As highlighted earlier, causes of intelligence failure in South Asia, Britain and the European Union are all the same. We have already reviewed the 1962 Indo-China war, the 1971 war between Pakistan and India, the Kargil war, war on terrorism in Afghanistan, waves of terrorism in Europe. In all these cases we can find the same causes of intelligence failure. Indian intelligence failed to predict Chinese invasion in 1962, Pakistan's intelligence failed to predict the fall of Bengal and Indian intelligence collaborated with Mukti Bahani group, the RAW failed to detect Pakistan's infiltration in Kargil. Intelligence failure can be expected in a robust democratic political system involving the ever-volatile mix of free speech, politicians, and the news media. Expert of intelligence analysis, John Hollister Hedley, (Learning from Intelligence Failures, International. Journal of Intelligence and Counterintelligence) has noted that notwithstanding weak, low quality, incomplete and contradictory intelligence is, decision is taken on that quality of information:

"No matter how incomplete, inadequate, uncertain, or contradictory the information on which a judgment must be made, the judgment is nevertheless expected and must be made. Making it necessarily entails a recognition of the risk that the judgment can miss the mark. This should go without saying, but it doesn't. (In intelligence work, having enough evidence to indict is common; but there's almost never enough to convict.) Would that all those who would take to task the makers of an erroneous assessment be somewhat more understanding of the intellectual risks that had to be taken, and the inevitability of taking them, but they aren't. The expectation after the fact is that the analysts should have gotten it right. Those who are caught up in the doing or studying of intelligence work should not be startled or dismayed about this. It should be expected and accepted, pure and simple, as a cost of doing business in a free country. There is no need to fall on one's sword or spend time lamenting the unfairness of the allegations. They are a fact of life, and in many cases deserved. For as long as foreign policy surprises occur, and for as long as open societies have free news media and ambitious politicians, allegations of intelligence failure are likely to be made, virtually as being part of the process. Perhaps "process" is too dignified a term, but failures and the attendant allegations—the "school of hard knocks"—is one from which lessons not only can be, but are learned".[1]

The EU and UK has been spending a substantial amount of money for strengthening their intelligence infrastructures, after they witnessed numerous instances of terrorist attacks. They now become prone to more terrorist attacks. Taking the cases of failure to prevent the 2015 attacks in Paris, Germany, Italy, Austria and the UK, this chapter focuses on intelligence failure and its causes. Expert of intelligence, Janani Krishnaswamy in her research paper (Why Intelligence Fails, The Hindu Centre-2013) documented caused of intelligence failure: "Whenever a terrorist attack happens, faulty or inadequate intelligence is cited as a major cause, regardless of whether there happen to be policy failures. However, there are a few exceptions. As a consequence of linking terrorist attacks with inadequate intelligence, the argument of an existing intelligence system not being capable of dealing with immediate threats arises all the time. This unbalanced approach of routinely establishing a strong link between intelligence and counter-terrorism policy is due to the assumption that intelligence analysis normally influences policy decisions leading to a natural deduction that the availability of good intelligence can only lead to effective policies and vice versa. However, this is not to dismiss the need for more capable intelligence machinery. The model inaccurately links flawed counter-terrorist policies to insufficient or erroneous intelligence. The helplessness of the intelligence community to defend any allegations of failure has only reinforced the claim made above. Such an unsound analysis will lead to questions such as why or how policy makers overlook available intelligence."[2]

After the Paris, Brussels and Berlin terrorist attacks, the EU member states realised to establish a strong unified intelligence and security network. However, things were not alike, which we sensed. There were different priorities, resources and levels of expertise within every state. Intelligence sharing among member states was not an easy task as it seemed that policy makers and secret services faced numerous legal, technical and political obstacles. Large states such as France, Germany, and the UK have established significant counterterrorism institutions and human resources to maintain sophisticated intelligence networks. Intelligence agencies in several other countries were fighting radicalization and extremism on national interests based strategies, and shared information with neighbouring states to further intercept terrorist attacks, control foreign espionage and external interference, but traditional security threat remained as a precarious threat to national security. From nuclear proliferation, and smuggling of dirty bomb materials to nuclear and biological terrorism, all challenges were being tackled by national security and intelligence agencies. Recent reforms in France, Germany and the UK are indicative of their professional approach to state security and professionalization of intelligence. Expert of intelligence and security, Janani Krishnaswamy (Why Intelligence Fails, The Hindu Centre-2013) has also highlighted dynamics of intelligence failure in her paper:

"The principal debate among Indian intelligence scholars starts with the assumption that counter-terrorist decision making is influenced by intelligence analysis. This approach of studying a failure of the intelligence community involves evaluating the accuracy of the intelligence analysis and critiquing either the intelligence producer or policy maker for not providing or not acting upon provided intelligence. Though intelligence agencies do play a vital role in policy making, pursuing this kind of a research agenda can be extremely difficult given the secretive environment of national security intelligence. Further, it cannot offer holistic solutions to the problems of the community. Instead, as Henry Kissinger explains in his article on intelligence failures, "Resetting the priorities of intelligence and adapting to the new realities of terrorism must start with an understanding of the problems requiring a solution." Besides shoddy tradecraft and problems arising from intelligence analysis, sources of intelligence failures may stem from a variety of factors, including (a) misunderstanding about what the intelligence community can reasonably provide and what some decision-makers or journalists expect, (b) organisational flaws within the community, and/or (c) implementation of faulty reforms. The answer as to why there is very less definitional clarity—within intelligence studies in India — is evident from the lack of methodology-driven studies that address the real dilemmas of the intelligence community and theory-driven discourses that explain the intelligence failures. Several studies focusing on intelligence reforms have emphasised the need for the intelligence community to interact with citizens at multiple levels, the need to provide for adequate whistle-blower protection mechanisms for those who report orders perceived as illegal and the need for effective legal and parliamentary oversight systems to monitor the performance of intelligence agencies".[3]

The UK intelligence agencies are facing numerous challenges due to the recent financial crisis, and the role of intelligence in fighting terrorism and foreign espionage. The exponentially growing graph of crime, extremism and radicalization has put intelligence on the ordeal. In a modern state, policing and intelligence mechanism is a diverse job, which requires a disciplined approach to counterterrorism and counterintelligence. Many intelligence agencies adopted different approaches like conduct of policy, and disciplinary procedure. We live in an age of risk mixed insecurities, anxieties about civilities and anti-social behaviour. We hoped that the EU and UK policing and intelligence forces would respond to all these torments and threats with a professional security approach in maintaining security and law and order, but they failed and our hopes vanished. The Snowden revelation regarding mass surveillance in European Union states and the UK generated an unending debate, while media in 2013 began publishing his documents to inculcate the civilian population about their illegal and shameless intelligence surveillance mechanism and the use of Facial Recognition Technologies. His revelations exposed several states spying on their own citizens. The NSA, BND and GCHQ came under severe criticism by mainstream society across EU and the US. There has been an intense debate in European electronic and print media about the underwhelming Achilles heel operational mechanism and tactics of their intelligence agencies. Assistant Professor Department of Political Science Towson University and Senior Research Scholar Centre for International and Security Studies at Maryland University, William J. Lahneman in his paper (National Intelligence Agencies and Transnational Threats: The Need for a New Intelligence Paradigm-27 January 2008) has highlighted traditional concept of information flow and threat perceptions:

"The traditional concept of information flows is still relevant when the IC performs its traditional mission of solving puzzles using secrets and OSINT. This suggests that, rather than abandoning the traditional view in favour of a totally new conception of information flows, traditional flows should be augmented by new types in order to perform adaptive interpretations. A trusted network is one in which all of the members are trusted to enter only validated information and to use network information responsibly. Within these constraints, network members can be any organization that can provide needed information. This will include government agencies, private firms, IGOs, NGOs, and even individuals in various informal communities of interest. Since their purpose is to address transnational issues and threats, trusted networks must be global in scope. The overriding principle is that members of a trusted network must agree to voluntarily share their own information to be able to access the network's contents. In short, the network depends on mutual trust among its members. Only the organizations that are members of the network have access to its information, and these organizations have access to all of the information in the network at all times. This means that trusted information is not open source information because it is not available to the public. Nor is trusted information classified information, since its distribution is not restricted to the minimum number of people possible. In fact, distribution will be impossible to control, since members are free to use network information for any responsible purpose. Such uses would include use by a country's intelligence organizations".[4]

The involvement of EU agencies in power abuse, over-activation, politics, and corruption has made their performance absurd. Policy experts and intelligence analysts across Europe have recognized the motives of lone actors, and proposed wide-ranging security measures to counter emerging threats. The EU border existence is now in crisis after the terrorist attacks in Germany. France is facing waves of Middle East-bound terrorism, and Germany has border problems with Poland. Spain is in deep water. The country has not been exempted from lone-wolves attacks. The Russian intelligence operation and American intelligence failure are two lessons learnt to understand the role of intelligence in war and peace. Intelligence failure often occurred as a result of weak and wrongly designed strategies. Poor understanding capabilities, and information processes by policy makers are the main reasons intelligence failed. Intelligence is being collected by five means: HUMINT, SIGINT, Imagery Intelligence (IMINT), and Open Source Intelligence (OSINT). Without clear coordination and process failure, intelligence is failed. Intelligence failures are unfair in that they derive from ignorance of the facts and from unrealistic expectations. Expert and analyst, John Hollister Hedley (John Hollister Hedley (2005) Learning from Intelligence Failures, International Journal of Intelligence and Counterintelligence) has identified causes of the failure of intelligence:

"The statement that intelligence failures are inevitable has the certainty of a law of physics. No one person or organization can be right on all subjects at all times, nor is it reasonable or realistic to have such an expectation—either in making an intelligence assessment or in passing judgment on it after the fact. To do their job well, intelligence analysts must be willing to take risks. No matter how incomplete, inadequate, uncertain, or contradictory the information on which a judgment must be made, the judgment is nevertheless expected and must be made. Making it necessarily entails a recognition of the risk that the judgment can miss the mark. This should go without saying, but it doesn't. (In intelligence work, having enough evidence to indict is common; but there's almost never enough to convict.) Would that all those who would take to task the makers of an erroneous assessment be somewhat more understanding of the intellectual risks that had to be taken, and the inevitability of taking them, but they aren't. The expectation after the fact is that the analysts should have gotten it right.

Those who are caught up in the doing or studying of intelligence work should not be startled or dismayed about this. It should be expected and accepted, pure and simple, as a cost of doing business in a free country. There is no need to fall on one's sword or spend time lamenting the unfairness of the allegations. They are a fact of life, and in many cases deserved. For as long as foreign policy surprises occur, and for as long as open societies have free news media and ambitious politicians, allegations of intelligence failure are likely to be made, virtually as being part of the process. Perhaps "process" is too dignified a term, but failures and the attendant allegations—the "school of hard knocks"—is one from which lessons not only can be, but are learned".[5]

There are different perceptions about intelligence failure in Asia and Europe, which diverted attention of states and governments towards professionalization of security sectors, in order to eradicate extremism and radicalization. During the President Trump era, we have seen US intelligence agencies fighting against each other, and supporting politicians of their own choice, this war of strength continues with full strength. This internal turmoil caused the failure of the US army to stabilise Afghanistan. Intelligence failures occur for more reasons than just sloppy tradecraft and are often attributable to decision-makers as well as to the intelligence community and the benefits and disadvantages of conducting inquiries immediately after the intelligence failure. Keeping in mind consecutive intelligence failure, the French intelligence leadership and successive governments introduced intelligence and security sector reforms to fight terrorism and radicalization with news strategies. Assistant Professor Department of Political Science Towson University & Senior Research Scholar Centre for International and Security Studies at Maryland University, William J. Lahneman in his paper (National Intelligence Agencies and Transnational Threats: The Need for a New Intelligence Paradigm-27 January 2008) has documented traditional state-based security challenges:

"While traditional state-based security challenges remain important, the most serious threats to international security come increasingly from transnational phenomena. Transnational terrorism is the most visible current threat of this type, and governments are all too aware of the problems of fighting such a networked opponent that operates across borders, skilfully capitalizing on the increased travel, multifaceted communications, and expanded financial capabilities resulting from the process of globalization. Transnational criminal networks pose another serious threat, albeit one that lacks the visibility of terrorist networks because criminals seek financial gain rather than mass casualties. These threats have one thing in common beyond their potential for destructiveness: all are transnational. As such, none can be understood—let alone defeated or reduced in intensity—by the actions of single states. In an ideal world, all states would cooperate to deal with these common threats. Cooperation would take many forms, depending on the specific circumstances and nature of the threat, but the need to share large volumes of information and knowledge would be a common thread running through these efforts. In the real world, there are significant impediments to sharing on this scale. This is because the knowledge and information in question fall into two broad categories. First, there is information and knowledge that virtually all governments and other actors have an interest in sharing voluntarily, although they might not recognize this fact. Second, there is information and knowledge that governments desire to keep secret. It is difficult for single institutions to deal with both types equally well. Intelligence agencies are the part of national governments charged with making sense of future security challenges. However, intelligence agencies' traditions and organizational cultures emphasize secrecy, not knowledge sharing".[6]

Intelligence has been defined in many ways. Some define it as the ability to learn about, learn from, understand and interact, but intelligence expert Michael Herman (2011) understands that intelligence is a classified knowledge that supports its own state's information security by advising on and setting standard of defensive, and protective security measures. In his recent book, he describes intelligence in these words: "Intelligence supply assessments of intelligence threat; engages in counter-espionage; and seeks evidence of hostile countries' intelligence successes through counterintelligence penetrations of their organisations." In the case of former Afghan intelligence agencies, and Pakistani intelligence agencies, we observed that they never adopted these and other measures of intelligence and counterintelligence to lead the government and policymakers in the right direction. There are countless articles and papers highlighting failure of the French intelligence during the Paris terrorist attacks. In fact, France's intelligence services were struggling to meet the challenge in 2015 before the ISIL translated its anger into a violent action, but failed to coordinate with law enforcement agencies. However, the magnitude of this challenge means that analysts in one intelligence agency will need to share information with analysts in other parts of the intelligence community. After the ligature of bombing in Paris, French intelligence was preparing for a strong response to the ISIS and other groups. Analyst and experts, Bruce Crumley, in his

Al Jazeera article (Were the Paris attacks a French intelligence failure? Al Jazeera (November 17, 2015) noted activities of terrorist and extremist organizations in France and operational mechanism of French intelligence:

"Reports that France was warned by the United States and Iraq before the Paris attacks that an ISIL assault was imminent have prompted many to ask how security services could have missed the plot. Such incredulity was heightened by the fact that a number of those involved were on the radar of French authorities as radicals and potential threats—with at least one charged in a terrorism-related case. Such a scenario might seem unthinkable in the U.S., but the reality is that neither France nor its European Union partners have the forces, assets, funding or legal provisions to take sweeping preventive measures—often based on sketchy intelligence—that the U.S. can. And fail-safe operational monitoring of the sheer number of potential threats on European soil, in the form of sympathizers with groups like the Islamic State in Iraq and the Levant (ISIL), many of whom have travelled to Syria and spent time with the group, is beyond the capacity of any security service......The emergence of ISIL, which has raised its flag over huge stretches of territory in Syria and Iraq that are relatively easily accessible from Turkey, has dramatically altered the challenge facing European security services whose primary problem was once Al-Qaeda. That's because Osama bin Laden's group preferred to operate from the shadows as a more professional elite force, whereas ISIL is far more accessible to young would-be radicals traveling from the West".[7]

British former Home Secretary, Teresa May once warned that the law enforcement agencies must be prepared to tackle expected lone gunman or Mumbai-style attacks on the streets of Britain. Extremist and terrorist networks are very strong and often challenge the national security of the country, but the Home Secretary and her administration had failed to control the subversive activities of extremist forces in Britain. Recent wave of sectarian violence in Northern Ireland has now become a bigger national security challenge, where terrorists and anti-state elements target the police and innocent civilians. Racial walls have never been considered an instrument of peace in any religious conflict in modern history. Walls cannot separate brothers from brothers, mothers from sons and friends from friends. Walls cannot divide minds, hearts, ethnic and linguistic relations. We can separate human beings by any means but we cannot undermine human values, relationships and a traditional way of life. Walls in Northern Ireland are an ugly blot on the face of Britain's intelligence agencies that failed to stabilize the region. In 2015 and 2016, terrorists launched attacks in different European states. On 13 November 2015, terrorists launched coordinated attacks on civilian targets in central Paris, and killed 132 people and injured 352. Unfortunately, they were three groups of 9 terrorists while three terrorists attacked national sports stadium then fired at people outside several cafes and restaurants, and gunmen entered the Bataclan concert hall where they killed tens of people before detonating their suicide vests. Analyst and expert, Dr. Emmanuel Karagiannis in his article (Were the Attacks in Paris and Brussels an Intelligence Failure? Defence-in-Depth, the research blog of the Defence Studies Department, King's College London) noted terrorist attacks by nine terrorists in Paris, where they killed innocent civilians:

"During 2015-2016, ISIS cells and ISIS-inspired lone wolves launched a series of terrorist attacks against European cities. On 13 November 2015, a group of ISIS assailants launched coordinated attacks on civilian targets in central Paris. They killed 132 people and injured 352. It appears that there were three teams of nine gunmen. Three suicide bombers attacked the national sports stadium during a friendly match between the national soccer teams of France and Germany. Then attackers shot at people outside several cafes and restaurants. Finally, gunmen entered the Bataclan concert hall and killed tens of people before detonating their suicide vests. Most of the gunmen were Belgian or French citizens. Next day ISIS claimed responsibility for the attacks....Intelligence failures can be determined by the lack of information or the lack of information accuracy, which determines a distortion of the analytical process. This can occur either through ignoring or through the mistaken interpretation of data. The analysis of the terrorist attacks in Paris and Brussels suggests there is a new form of terrorism, leading to an unpredictable intelligence failure. The asymmetric character of jihadi attacks means that the success of combatting terrorism no longer relies just on the magnitude of available resources. Unlike other fields, the identification of the causes of errors of intelligence activity is especially difficult, given that their main resource–information–is difficult to quantify. Thus, one can legitimately ask the question – are we talking about a failure of the intelligence services or of a failure of public policies that determine the direction of action of these organizations?"[8]

Significant failures of the local administration in tackling the issue through negotiation and community level in the past caused further misunderstandings about the conflict resolution mechanism of the central government. Low quality religious education, sectarian feelings at schools and colleges level, terror attacks, bomb blasts, and all these unwanted misadventures caused violence in the streets, markets and parks. The danger is approaching as the issues of ethnicity, racism and sectarianism have taken root across the country. Religious violence and racism causing the death of innocent lives are well documented, and the killings of policemen and innocent civilians are not new. The EU faces an increasingly insecure and unstable neighbourhood. The war in Syria, Iraq and Afghanistan, humanitarian crisis in the region and the weakening of state structure have created many problems like the invasion of refugees and infiltration of extremist and terrorist forces into the region. The EU may further face a deteriorating security environment and an unprecedented level of threat, while Brexit has made the security of the project complex.

Moreover, recent independent and government reports indicate that the threat of sectarian terrorism remains serious. Violence in Northern Ireland is complicated and cannot be separated from political, geographical and cultural contexts. There are many ways of reconciliation and elimination of violence and the deepening social crisis if the local government adopted a multidimensional security approach. Germany and France faced a wide range of security challenges including the lone wolf attacks and radicalization, which prompted wide-ranging legal and administrative reforms in these two states. In December 2016, Germany, France and Italy proposed a multilateral cooperation in the field of intelligence sharing to counter extremism and radicalization in Europe. The EU member states collectively established three competent institutions to make the process of intelligence sharing. Berne Group, Europol and the EU Military Staff, but never thought to tackle the crisis of mistrust. The recent Paris, Brussels and Istanbul attacks, and extensive intelligence war in Britain also raised important questions on the credibility and unprofessional demonstration of intelligence and counterterrorism agencies across Europe.

It is clear that intelligence and law enforcement in some European Union (EU) member states are characterised by variety, being the product of their specific history and culture. Majority of states still live in the cold war era while awareness about national security, intelligence and law enforcement is underwhelming. In Central and Western Europe, some states introduced major reforms in the field of law enforcement and intelligence, but the way their intelligence agencies were operating was not professional due to their consecutive failure to tackle national security threats in yesteryears. These reforms have had mixed results; sometimes states adopted a democratic model, and at times, it looked as though hardly anything had changed. Every state adopted its own culture of national security mechanism, which prevented them from adopting a common security approach. Now the case of intelligence sharing has become complicated as all member states face deep political and military crises. However, Radicalization in Europe emerged in all member states where terrorist and extremist groups operate with impunity. Newspapers and journals reported terrorist attacks in cities and towns. Large proportion of home-grown extremists and radicalized groups developed their violent skills, or habitus, through involvement with local street culture, and local prisons. Expert and analyst, Robin Andersson Malmros in his paper (Prevention of terrorism, extremism and radicalisation in Sweden: A sociological institutional perspective on development and change, 07 Sep 2021) has noted some aspects of jihadism and role of intelligence in Sweden:

"The primary role of the Intelligence and Security services is to evaluate, prevent and repel threats to Sweden and Swedish interests. They examine adversaries' intentions, and the ever-changing and developing situation in the world. Through advice, training and review, the services ensure that possible threats – in Sweden and internationally–are understood accurately, that standards and rules are followed, and that all personnel maintain the appropriate levels of security. The Intelligence Service collects and processes information and then informs the relevant people. This information relates to areas such as global political developments, and external threats to Sweden and Swedish interests. With the help of such information, the service seeks to predict what steps an adversary may take, in order to prepare a military response accordingly. The service also uses open sources such as media outlets and websites to build a picture of global trends. The task of the Security Service is to prepare and protect the Armed Forces from security threats. It works pre-emptively to assess security threats, and to shape and take security measures if necessary. The service follows up and counters different types of threats; the most common threats emanate from the work of foreign intelligence services, organised crime, subversion, sabotage and terrorism. The Intelligence and Security services are subordinate to the Military Intelligence and Security Service (MUST). Training of intelligence and security personnel is conducted, in part, at the Armed Forces' Intelligence and Security Centre".[9]

In Europe, there is the general perception that as extremist and sectarian groups have already used some dangerous gases in Iraq, Afghanistan and Syria, therefore, they could use biological weapons against civilian populations in Europe. If control over these weapons is weak, or if their components are available in the open market, terrorists can inflict huge fatalities in the region. Experts recently warned that the availability of such materials in the open markets of some European states can fall in the hands of local terrorist organisations, which may further jeopardise the security of the region. Two Belgian nuclear power plant workers had joined ISIS, leading to fears that jihadists had the intelligence to cause a meltdown disaster. Before the suicide attacks in Belgium, security agencies were fearful that perhaps ISIS operatives had been looking to target a nuclear plant as it emerged that two workers from a plant in Doel fled to Syria to join ISIS. Belgian Interior Minister Jan Jambon said at the time that authorities had determined there was a threat "to the person in question, but not the nuclear facilities." In the wake of the terrorist attacks in Brussels, security experts raised the question of intelligence-sharing failure, which caused huge infrastructure destruction and the killings of innocent civilians. Terrorists killed more than 34 innocent people and injured over 200 in Brussels. President of the EU Council said: "I am appalled by the bombing at Zavantem airport and the European District in Brussels, which have cost several innocent lives and injured many others. Experts, Manne Gerell, Joakim Sturup, Mia-Maria Magnusson, Kim Nilvall, Ardavan Khoshnood and Amir Rostami in their research paper (Open drug markets, vulnerable neighbourhoods and gun violence in two Swedish cities-19 March 20212) have highlighted the gun culture in Sweden:

"Gun violence increased substantially in Sweden between 1996 and 2015 (Khoshnood, 2018; Sturup et al., 2018b). The increase appears to have continued since, with 43 cases of gun homicides in 2017 amounting to about twice the rate which was found from the 1990s up until the early 2010s (National Council for Crime Prevention, 2018; National Council for Crime Prevention, 2017). Between 2011 and 2017, Sweden witnessed 192 case of gun homicides, making it 2.0 gun homicides per 1,000,000 inhabitants (Khoshnood, 2019). This increase is unevenly distributed among the population, however, with lethal gun violence against women recording a decrease (Caman, Kristiansson, Granath, & Sturup, 2017), lethal gun violence against children reduced (Hedlund, Masterman, & Sturup, 2016), and most of the increase among men located in the younger age strata (Sturup et al., 2018b). In terms of the context of gun homicides, the increase is mostly attributed to criminal conflicts, while family- or partner-related homicides have decreased (National Council for Crime Prevention, 2015b; Sturup, Rostami, & Appelgren, 2011). This is paralleled by the decreasing share of gun homicides that are perpetrated with legally owned weapons, dropping from 25% in the early 1990s to 11–12% in the 2000s (National Council for Crime Prevention, 2015b). The increase in gun violence is also tied to deprived neighbourhoods with one study noting that almost the entire national increase between 2006 and 2014 in gun violence took place in such neighbourhoods (National Council for Crime Prevention, 2015a). In summary, gun violence has increased substantially, and much of the increase is tied to young men, deprived neighbourhoods, and criminal conflicts and with illegal weapons being used. This parallels a development of growing street gangs in vulnerable neighbourhoods, which are often linked to incidents of gun violence (Police Authority, 2017)".[10]

On 30 March 2022, in its year book, Swedish intelligence and Security Service warned that Sweden's security was being challenged on several fronts. "We are facing a wider and rapidly changing threat from hostile states and violent extremism, a threat that has therefore become more complex. This complex threat is manifested in frequent activities and attacks, legal and illegal, targeting individuals as well as Sweden itself. The threat actors are prepared to go to extreme lengths to achieve their goal". In conjunction with Cyprus, Ireland, Austria and Malta, Finland and Sweden never demanded membership of the NATO organization. The two states have been neutral since World War-II, while the end of the cold war and emergence of myriad security challenges, Finland and Sweden needed more protection as they have been facing the threat of Russian aggression for years. Experts and analysts, Robin Forsberg and Jason C. Moyer in their paper (Sisters but Not Twins: Prospects of Finland and Sweden's NATO Accession-02 February 2022) have argued that in December, 2021, Russian Ministry of Foreign Affairs put forward an eight-point draft treaty with a list of security demands of the Western alliance, and also noted neutral policies of Finland and Sweden and their efforts to join NATO:

"In December 2021, the Russian Ministry of Foreign Affairs put forward an eight-point draft treaty with a list of security demands of the Western alliance. These include reverting NATO forces to 1997 positioning, banning new members from joining the alliance, and limiting NATO's presence in Eastern Europe. Washington responded that these points were unrealistic as they would entail the removal of multiple Eastern European countries from the NATO alliance and capitulate to Russia's desire for a greater sphere of influence over its neighbours. In a show of force, Russia positioned an estimated 100,000 troops along its border with Ukraine, with many fearing an imminent invasion of Ukraine. Renewed debates over NATO's Eastern European enlargement ambitions, the potential for further Russian aggression, and uncertainty over Ukraine's future have led other countries to reconsider their engagement with NATO – including

Finland and Sweden. Together with Austria, Cyprus, Ireland, and Malta, Finland and Sweden are the only EU states that are not members of NATO. Both have been militarily neutral since World War II, although the end of the Cold War reignited the NATO question in both countries...Finland is militarily non-aligned with an emphasis on a credible national defence. Politically, Finland has been a member of the European Union since 1995 and is bound by the common foreign and security...Sweden, by contrast, does not share a border with Russia. In public statements, the Swedish government declares it has a non-alignment policy that differs slightly from neutrality, yet is predicated on it. It sees this policy of non-alignment as a source of stability and security in the region, and enjoys widespread public support of this stance".[11]

The drug and gun culture in Sweden has threatened the lives of peaceful citizens. Every day this dangerous culture is prevailing in cities and towns, but police and law enforcement authorities are facing a precarious threat of gang war. Criminal gangs from Africa, South Asia and the Middle East have established business contacts with criminal and radicalized elements across the border. Smuggling, shootings around open drug markets in vulnerable neighbourhoods exhibiting a 30 times higher density in Malmö than for the city as a whole. Since the 2000s domestic radicalization has become a great concern in Europe's security agencies that radicalized groups might attack businesses and government installations. However, the number of people who have adopted radicalization have also engaged in serious organized crimes. Analysts and experts, Rune Ellefsen and Sveinung Sandberg in their paper (Everyday Prevention of Radicalization: The Impacts of Family, Peer, and Police Intervention, Studies in Conflict & Terrorism) have highlighted the scourge of radicalization in Norway:

"After the civil war in Syria erupted in 2011, the concern over radicalization of Muslims escalated dramatically in Europe. The war in Syria was a transformative event that mobilized Muslims globally, but only a minority radicalized to the point of actually leaving for Syria and taking part in extreme violent acts and terrorism. About 5,000 European Muslims travelled to Syria and Iraq to engage in the conflict, among them 100 Norwegians, while a much larger number considered doing so. As the Islamic State in Iraq and the Levant (IS/ISIL) launched armed insurgency in Syria, they initially attracted wide support among young Muslims across the world. However, as time passed, their support fell dramatically, following news reports of their atrocities and their eventual failure to maintain territorial control..... Policies to prevent radicalization and violent extremism have increasingly emphasized working closely with the families of radicalized individuals. Germany pioneered family support as part of their strategy against radicalization, and there are several other examples of government programs where police engage with the parents of potential terrorists. Involving families is also highlighted in recent governmental action plans to prevent radicalization and violent extremism in the Nordic countries. While police officers in Norway have emphasized the importance of engaging with family in their preventive work, actual engagement was still unusual because of what officers describe as a lack of access. Radicalization and terrorism scholars similarly emphasize the role of families for efforts to de-radicalize or disengage from violent extremism".[12]

The waves of extremism and radicalization in Austria are exacerbating by the day, while political leadership stress the need for legal options to fight extremism and introduce intelligence reforms. David Rising and Philipp Jenne have reported to Associated Press (Austria plans intelligence agency reforms after attack: Austrian leaders are calling for more legal options to fight extremism and for an overhaul of the country's domestic intelligence agency in the wake of this week's deadly attack blamed on an Islamic State sympathizer-5 November 2020) that Austria's leader had called for more legal options to fight extremism. Moreover, the Federal Agency for State Protection and Counterterrorism BVT is one of the most powerful institutions in Austria. Emerged from the working group on retained data Austria that has been active in Austria since 2010, picenter. works in its website comment (State Protection Act Resistance against the New Austrian Domestic Secret Service noted: "In order to carry out a corresponding reform, the BMI created the "BVT new" project, which is intended to realign the police intelligence service and state security in accordance with international standards. The Austrian Office for the Protection of the Constitution is to be reorganized and professionalized in terms of content due to international requirements and the events in recent years involving the Federal Office for the Protection of the Constitution and Counter-Terrorism."[13] However, Epicentre. Work in its recent report (12 benchmarks for the reform and oversight of intelligence services in Austria. February 10, 2021) noted new domestic secret service with far reaching surveillance powers:

"The Federal Agency for State Protection and Counterterrorism (abbreviated BVT in German) is one of the most powerful institutions in Austria. Yet there are hardly any other organisations of similar disrepute. There is no party which does not address deficiencies and the need for improvement.

Foreign intelligence services already restricted cooperation with the BVT years ago and abroad considers Austria a "security gap". An investigation committee on the house search in the BVT during the Kickl era and the terrorist attack in Vienna on 02 November 2020 have put plans for a reform on the agenda. Legislative proposals were announced for December, therefore they cannot build upon the expert commission's investigation and examination of the attack. When intelligence services fail to prevent terrorist attacks, they are usually rewarded with new surveillance powers. The anti-terror legislative package includes an ankle monitor for persons who pose a threat to public safety. This was already discussed in 2017, but when the Minister of Justice Brandstetter prevailed against minister of the interior Sobotka – both from the right-wing conservative party (ÖVP)–the issue was finally dropped. However, the BVT reform entails several substantial and highly complicated problems, even without new surveillance methods. There is no country in the world where the oversight of intelligence services is solved how we would like it to be, but there are many international best practices. In the following, epicenter works want to use these best practices to establish benchmarks, against which the new reform of the BVT must be measured. The present benchmarks are not civil society's wish list, but rather they are strongly guided by international standards and jurisdiction, which Austria is subject to and which are currently not met. The ruling Schrems II showed once again that the right to privacy in the digital age cannot be enforced unilaterally with regard to national security. Therefore, experts meanwhile call for an international standard in democratic intelligence practice, so that democratic states do not violate each other's human rights and undermine democracy".[14]

The United Kingdom is offering technical ways and mechanisms for peaceful resolution of ethnic and sectarian conflict to several Asian states including Afghanistan and Pakistan, but the country's successive governments have never been able to eradicate the roots of extremism, international terrorism, racism, ethnic and sectarian violence in Northern Ireland and Scotland. We often read heart-breaking statements of police and intelligence chiefs about the looming threat of international terrorism, cyber-attacks and experienced numerous changes in the National Security Strategy since 2007, but no proper solution has so for been sought. In 2018, The UK former Foreign Minister Boris Johnson warned that 'the issue of the Northern Irish border was being used politically to try to keep the UK in the customs union, effectively the single market, so we cannot really leave the EU'. Expert and analyst, Neil Dooley (2022) in his research paper (Frustrating Brexit? Ireland and the UK's conflicting approaches to Brexit negotiations, Journal of European Public Policy) has highlighted issues relating to Northern Ireland and the Brexit:

"Existing literature on Brexit negotiations has not focused explicitly on Ireland's negotiating success, and accordingly, the UK's negotiating failure regarding Ireland. It's possible that there is no puzzle to explain here. Why wouldn't the EU defend Ireland's interests against a country that was leaving? An unaccommodating stance towards the UK vis-à-vis Ireland can be viewed as an effective strategy of discouraging other EU member states from considering their own exit. Whether motivated by solidarity or a desire to 'frustrate Brexit', this explanation takes for granted EU support for Ireland. We don't need to spend time examining the relative successes or failures of Ireland/UK's own negotiating strategies. This explanation cannot tell the full story for the following reasons. First, the EU did not really need Ireland as leverage. It was already in a strong position to send a signal to member states about the negative consequences of an exit. The UK made major concessions to the EU, in the sequencing of negotiations, in a financial settlement, and access to the Single Market. The market and institutional power of the EU dwarfs the UK, and 'no deal' rhetoric aside, access to the EU market was always going to be too important for the UK to abandon without some form of a deal (Schimmelfennig, 2018)".[15]

Northern Ireland is a challenging province for the UK where war brought destruction and catastrophe. During the last 30 years of internal war, more than 3,500 people were killed. Finally a peace agreement was signed to establish a power-sharing government that included political forces aligned with armed groups. Central to Ireland's negotiating success was its strategic early and intensive diplomatic campaign. However, expert and analyst, David Ehl in his DW analysis (Northern Ireland's peace faces new Brexit threats: The 1972 Bloody Sunday massacre was a turning point in Northern Ireland's conflict. Peace has prevailed for a quarter of a century. That is a success that must now be defended against new threats-30 January 2022) documented historical events of war, fatalities and the signing of the Good Friday Agreement in Northern Ireland. Writer Ehl also noted the first report that was written hurriedly in April 1972 that exonerated the soldiers involved in the killing of innocent civilians. But the Saville Report, presented 38 years later, meticulously reconstructed the course of events of the massacre:

"The events of January 30, 1972, in Northern Ireland's second largest city, Londonderry, were a turning point, however: In an already politically charged atmosphere, British soldiers shot two dozen unarmed people at a protest. We know now that the commanders' aim was to show toughness and demonstrate the state's monopoly on the use of force. The result, however, was that the conflict between the Irish Catholic nationalists and the mostly Protestant unionists spiralled further. The IRA registered a large number of new members and continued to stoke the violence: 1972 became the bloodiest year in the entire conflict, with almost 500 deaths. Bloody Sunday is the only event in British history that has been investigated by two judicial commissions. The first report, hastily written in April 1972, seemed to mostly serve the purpose of exonerating the soldiers. But the Saville Report, presented 38 years later, meticulously reconstructed the course of events of the massacre and leaves no doubt about the interpretation: The paratroopers fired on civilians, none of whom posed a threat, and 14 British citizens were ultimately murdered in an operation commissioned by the state. In 2010, after the report was completed, Prime Minister David Cameron asked for forgiveness. For the bereaved families, who had fought for so long against the prejudiced portrayal of the first report, this was an important victory. But today, 50 years after the fateful day, it is more uncertain than ever whether even one of the shooters will ever be prosecuted. The greatest threat for the further investigation of Bloody Sunday and all other atrocities of the Northern Ireland conflict comes from the British government: Prime Minister Boris Johnson, who admittedly has quite different concerns right now, wants to put the conflict in the past. In 2021, the government published key points for a statute of limitations to end all prosecutions."[16]

The United Kingdom is facing numerous political, social and economic challenges since the Brexit referendum in June 2016. Relationships with the EU member states remain in strain, while internal political turmoil and disagreement between opposition and ruling coalition on the triggering of article 50 prompted wide-ranging debate in print and electronic media across the country. With the commencement of year 2022, British Prime Minister has been in muzzy and some of his party members raised important questions about the loss of the single European market after withdrawal from the project. The British economy appears to have weathered the initial shock of the referendum vote in 2016, and the value of Sterling Pound remained near a 30-years low. The EU single market is seen by its advocates as a great achievement but the present political and financial ruckus across the continent has put it in danger. The market which was completed in 1992 that facilitated free movement of goods and other related materials across Europe, but recent borders restrictions and terrorist attacks in some EU member states, the future of single market has become bleak. Major political, economic, and technological developments in the continent and distrust between Britain and the EU project has prompted a questionable situation in the trade market of the country, which is very much dependent on imports from the European Union. Experts and analysts, Dr Hager Ben Jaffel and Dr Jeremy Pearson have reviewed the relationship between the UK and European Union in their article (Intelligence, law enforcement and Brexit, UK in a Changing Europe. 26 Feb 2021):

"Despite what politicians say or want about Brexit, the need to ensure post-Brexit cooperation caused UK policing to embark upon a significant programme of engagement with European law enforcement agencies in the months prior to EU exit. This signalled that they sought to pragmatically manage any disruption that Brexit might have brought and ensure continued mutual cooperation. During the period leading to EU exit, the potential loss of access to policing tools such as the Schengen Information System (SIS II) and the European Arrest Warrant (EAW) caused UK policing bodies to critically evaluate international policing mechanisms and to identify contingency measures that would mitigate any potential loss of capability. Significant investment was committed to building policing structures that would provide operational support to police forces across the UK and to better manage international requests for operational support. The creation, in 2018, of the International Crime Coordination Centre (ICCC) is the most obvious example of these efforts. The long history of joint intelligence sharing and existing networks, such as the UK liaison officer network within Europe, provide a solid base upon which expanded future cooperation arrangements must be built. Moving forward, the law enforcement mission must be to ensure that future cooperation is as seamless as possible. For a number of years, the UK has marginalized Interpol in favour of Europol. The post-Brexit loss of SIS II and other European policing tools has caused British law enforcement agencies to once again see the importance of this long-established international policing organisation".[17]

On 23 June 2016, the United Kingdom held a referendum which left deep impacts on the business industry in both Europe and the UK. Now, with this act of the British government, the EU would apply its external customs duties on the UK goods, and it may possibly introduce non-tariff hurdles for goods. However, Brussels can also restrict the UK's ability to conduct euro transactions and euro-derivatives transactions, and thereby undermine the position of the London city as the financial centre of the world. The UK citizens can also lose their right of open trade in all EU member states. Moreover, there are many factors of Brexit that can impact the UK based business organizations while some EU member states like Germany, Italy and Spain want integration. Brexit may also cause political instability in the UK and EU or the collapse of the European Union, inflame anti-EU sentiments in the UK and can empower nationalist and Eurosceptic forces. Brexit would not only be bad for Britain, it will also affect the EU markets. After a successful campaign, former Prime Minister David Cameron resigned on the pretext that he was against Brexit, while the fact of the matter is, he was behind the whole story, in which he played a crucial role. As a Prime Minister, David Cameron was very upset by the underwhelming attitude of EU leaders. They never allowed him to act independently, and challenged many internal policies of his government. These and other disagreements prompted the withdrawal of Britain from the European Union. Expert Dr Stefania Paladini has noted in her comment (Intelligence and National Security. Birmingham City Business School) the consequences of Brexit and intelligence relationship between the UK and European Union:

"The exit of the United Kingdom from the European Union should not pose any special challenge under these regards: the UK and most EU members will remain member states of NATO, with the ensuing obligations in matters of defence and reciprocal obligations. A UK exit out of Eurojust will make all the procedures less effective and more time consuming, in the case of extradition outside the EAW framework. While it is difficult to forecast at this stage which kind of alternative will be devised to address similar issues, there will be an enhanced need for additional coordination that will be carried out under a different framework. In terms of people's movement across the EU, one of the contentious areas of the Brexit, there will be certainly be an impact on immigration rules, policies, border security practices on both sides of the Channel: UK borders will become tighter rather than more porous, during the negotiations and at the end of a Brexit process, but, a diminished cooperation between the border police enforcement agencies across the Channel might will probably create a series of issues and make more challenging the exchange of critical information".[18]

In the Netherlands, jihadism has spread across the country into a complex and dynamic movement, which poses a precarious challenge to the national security of the country. A recent report of Dutch intelligence, AIVD, was a stern warning to the law enforcement authorities and to the government in power that terrorist networks posed serious security threats. Wars in Afghanistan, Syria and Yemen provoked violent forces in the country. Home-grown extremism has also forced the government and law enforcement agencies to introduce laws and reorganise preventive measures. Major political, economic, and technological developments in the continent and distrust between Britain and the EU project has prompted a questionable situation in the trade market of the country, which is very much dependent on imports from the European Union. The UK's 58 percent exports go to EU, which is the biggest trade volume in the continent. Germany, Netherland and France are its bigger trade partners, while the United States also boosts the UK market by investing billions of dollars in various sectors. International trade is undoubtedly the exchange of capital, products and import and export-related activities across borders, but as is evident from the fact, the UK economy is dependent on foreign trade, for that reason the country is active in multifaceted trade activities worldwide. There are hundreds of largest international trade and investment corporations operating here of which more than 60 belong to the US investors.

Writer and analyst, Mark Galeotti in his analysis (The secret battlefield: How the EU can help Georgia, Moldova, and Ukraine protect against Russian subversion. Policy Brief 15 December 2021, European council on foreign relations 15 December 2021) has highlighted how the European Union can protect Georgia, Moldova, and Ukraine against Russian invasion: "Various bilateral intelligence-related agreements and joint projects exist between particular EU member state agencies and Georgia, Moldova, and Ukraine. These tend to relate to law enforcement work, counter-intelligence, and cyber-security. They are often quite limited in scope, and are strictly bilateral in nature. Georgia, Moldova, and Ukraine also have agreements with Europol, and liaison officers in that organisation. However, across the region, this is a propitious moment for the EU to develop a collective intelligence partnership with these three states. When Ukraine's president, Volodymyr Zelensky, asserted earlier this year that "there is no alternative to the reform of the [Security] Service, and there will never be," he committed Ukraine to serious intelligence reform. He also dismissed a number of key figures within the SZV and the Security Service of Ukraine (SBU). This was in preparation for the final passage of a law that would reduce the size of the SBU and, in particular, transfer the investigation of organised and financial crimes to a new Bureau of Economic Security (BES), as well as the National Anti-Corruption Bureau and the National Police. This is therefore a good opportunity for Europe to support a country of which Borrell has said "your security will be our security" and seize a moment when Kyiv is likely to be especially receptive to partnership and advice. In Moldova, just weeks before incoming president Maia Sandu took office at the end of 2020, parliament made attempts to strip her of control of the Security and Intelligence Service (SIS; also widely known as the SIB, from its title in Russian). The law passed, but a legal ruling declared it unconstitutional in April 2021. Ironically, this incident pushed the question of reform of the sector up the political agenda, with protesters taking to the street in support of the president. At her speech commemorating the SIS's thirtieth anniversary, in October 2021, Sandu singled out the need for both practical and political reform of the service".[19]

# Chapter 3

# The UK Big-3: Challenges of Foreign Espionage, and Intelligence Cooperation with European Union

The British intelligence agencies are operating in miscellaneous political and social environments to protect the interests of the country. They are dancing professionally and acting legally when they come to the security and protection of national and economic assets. During the Iraq war, political leadership misused their power and expertise to find weapons of mass destruction but failed. Without authentication and page proof of the existence of weapons of mass destruction, invading a poor country and destroying its military infrastructure was unsubstantiated, groundless, and unsupported by the international community. It has since become clear that the US and British governments had only a wrong understanding of Iraqi's so-called weapons of mass destruction, and they were unable to characterize the scale of the Iraqi effort that they described as a key motive for the conflict. The British and US leadership failure over Iraq's weapons of mass destruction (WMD) is one of the most intense investigations in recent times. There was a chain of debates in the UK parliament to discuss the catastrophe inflicted on Iraqi Muslims. The destruction of Libya was an act of revenge, and tit for tat while invasion of Afghanistan was to control its mineral resources. In all these conflicts, the UK and US Armed Forces failed to bring home-roasted Gallus-Gallus.

Most of the current intelligence challenges of the UK and European Union, whether they relate to predicting surprise attacks, the politicization of intelligence, or questions of ethics and privacy, are old conundrums. However, it is hard to escape the feeling that closer attention to obvious lessons from the past would have assisted intelligence sharing of these states in avoiding the Taliban, ISIS and other ethnic and sectarian group's attacks on civilian and military installations. Bureaucratic control of unreformed intelligence operations, government and private stakeholders, and ethnic and sectarian factors are the most important aspects of any intelligence infrastructure in a state, where these conflicting developments paralyze an intelligence agency. Expert and analyst, Christiaan Menkveld (Understanding the complexity of intelligence problems) in his research paper noted that effective intelligence and security services need to take the complexity of an intelligence problem into account when determining the aims of their investigation, the strategy of intelligence collection and its analytic approach:

"The complexity of an intelligence problem (required intelligence assessment on a certain subject) determines to a great extent the certainty that intelligence and security services can provide on such an assessment. Even though this claim sounds almost obvious, its implications are significant, because it means that the public value of an intelligence service can vary depending on the complexity of an intelligence problem. This ranges from providing 'actionable' intelligence that can lead to interventions (legal, military, interruption operations, etc.), to providing insights that can be used as input for policymakers and as context for interventions. Therefore, to be effective, intelligence and security services need to take the complexity of an intelligence problem into account when determining the aims of their investigation, the strategy of intelligence collection and its analytic approach. This also means that intelligence clients and oversight officials and legislators should take the complexity of intelligence problems into account when directing and appraising the performance of services."[1]

In the UK parliament, debate on the Afghan crisis and Ukraine raised important questions including failure of intelligence to assess the real elements of state collapse. Clarifying his position on Afghanistan, the British Foreign Secretary said he did not call his Afghan counterpart to assist the evacuation of Afghan translators who worked with the UK because he was prioritizing the security of Kabul airport. "The UK government's overriding priority has been to secure Kabul airport so that flights can leave," Dominic Raab said in a statement. He was facing mounting calls to resign over his alleged lackluster response to the collapse of the Afghan government and the Taliban's power grab. The debate (MPs "ashamed" of aspects of the UK. withdrawal from Afghanistan and concerned about parallels emerging in the UK's response to Ukraine on 4, March, 2022) criticised government for its failed approach to work effectively supporting the Afghan people: "The UK Government failed to work effectively or quickly enough to provide support for aid workers and the Afghan people, a new report from the International Development Committee–Afghanistan revealed. Furthermore, the Committee was concerned about the pace at which the UK Government had disbursed pledged UK aid to Afghanistan and whether it will act swiftly enough to disburse pledged UK aid to Ukraine. The Chair of the International Development Committee, Sarah Champion said: "We are deeply grateful to aid workers-be they British, Afghan or of other nationalities–for all they have done for the people of Afghanistan. The work that they do is phenomenal. "But we are ashamed that the Government did not give them the support that they needed during the UK's withdrawal, or now, during the complex task of delivering an aid programme under Taliban rule. "More than 23 million people, over half the population of Afghanistan, are facing starvation. The Government must provide the support and the clarity that people working in the aid sector in Afghanistan have told us that they need."[2]

Analyst and expert Bowman H. Miller, in his research analysis (U.S. Intelligence Credibility in the Crosshairs: On the Post-War Defensive) documented failure of British and American intelligence agencies in Iraq and Afghanistan to authenticate weapons of mass destruction and international terrorism in Afghanistan: "Leaks in the U.S. Intelligence Vessel Equally, if not more, damaging to the reputation of both U.S. intelligence and American diplomacy have been the mammoth, unlawful disclosures of diplomatic reporting by U.S. Army Specialist Bradley (now Chelsea) Manning via Wikileaks and the haemorrhaging of even more costly leaks by Edward Snowden exposing a variety of sensitive U.S. intelligence efforts and capabilities. These two millennials, claiming high-minded motivations for their criminal behaviour and violation of public trust, have caused untold harm to U.S. national security with their actions. Regardless of their reasoning, the fact remains that some in the United States and many abroad, particularly in political, parliamentary, and media ranks, were all too pleased to have access to such supposed "hard evidence" of alleged U.S. intelligence malfeasance and illicit activity. Tales of espionage, snooping, and such make for lively press, if not media sensationalism, but there is ample fire behind the smoke to make many of these recent accounts and accusations of U.S. misdeeds and violations of trust appear accurate. The Snowden case and its revelations continue. The fact that reporters for the Guardian in Britain write about them and draw from them not while on British soil but writing from Brazil—beyond the normal reach of UK intelligence and security agencies MI5 and MI6—is testimony to the supposition that their publication is most likely in violation of the UK Official Secrets Act's provisions. The "temporary" Russian exile of Snowden likewise attests to similar fugitive status in his own case but also perhaps, for a while at least, After the Wars 207 to Snowden being a welcome and apparently informative house guest of the Federal Security Service (FSB), a KGB successor agency."[3]

Xinhua News Agency (British security tactics proved ineffective, outdated. March 1, 2015) reported former shadow Home Secretary David Davis that Britain's intelligence services had long utilized tactics that had proved "ineffective, "with a series of security failures showing a "worrying pattern". "One of the results of this policy was that it left known terrorists both to carry out evil deeds and to recruit more conspirators. As a result, the problem on the street grown progressively larger," Davis wrote in the Guardian newspaper. He said it was "extraordinary" that Mohammed Emwazi, the masked "Jihadi John" who was pictured in a number of videos released by the Islamic State (IS) showing beheadings of western hostages, "escaped the attentions of the security services." Mohammed Emwazi, a university-educated Briton from west London, was believed to have been known by British intelligence services before he fled to Syria and joined the IS. "These failures are part of a worrying pattern," Davis said, citing similar cases in connection with the 9/11 attacks in the United States in 2001, the 7/7 London bombings in 2015, and the Charlie Hebdo shooting in Paris this year. Xinhua reported.[4] Expert and research scholar Robert Jervis in his research paper (Reports, Politics, and Intelligence Failures: The Case of Iraq) has highlighted in detail the failure of UK and UK's intelligence in Iraq to find weapons of mass destruction:

"If intelligence services do not stand out in having a hard time reforming themselves, they are unusual in that their major errors are believed to be so consequential. In fact, the relationships between policy and intelligence in Iraq and elsewhere are complex and often unclear. One argument (analysed in the reports and discussed below) is that the intelligence was politicized – i.e., illegitimately influenced by the IC's knowledge of the answers the policy-makers wanted to hear. More obviously, causation is believed to run the other way, as intelligence informs policy. The fact that only those countries that supported the war held investigations is consistent with this view (although another possible reason is that intelligence is not seen as important in France and Germany), and most of the investigations imply a link between intelligence and policy. They almost have to: if there were none, why bother with the investigation? The most obvious sense of intelligence failure is a mismatch between the estimates and what later information reveals to have been true. This is simultaneously the most important and least interesting sense of the term. It is most important because this is what policy-makers and the public care about. To the extent that policy depends on accurate assessments, almost the only thing that matters is accuracy. In two ways, the brute fact of the intelligence failure is uninteresting, however. First, it does not take intensive probes to decide that there was a failure here; all that is required is the knowledge that what was found in Iraq did not match the assessments. Second, the fact that intelligence often is in error does not surprise scholars and should not surprise policy-makers."[5]

The three pillars of the UK intelligence machinery are Big-3 with important work carried out by Defence Intelligence and the Joint Terrorism Analysis Centre. Since 2016, the word global Britain has been appearing in British and international media that Britain wanted to have an independent voice, but things evolved differently while it faced a different political and economic crisis. Altercation with the European Union over the border of Northern Ireland further caused mistrust. Experts and analysts, Anisa Heritage and Pak K. Lee, (Global Britain': The UK in the Indo-Pacific: While its involvement is broadly welcomed in the region, the U.K. must first clarify what its Indo-Pacific presence will entail. The Diplomat--January 08, 2021) in their paper highlighted challenges faced by the UK after the announcement of Brexit referendum:

"Since 2016, the phrase "Global Britain" has been used to signal the ambition and intent of the United Kingdom to seek "an independent voice" in international diplomacy outside and beyond the European Union. But to date the phrase remains deliberately vague.....The current Integrated Review of Security, Defence, and Development Policy, the most comprehensive review of its kind undertaken in the U.K., was heralded by Prime Minister Boris Johnson as a much-needed overhaul that would consider "the totality of global opportunities and challenges the U.K. faces and determining how the whole of government can be structured, equipped and mobilized to meet them." The first House of Commons report on the integrated review in August 2020 acknowledged that Brexit and a more isolationist U.S. have challenged the U.K's position as the bridge between the EU and the United States. The report also recognized the vulnerabilities of a middle power navigating an increasingly competitive and tense international environment. Although the U.K's foreign policy strategy will be officially revealed later in 2021, evidence already points to a substantial orientation of its security, development, and trade policies toward the Indo-Pacific–a tilt welcomed by many U.K. partners in the region. Prior to the U.K's official exit from the EU, the Johnson government started pursuing partnerships and initiatives beyond EU-27 collective positions.

It issued a joint statement on Hong Kong in coordination with other Five Eyes partners in May 2020, before the EU released its own statement in July. Johnson is also leading an initiative to build a "D10" alliance of democracies–the G-7 plus Australia, South Korea, and India–to create alternative suppliers of 5G equipment and other technology to reduce China's domination of global digital infrastructure. It is as yet unclear how the proposed D10 arrangements might synchronize with U.S. President-elect Joe Biden's plans to convene a Summit for Democracy".[6]

There are a multitude of perceptions about the work, popular and communal relationships, and the course of action of British intelligence agencies (The Big-3), the policing and their private partners in research papers, newspapers, journals and books that spotlight their course of action and weaknesses in domestic and international fronts. There are countless books available in markets and libraries that discuss professionalization and controversies, and elucidate the operational mechanism of the Big-3 and the whole body of other horses who rum sometimes in unknown directions. From Iraq to Afghanistan, Syria and Ukraine, experts and scholars raised different questions in the realm of strategic and technological intelligence operation, and its relevance to parliament and policy makers. The reason that the Big-3 have often been reluctant to engage directly with the public due to concerns surrounding their secrecy. They are being represented by print and electronic media to convince communities and policy makers that everything was going on in right direction. The facia near to the Big-3 demonstrates differing approaches to openness and secrecy, with Britain seemingly favouring the latter when compared to her American counterpart. Now they are more open in the media in their professional and sometimes political statements. We read political statements of the Big-3 leadership in newspapers and electronic media every day. They demonstrate like political leaders and dance like military commanders, but we cannot judge what Gallus-Gallus they roasted and what their share with policymakers is. Expert and PhD Scholar, Abigail Julia Blyth in his thesis (The British Intelligence Services in the public domain: Thesis submitted in partial fulfilment of the requirements for the degree of PhD. Department of International Politics Aberystwyth University 2019) highlighted how the relationship between the Big-3 and the public is conducted:

"The Intelligence accountability literature increasingly acknowledges how the relationship between British Intelligence and the public is conducted by the media, and specifically news journalism. However, despite the centrality of this relationship, Richard Aldrich rightly argues it has received minimal analysis. This is slowly changing, as those specialising in intelligence accountability such as Claudia Hillebrand, Cris Matei, Karen Lund Petersen, Sir David Omand, Mike Goodman and Robert Dover examine the relationship between intelligence and the media, this thesis will contribute to the growing discussion due to the contemporary analysis undertaken. Hillebrand's analysis of news journalists reporting on intelligence proved a useful starting point, as she explores how they are crucial to inform and educate the public in the realm of intelligence. However, news journalism's scrutiny of intelligence matters remains indirect, informal and infrequent, arguably due to the media strategies adopted by the Intelligence Services and their Governments. Hillebrand argues that these actions include the use of excessive secrecy which acts as a blanket to conceal abuse, corruption, or incompetence, only providing sporadic information from insiders, and the Intelligence Services simply refusing to respond to stories which journalists are reporting on. All of these contribute to the limited coverage of intelligence issues by restricting the work of news journalists".[7]

The Big-3 are in full cooperation with domestic and international security actors, share intelligence, receive reciprocity and enjoying the whole recipes to ensure their taste is better. Small and private actors are doing their entrusted job to help the Big-3 against complex and globalised threats. The Police is dancing well and shares its tast with the Big-3. In world wars, the Big-3 were playing excellent role, in cold war they played against communist bloc magnificently, but after the cold war, their way of operation and perceptions of war on terrorism in Iraq, Libya and Afghanistan changed. The Big-3 was in full cooperation with the CIA, Eyes Five and Pentagon in their bad business in Iraq and Afghanistan. All round their history, colours of military influence on their operational mechanism in Iraq, and Afghanistan were crystal clear, and that course of operations manufactured their military perception of intelligence operation. Different merits including facets of the military were engaged with the Big-3 leadership. Recent research found that these engagements prompted militarization of operational mechanism of the Big-3. Expert and scholar, Abigail Julia Blyth in his thesis (The British Intelligence Services in the public domain: Thesis submitted in partial fulfilment of the requirements for the degree of PhD. Department of International Politics Aberystwyth University 2019) explained capabilities of the Big-3 during the Second World War:

"Following the end of the Second World War, Britain sought to ensure their intelligence capabilities remained, albeit in a more cost-effective and centralised manner which created the Joint Intelligence Bureau. They had responsibility for a myriad of intelligence activities, including topographic, economic, industrial and scientific intelligence. These would not only have aided the military at a time of rising tensions with the Soviet Union, but also the wider Government and in particular the Big 3, who were also seeking to counter the Soviet threat. Therefore, the forerunner to DI would have had close cooperation with the Big 3 due to the nature of the work undertaken, and this is something that undoubtedly continues. The London headquarters of both MI5 and MI6 are also surrounded by high levels of security, with the MI6 headquarters surrounded by high gates, with guards stationed at them. Although, unlike armed forces personnel, the staff of MI5 and MI6 do not wear uniforms, the latter are nevertheless clearly part of a professional community set apart from other civil servants. This is perhaps furthered by the amount of secrecy which governs their work, something the former DG Dame Stella Rimington has referred to. She stated that during her time in MI5, she was part of a separate and distinctive community, characterised in part by the prohibition on discussing work matters with outsiders. In practice, this meant that MI5 staff socialised almost exclusively with one another, narrowing their social circle considerably, particularly evident in how the Big 3 all have clubs and societies for staff and their families to use. Phillip Knightley agrees, asserting that those working within the intelligence services tend to socialise predominantly with one another, as they are able to relax in each other' company, as opposed to being wary of anyone deemed an outsider".[8]

Following the 7/7 terrorist attacks in London, poor performance of Big-3 raised important questions including their underwhelming domestic security approach. Government established Joint Terrorism Analysis Centre with the appointment of MI5 staff, and policing experts to counter-terrorism in UK, but recent terrorist attacks exhibited that the Centre's performance has been underwhelming. The centre was accountable to the DG of MI5, but terrorist succeeded to carry out more attacks despite its preparedness. The London, Birmingham and Manchester attacks raised important question on the credibility of Joint Terrorism Analysis Centre and the MI5 who had failed to intercept terror elements before they translated their anger into violent attacks. Later on, the GCHQ extended its hand of cooperation to other government organizations, while the MI6 leadership acknowledged difficulties of its officers, and pointed to the fact that there were some failures. Expert Abigail Julia Blyth in his research thesis (The British Intelligence Services in the public domain: Thesis submitted in partial fulfilment of the requirements for the degree of PhD. Department of International Politics Aberystwyth University 2019) noted the intelligence dimension of numerous organizations in their work:

"Over the past 15 years, the British Government has created numerous organisations with an intelligence role, arguably due to the Government's desire to ensure a cohesive cross-Government approach to terrorism, as well as overcoming the problems surrounding the politicisation of intelligence following the Iraq War. The Joint Terrorism Analysis Centre (JTAC) sought to develop coordinated arrangements for handling and disseminating intelligence in response to the international terrorist threat. Whilst being an organisation within MI5, it is staffed by 16 different Government departments and agencies, suggesting that organisational difficulties could occur. This is also evident in the case of The Centre for Protection of National Infrastructure (CPNI), which is situated within the Cabinet Office and by working with the Government and the private sector, aids protection of Britain's critical national infrastructure. The newly established National Cyber Security Centre (NCSC) also uses the expertise of staff from across Government and its website clearly states how it is part of GCHQ. This is in conjunction with the National Technical Assistance Centre (NTAC), which manages intercepted communications data to those entities who have requested it, also being located within GCHQ, despite their extensive cooperation with the wider Government. This demonstrates how new organisations are continually created, with staffing coming directly from the Big 3 and other entities. Therefore, there are structural difficulties relating to ensuring the analysis and dissemination of intelligence in a timely manner".[9]

There are perceptions within different political, religious and government circles that the Big-3 is a male dominated establishment where all decisions are being taken by males while minority community's representation is underwhelming. In 2018, the Intelligence and Security Committee published a paper on diversity to highlight the percentage of BAME and LGBT within the Big-3. The report covers the issue of diversity and inclusion in each of the seven organisations overseen by the Intelligence and Security Committee. In its report (Intelligence and Security Committee of Parliament. Diversity and Inclusion in the UK Intelligence Community. Presented to Parliament pursuant to section 3 of the Justice and Security Act 2013. 18 July 2018) Intelligence and Security Committee noted efforts of different security organs to introduce new plan to recruit people from BAME community but there are some hindrances that need to be addressed:

"Whilst we are informed that over half of the vetting officers (the individuals who conduct vetting interviews) in SIS and MI5 are women, an aspect that was repeatedly mentioned was that the majority of the vetting officers across the wider intelligence community are still white, male and middle-aged. Anecdotally, it is apparent that they have a particular approach formed by their own personal experiences and background, both personal and professional. A number of individuals we spoke to from under-represented groups suggested that it would be helpful if all vetting officers were to receive specific training on cultural and behavioural norms – in areas such as personal relationships and finance, for example. We understand that vetting officers across the Agencies undertake professional development training on gender and identity awareness, and that active measures are being taken in some parts of the intelligence community to train and develop a more varied group of individuals to take on this important role. The Committee welcomes this initiative and will monitor progress on this important issue. The vetting process is, and will need to remain, an extremely thorough and intrusive process which, by necessity, investigates and evaluates every area of an individual's life. However, that is all the more reason why the officers undertaking this important work should themselves be more diverse. There is increasing collaboration across the intelligence community in terms of development and leadership programmes, with the delivery of Inspiring Women Leaders, Inspiring BAME Leaders, and Inspiring LGBT Leaders – programmes that draw on the expertise of external partners and have been developed for personnel working in the Agencies. The staff we talked to welcome the partnerships being developed with external organisations such as Stonewall and Business in the Community – this type of benchmarking was raising the profile of LGBT, race and gender issues across their organisations (and also proving a useful recruiting tool). Greater collaboration on diversity across the community and within the private sector would no doubt bring benefits".[10]

No doubt, the Big-3 and their partners are committed to be inclusive and diverse workplaces, a theme particularly emphasised by MI6. Recent statements and programmes of Big-3 indicated that they were going to introduce their leadership and workforce as a symbol of diversity. In yesteryears, there was no gay officials within intelligence agencies. A number of gay and homosexuals were hiding their sexuality for career purposes. Expert and Professor Daniel W. B. Lomas has highlighted this in his paper (Daniel W. B. Lomas. July 2021 Forget James Bond: diversity, inclusion and the UK's intelligence agencies, Intelligence and National Security, 36:7, 995-1017, DOI:10.1080/02684527.2021.1938370) the issue of diversity and efforts of Richard Moore to relax his organization's recruitment rules to allow applicants within dual UK nationality:

"In February 2021, The Times reported that Britain's foreign intelligence agency, the Secret Intelligence Service (SIS or MI6), was relaxing rules to allow applicants with dual UK nationality, or with one parent being a UK national or having 'substantial ties to the UK', to apply. Sources told the paper it was just the latest move to access a 'larger talent pool', adding: 'We want a diversification of thought, a diverse workforce, not people who all think in similar ways'. Later, marking LGBT History Month 2021, SIS's Chief ('C') Richard Moore followed other agency heads in apologising for the historical treatment of LGBT (Lesbian, gay, bisexual and transgender) officials and the bar to gay men and women serving in SIS. In a video shared on his Twitter feed, Moore said the ban deprived SIS of 'some of the best talent Britain could offer' and was 'wrong, unjust and discriminatory'. PinkNews also interviewed two LGBT SIS officers. 'I think the legacy of the ban has been ... helping people understand that LGBT+ people aren't inherently untrustworthy', said 'Leia', a member of SIS's LGBT+ Affinity Group. 'It's drawn a line in the sand', she added. The statements and media coverage mark just the latest in a series of announcements on the agency's commitment to diversity and change. In January 2021, tabloid newspapers reported on an SIS recruitment drive, specifically an advert, headlined 'Tell me a secret', calling for 'individuals with diverse skill sets and life experiences' to apply for part-time and consulting roles. Responding, Moore tweeted his service's commitment to 'flexible working' and 'diversity'. '#ForgetJamesBond', he added, acknowledging that Bond often shaped perceptions of the ideal intelligence officer. Sir Colin McColl, 'C' from 1989 to 1994, once described the fictional intelligence officer as, in his view, 'the best recruiting sergeant in the world', yet successive Chiefs, like Moore, have tried to distance themselves, seeing Bond's legacy as both a blessing and a curse. In October 2016, Moore's predecessor, Alex Younger, admitted he was 'conflicted' about Bond, on the one hand creating a 'powerful brand', although one that seemed exclusively white and male. 'For too long – often because of the fictional stereotypes I have mentioned – people have felt that there is a single quality that defines an MI6 officer', Younger told journalists in his first public speech in SIS's Vauxhall Cross headquarters, 'be it an Oxbridge education or a proficiency in hand-to-hand combat. This is, of course, patently untrue'. There was 'no standard MI6 officer".[11]

The Blair Government acknowledged that 'evidence of Saddam's weapons of mass destruction was indeed less certain and less well-founded than was stated at the time'. This means policymakers were kept in the dark. Mark Simmonds never discussed events leading up to the Iraq war, until after the publication of the much anticipated Chilcot Inquiry. Following the terrorist attacks of September 11, 2001, the CIA established secret detention centres known as "black sites," outside the United States, where Muslim were subjected to "enhanced interrogation techniques" that involved torture and other abuse. The US and NATO attacked Afghanistan just to plunder its natural resources, and train more terrorist groups in order to keep the fire ignited. The role of our intelligence agencies in kidnapping British citizens and handing them over to the CIA has been an underwhelming business during the last 20 years. In his Open Democracy article (The Belhaj case shows British intelligence agencies are out of control: Tony Blair's non-apology to the victim of 'extraordinary rendition'–and Jack Straw and Theresa May's attempts to draw a line under the issue–raise more questions than they answer.. Open democracy-22 May 2018), Richard Norton-Taylor Has noted the role of MI6, MI5 and GCHQ in war against terrorism:

"For years, Britain's three security and intelligence agencies – the Secret Intelligence Service, commonly known as MI6; the domestic Security Service, MI5; and GCHQ, the worldwide communications eavesdropping agency – have insisted they are accountable to ministers, that they are responsible to democratically-elected politicians. And for years, ministers have insisted that the agencies are properly accountable to them. We all now know what some of us have been saying for a very long time: such assertions are myths. The Prime Minister herself has admitted it. On 13 December 2005, Jack Straw, then foreign secretary responsible for MI6, told the Commons Foreign Affairs Committee: "Unless we all start to believe in conspiracy theories and that the officials are lying, that I am lying, that behind this there is some kind of secret state which is in league with some dark forces in the United States …There is simply no truth in the claims that the United Kingdom has been involved in rendition full stop, because we have never been". Straw added that the British government was not compliant in rendition, nor did it turn a blind eye to it. This was not true. On 18 March 2004 – nine months before Straw gave his denials to MPs – Mark Allen, head of MI6's counter-terrorism section, wrote to Moussa Koussa, foreign intelligence chief of the Libyan dictator, Muammar Gaddafi, congratulating him on "the safe arrival" of Abdel Hakim Belhaj – the Libyan national in the news last week after Theresa May was forced to apologise to him and his wife for Britain's role in their rendition. Faced with such clear evidence of British involvement in rendition operations, Straw told the BBC on 5 September 2011: "No foreign secretary can know all the details of what its intelligence agencies are doing at any one time." The Metropolitan Police opened a criminal investigation and questioned Straw and Allen. After four years they handed a file to the Crown Prosecution Service (CPS). In 2016, the CPS announced that neither Straw nor Allen would face charges because of insufficient evidence".[12]

Moreover, BBC (28 October 2010) reported head of MI6, Sir John Sawers assertions that torture was illegal and abhorrent and defended the service's need for secrecy. He said his organisation faced "real, constant operational dilemmas" to avoid using intelligence which had been gathered by torture. He also said secrecy was not a dirty word and played a crucial part in keeping Britain safe and secure. The issue of torture came to prominence with the case of Binyamin Mohamed, particularly when he was returned to the UK in early 2009. He had been held in Pakistan in 2002 before US agencies moved him to Morocco, where he was severely tortured and then ended up in Guantanamo Bay. BBC reported. Adam Brown in his article (Secret affairs with radical Islam: why Britain's covert foreign policy needs to change. November 8th, 2010) reported the condemnation of Binyamin Muhammad case by a British most senior judge:

"Earlier this year the case of Binyam Mohamed resulted in the severe condemnation, by one of Britain's most senior judges, of Britain's Security Service, finding that they had "failed to respect human rights, deliberately misled parliament and had a "culture of suppression" that undermined government assurances about its conduct." It was shown that MI5 officers were complicit in the ill-treatment of a British resident, causing him "significant mental stress and suffering" – he had been tortured. Such was the severity of Judge Neuberger's draft judgement, that MI5 lawyer Jonathan Sumption QC, privately wrote to the court asking that the judgement be reconsidered before being handed down. The British government's response to this case was denial and attempts to judicially suppress the classified information exposed by the case from the public. American CIA agents were also implicated in the human rights violations and as foreign secretary David Miliband argued, the case was causing a "great deal of concern" in the US and that the release of such material could endanger intelligence sharing between the two countries. The West has been activity fostering and aiding Islamic terrorists and groups, for over fifty years. However, rarely has this information entered the mainstream debate on terrorism and its causes. The media often portray the emergence of terrorism, particularly Islamic terrorism, as an anomaly, born out of a new post-Cold War era. Like most things, however, it has not appeared out of thin air."[13]

On 16 December 2020, the Investigatory Powers Tribunal revealed that the UK intelligence unilaterally assumed the power to authorise agents to commit crimes in the UK–potentially without any legal basis or limits on the crimes they can commit. Reprieve, the Pat Finucane Centre, Privacy International, and CAJ were challenging a secret policy under which MI5 authorised covert agents, known as covert human intelligence sources or CHIS, to commit crimes in the UK.[14] The Committee on the Administration of Justice which was established in 1981 as an independent non-governmental organisation in its recent comment expressed deep concern that intelligence agencies of the UK may get authorization to commit crime. The Committee also reported in its comment that in 2020, British foreign intelligence was forced by the Tribunal to apologise when its officers wrongly sought to stop independent judges from scrutinising the agency's activities: "These revelations come only a day after the Investigatory Powers Commissioner severely criticised MI6 for "several weaknesses" in its agent-running within the UK, leading to "several errors". It found that MI6 needed to "better recognise" and "authorise activity in compliance with" the law in the UK. The Johnson Government sought to put these practices into legislation with the Covert Human Intelligence Sources (Criminal Conduct) Bill, which at present contains no expressed limits on the crimes covert agents may be permitted to commit, even against torture, murder, or sexual violence. Maya Foa, Reprieve's Executive Director, said: "We've learned today that MI6 unilaterally assumed the power to authorise unchecked agent law-breaking on UK soil, going far beyond the rules set for them by Parliament. In light of this secret power-grab, Parliament should think twice about giving assent to the Government's CHIS bill, which places no express limits on agent lawbreaking even for crimes like murder, torture, or rape".[15]

# Chapter 4

# Terrorist Attacks, Radicalization and Security Sector Reforms in the UK and European Union

Intelligence cooperation between the EU and Britain has never been fair-minded since the announcement of the Brexit referendum in 2016 by the former British Prime Minister Theresa May. That announcement caused distrust and wariness. Research reports, books and newspapers articles have often spotlighted weak and misunderstood approaches of intelligence leadership to national security challenges. No state wanted to share its national secrets with another state about terrorism and extremism. In yesteryears, debate on Brexit generated further misunderstanding that Britain no longer wanted the EU instruction and dictations on its foreign and domestic policy. Britain also wanted an independent judiciary and human right approach to decide the fate of war criminals living in the country. Experts and analysts, Dr Hager Ben Jaffel. Dr Jeremy Pearson (Intelligence, law enforcement and Brexit-26 Feb 2021) have highlighted several aspects of the issue in their article:

"In the field of security, the most recent example is that of the UK opt-out from Justice and Home Affairs (JHA) in 2014. At that time, the British Government decided to leave some JHA measures on police cooperation and criminal justice, and later re-joined selected ones after discussion with the EU. Brexit is a mechanism similar to that of the opt-out: it's an in-and-out process which involves leaving the EU while forging a new relationship with the EU on security issues. This is demonstrated by the deal reached last December, which retains the participation of UK law enforcement in a number of EU arrangements. Second, we need to think about how UK law enforcement responds to a political decision like Brexit. Brexit, like the opt-out from JHA, suggests that security issues are also political.....During the period leading to EU exit, the potential loss of access to policing tools such as the Schengen Information System (SIS II) and the European Arrest Warrant (EAW) caused UK policing bodies to critically evaluate international policing mechanisms and to identify contingency measures that would mitigate any potential loss of capability. Significant investment was committed to building policing structures that would provide operational support to police forces across the UK and to better manage international requests for operational support. The creation, in 2018, of the International Crime Coordination Centre (ICCC) is the most obvious example of these efforts. The long history of joint intelligence sharing and existing networks, such as the UK liaison officer network within Europe, provide a solid base upon which expanded future cooperation arrangements must be built. Moving forward, the law enforcement mission must be to ensure that future cooperation is as seamless as possible. For a number of years, the UK has marginalized Interpol in favour of Europol. The post-Brexit loss of SIS II and other European policing tools has caused British law enforcement agencies to once again see the importance of this long-established international policing organisation".[1]

The failure of EU intelligence agencies to intercept or identify terrorists before carrying out attacks against civilians in Germany, France and the UK, the counterterrorism approach of Brussels, Germany and French remained in question. There were so many hindrances due to which the EU member states couldn't move ahead with a single voice. The speculation that the security assurance of all member states within the EU was mere hyperbole as complaints of some Eastern European allies about the Brussels attitude raised several questions. The Netherlands, Denmark, Moldova and Baltic states felt threatened. Their complaints against the weak intelligence-sharing mechanism were a matter of great concern. Expert and research scholar at the Centre for Security Studies, Metropolitan University, Prague, Oldrich Bureš, in his paper (Intelligence sharing and the fight against terrorism in the EU: lessons learned from Europol, European View (2016) 15:57–66. DOI 10.1007/s12290-016-0393-7. Published online: 03 May 2016) discussed security management and attacks of Muslim radicalized elements:

"The recent terrorist attacks in Belgium and France have once again highlighted the contradiction between the seemingly free movement of terrorists across Europe and the lack of EU-wide intelligence sharing. Due to their earlier criminal activities, most perpetrators of the attacks in both Paris and Brussels were known to the various security agencies in several EU member states. For instance, the Abdeslam brothers had run a café in Brussels that was notorious for drug peddling. In early 2015, Belgian police questioned them about a failed attempt to travel to Syria, but they were not detained. Soon after, Dutch police stopped them during a routine traffic check, fined them €70 for carrying a small quantity of hashish and then released them because they were not listed in their national information system. Allegedly neither the French security agencies nor the EU coordinating agency, Europol, were informed of either of these incidents prior to the Paris terrorist attacks in November 2015 (La Baume and Paravicini 2015). Similar stories of information non-sharing have emerged in the aftermath of other major terrorist attacks in Europe since the Madrid bombings in 2004. In response, EU policymakers have repeatedly promised to improve intelligence sharing across Europe, and some have even floated the idea that Europol should be turned into a centralised EU criminal intelligence hub, akin to the US Federal Bureau of Investigation (FBI) (Zimmermann 2006, 135)".[2]

Growing radicalization, extremism and the terrorist incident caused misunderstanding between Muslim and Christian communities in Europe. Muslim radicalized elements promoted their business of killing and torture in France, Germany and Netherlands, while White Supremacists targeted Muslims. They established their own radicalized organization linked to Al Qaeda, Al Shabaab, a Somalia-based terrorist jihadist fundamentalist group, Taliban and the ISIS terrorist infrastructure in all European states. In 2010, former British Prime Minister David Cameron, former French President Nicolas Sarkozy and former German Chancellor Angela Merkel took turns denouncing multiculturalism as a "failure" and assigning to it a large part of the responsibility for the wave of terror attacks that Europe had experienced since 2005. In France, terrorist groups and jihadist infrastructure challenged secularism and authority of the state. A lecturer of history and geography was killed in the city of Conflans in October 2020, the church of Nice was also attacked thirteen days later. Senior associate fellow, Institute for Statecraft-London, Fatima Lahnait in her paper (Combating radicalisation in France: from experimentation to professionalization. (Lahnait, Fatima. "La lucha contra la radicalización en Francia: de la experimentación a la profesionalización". Revista CIDOB d'Afers Internacionals, issue 128 (September 2021), Fatima Lahnait) noted some aspects of wave of terrorism and radicalization in Europe:

"The French approach was soon at odds with its European neighbours'. Around the end of the 1990s, the Dutch intelligence services developed a new understanding of terrorism: from a purely law enforcement perspective, it was framed as a problem of "radicalization" of certain sectors of society (Muslim communities, right-wing groups). As the

Netherlands and the UK experienced their first wave of terror attacks with the murder of Theo van Gogh in 2004 and the London bombings of 2005, the reflexion intensified in intelligence circles, and by 2005, governments on both sides of the Channel adopted policies aimed at "countering" or "preventing" violent extremism (C/PVE): the UK with the PREVENT part of the CONTEST strategy, and the Netherlands with the officialization of the "Comprehensive Approach" to counter-terrorism and security. Under the leadership of the UK presidency of the European Union, the EU adopted the European Counter-Terrorism Strategy (Council of the European Union 2005a) and the Strategy for Combatting Radicalization and Recruitment to Terrorism (Council of the European Union 2005b) in 2005: the approach was mainstreamed at the EU level, but France continued to resist, claiming that laïcité prevented it from joining the change..... Before the murders committed by Mohammad Merah in 2012, the French authorities dealt with terrorism almost exclusively as a problem of public order. Hence the country was late in producing measures to prevent radicalisation and violent extremism....In March 2012, Mohamed Merah, a 23 year old with dual French-Algerian citizenship, killed three soldiers and four Jewish civilians, three of them young children, in Toulouse and Montauban (South of France). Merah's rampage and the terrorist attacks that followed–Paris in 2015 and 2020, Nice in 2016, Strasbourg in 2018 to mention a few - are still painfully fresh in public memory. Until mid-2021, more than 260 people have been killed by terrorists, most of them home-grown, claiming allegiance to or inspiration from Al Qaeda, ISIS, or Islamist religious fanatics"[3]

Radicalized members of Al Shabab, ISIS, Boko Haram, Lashkar-e-Taiba and Taliban forced the French authorities to introduce countering strategies and plans in 2014, to address challenges of national security and domestic governance. French intelligence and policing infrastructure were enforcing government strategies to make sure protection of critical national infrastructure. At present, the European Union and Britain face challenges of extremism and foreign espionage. Dick Zandee, Adája Stoetman and Bob Deen in their research paper, (The EU's Strategic Compass for security and defence squaring ambition with reality. Clingendael Report, May 2021. Netherlands Institute of International Relations 'Clingendael') have discussed in detail security challenges of the European Union: "Security challenges posed have set the three strategic priorities for the EU's CSDP: to respond to external conflicts and crises, to support partners to provide security for their own population, and to protect the Union and its citizens. In order to do so, the EU is developing a Strategic Compass for security and defence, to be ready by March 2022. It is expected that the Strategic Compass will contribute to the development of a coherent and strategic approach to the existing initiatives and will bolster the EU's security and defence policy, taking into account the threats and challenges the EU is currently facing. The goal is that the Strategic Compass, building forth on a common European threat analysis completed in November 2020, will define the policy orientations and specific objectives in four dimensions, or so-called 'baskets': (1) crisis management, (2) resilience, (3) capability development and (4) partnerships. Additionally, the Strategic Compass aims to advance the development of a common European security and defence culture".[4]

On 23 June 2016, the British Prime Minister announced the Brexit referendum to leave the European Union and become independent, but things evolved differently when cooperation between the UK and European Union disenfranchised and marginalized due to the slow process of intelligence and security cooperation. Statements of the British Prime Minister and his Ministers further caused misunderstanding and distrust. Britain's decision to leave the EU could have a significant impact on the Union's ability to help nations on its Eastern borders implement political and economic reform, or to respond to Russia's determined efforts to expand its sphere of influence. After the Paris, Brussels and Berlin terrorist attacks, the EU member states realized to establish a strong unified intelligence and security network, but things were not alike that we sensed as there were different priorities, resources and level of expertise within every state. Intelligence sharing among 28 member states was not an easy task as it seemed, policy makers and secret services faced numerous legal, technical and political obstacles. However, limited cooperation on security issues among all 28 states was a reminder that even after six decades of integration; the EU remained a weak project. Intelligence cooperation and adverse relationships between the EU and UK couldn't cease after Brexit as the UK contributes a lot in the field of intelligence and law enforcement. Experts and analysts, Danny Pronk and Claire Korteweg (Sharing the Burden, Sharing the Secrets: The future of European intelligence cooperation. Clingendael Report-September 2021. The Clingendael Institute, the Netherlands) have highlighted security measures of European Union:

"There are also major obstacles which can stand between ambitions and actual outcomes and which can obstruct cooperation even in cases where governments favour it. In the case of Europe, the most potent barrier has been national intelligence staffers whose interests were challenged by suggested schemes for increasing intelligence cooperation, formalisation and centralisation. Perhaps the most striking example of this kind of 'bureaucratic resistance' is Europol and its role in counter-terrorism. European governments have called repeatedly for increased intelligence support for Europol from national security services, but these calls went largely unheeded. Even legal instruments to boost intelligence sharing were largely ineffective in this area. Furthermore, existing institutions such as Europol may simply fail to overcome the common mistrust of the member states, which can inhibit intelligence sharing. As one of today's global powers the EU continues to be confronted with situations of violent conflict all around the world. To step into its desired role of security actor, the EU needs to engage with early warning and crisis prevention, or it will risk playing catch-up too often. In order to strengthen the EU's predictive and preventive capabilities, the EEAS and European Commission rolled out the EU conflict Early Warning System (EWS) in 2014. In the context of intensified collaboration between the EU and NATO, it is important to look at areas where both organisations might learn from each other. This section, therefore, describes the process of this particular early warning system and compares it to the NATO Intelligence Warning System (NIWS) in order to assess how the EU can strengthen its EWS by infusing it with elements from the NIWS. The EWS is a risk-management tool that has been set up to identify conflict prevention and peace building opportunities in conflict-prone regions."[5]

On 04 March 2018, former Russian military intelligence officer, Sergei Skripal, and his daughter, Yulia Skripal fell together abruptly in Salisbury-United Kingdom after taking poisonous food in a restaurant. This assassination attempt authenticated two things; first, the UK intelligence failure to counter Russian intelligence, and second, networks of foreign intelligence agencies were well-established in the country, and they could target every critic. We are witness to Indian, Pakistani and Bangladeshi military establishments who established suchlike terrorist and intelligence unit to easily target their critics and opponents in Europe and the UK. The use of Novichok against a retired man and his daughter on UK soil was underwhelming that the Russian civilian and military intelligence network was so strong in the UK. Experts and analysts, Peter R. Chai, Bryan D. Hayes, Timothy B. Erickson & Edward W. Boyer in their research paper (Novichok agents: a historical, current, and toxicological perspective. Peter R. Chai,Bryan D. Hayes, Timothy B. Erickson & Edward W. Boyer (2018) Novichok agents: a historical, current, and toxicological perspective, Toxicology.DOI: 10.1080/24734306.2018.1475151) have highlighted some important aspects of the Salisbury Novichok attack and response of the UK government:

"The fact that Sergei and Yulia Skripal survived poisoning from a Novichok agent is a testament to the astute diagnostic skills of the responding clinicians. This case underscores the importance of recognizing the cholinergic toxidrome, understanding its etiologies and causative agents, instituting proper decontamination measures, and promptly administering antidotal therapy. As toxicologists, we are well-positioned to educate our colleagues in the recognition and treatment of nerve agents. Additionally, our role as advocates for our patients must continue—in a world where chemical weapon assassinations and brazen nerve agent attacks against innocent civilians appear to be becoming frequent, we must use our voice to condemn the use of these and other banned chemical weapons. Furthermore, we should also be cognizant of the confounding manipulation of scientific literature and lay media to distort the lens in which we view chemical weapons. Like the publication of peer-reviewed manuscripts potentially used to mask research and development of Novichok agents in the 1990s, today's modern media can be used to distort the facts of chemical weapon incidents. In a world where news of assassinations and chemical attacks is rapidly disseminated, we will increasingly be called upon to lend our expertise in the education, diagnosis, and treatment of nerve agents. We urge our fellow toxicologists and clinicians to continue to speak out, defend, and develop policies against the use of chemical weapons."[6]

On 12 March 2018, following the former Prime Minister Teresa May's statement concerning the attack in Salisbury, newspapers reported that this was a military attack against the UK. The circumstances of the incident and the response of the UK government raised important questions of international law. On 17 April, the G7 Foreign Ministers issued a statement condemning the nerve agent attack and agreeing with the UK's assessment that it was highly likely that the Russian Federation was responsible. On 13 April, the UK National Security Adviser, Sir Mark Sedwill sent a letter to Jens Stoltenberg, the NATO Secretary-General, setting out further information on how Russia had the technical means, operational experience and the motive for the Salisbury attack. The UK Ambassador to Russia gave a briefing to the international diplomatic community. On 12 April, the Organisation for the Prohibition of Chemical Weapons (OPCW) published their report. It confirmed the UK findings: the toxic chemical used in the attempted assassination of Sergei and Yulia Skripal was a military-grade nerve agent–a Novichok. The Foreign Secretary gave a statement on the OPCW report and the Head of UK Delegation updated the Organization for Security and Co-operation in Europe. Al Jazeera news on 05 September 2018 (UK: Russians charged with Skripal nerve-agent poisoning: Prosecutors name two Russians as suspects in an attempted assassination of ex-spy) reported:

The UK charged two Russian men for the Novichok nerve agent attack on a former spy and his daughter in the English city of Salsibury, accusing them of being Russian military intelligence officers. British prosecutors issued arrest warrants on Wednesday for Alexander Petrov and Ruslan Boshirov, charging them with conspiracy to murder and attempted murder of former double agent Sergei Skripal and his daughter, Yulia. Both were poisoned with the military-grade nerve agent – developed by the former Soviet Union in the 1970s and '80s – in March but survived after spending weeks in hospital. The failed attack sparked an international diplomatic crisis with Russia being accused by several countries – allegations Moscow has repeatedly denied. Based on the body of intelligence, the government has concluded that the two individuals named by the police and the Crown Prosecution Service are officers from the Russian military intelligence service, also known as the GRU," British Prime Minister Theresa May told parliament. "This was also not a rogue operation. It was almost certainly approved outside the GRU at a senior level of the Russian state," she said. Britain will present its evidence at a UN Security Council meeting on Thursday, a spokesman for May told reporters. "We have called for a Security Council meeting to take place on Thursday so we can update the council on the progress of the Salisbury investigation," he said. Al Jazeera reported.[7]

However, the UK Counterterrorism on 21 September 2021 confirmed that charges were authorised against a third Russian person in relation to the investigation into the Salisbury Novichok attack. Detectives from Counter Terrorism Policing continued to investigate the attack on Sergei and Yulia Skripal as well as the murder of Dawn Sturgess and poisoning of Charlie Rowley in Alesbury in June 2018. As a result of these continued enquiries, a third man known as 'Sergey Fedotov' was identified. The lesion learnt from the Salisbury attacks, experts view it as an intelligence failure to intercept the attackers. In the EU, some states, such as Germany, Romania, Poland, and France, civilian intelligence infrastructure tackle domestic and foreign threats, while some states have given to law enforcement agencies intelligence powers to fight against corruption and terrorism. This is not a new story because every state wants to involve intelligence in law enforcement operations, or in policing. In majority Asian and African states, intelligence is fully involved in law enforcement operations, and led the police in the fight against serious organized crime. The growing distrust, and dilapidating security situation in Britain and the EU is a matter of great concern where radicalized groups and lone wolves have established secret cell, recruit young people and carrying out attacks against civilian and government installations.

The growing distrust, and dilapidating security situation in Britain and EU is a matter of great concern where radicalized groups and lone wolves have established secret cells, recruit young people and carry out attacks against civilian and government installations. Expert and research scholar at the Centre for Security Studies, Metropolitan University, Prague, Oldrich Bureš in his paper (Intelligence sharing and the fight against terrorism in the EU: lessons learned from Europol, European View (2016) 15:57–66. DOI 10.1007/s12290-016-0393-7. Published online: 03 May 2016) discussed attacks of Muslim radicalized elements: "Intelligence sharing has arguably been one of the most problematic areas of the EU's counterterrorism efforts. While there appear to have been gradual improvements over time, Europol has certainly struggled to transcend the traditional obstacles to intelligence sharing, and national security and law enforcement agencies are still too often reluctant to share 'high-grade', real-time intelligence on terrorism that can be acted on immediately. This is primarily due to the persistence of nationality in international policing and intelligence. Although numerous Council decisions and Commission proposals include an obligation for EU member states to share information, in practical terms, this duty has had little impact because it cannot force member states' authorities to share more information, that is, intelligence that has not previously been disseminated".[8]

The crisis of EU intelligence is irksome due to sectarian and ethnic divide. European intelligence agencies lack the confidence of political parties on their mass surveillance system. In Germany, intelligence law does not allow the Federal Intelligence Service (BND) to support police or involve itself in policing business, while in Estonia and Latvia, intelligence plays an important role in policing communities. Targeted surveillance in all EU states is being conducted on different lines. Intelligence agencies of the member states use surveillance but also give importance to human intelligence. In Brussels, Denmark, Finland, France and Italy targeted surveillance of groups and individuals has strong roots in society. Experts and analysts, Danny Pronk and Claire Korteweg (Sharing the Burden,

Sharing the Secrets: The future of European intelligence cooperation. Clingendael Report-September 2021. The Clingendael Institute, the Netherlands) have documented challenges of the UK and EU after the Brexit:

"While the British political decision to leave the EU generated much debate and concern about Britain's future in Europe, Brexit so far hasn't really impacted the intelligence and security ties between Britain and Europe. Especially in matters of counter-terrorism, Britain is firmly bound to Europe. It is everyday, 'bread-and-butter' intelligence cooperation that indicates the effective participation of Britain in the European space of counter-terrorism cooperation.....A comparative study of collaborative security regimes post-Brexit based on the overlap in national strategic documents found that there is potential for future convergence between EU and the UK at the industrial level, in internal security matters and in military missions. So, while there are good reasons to maintain practical cooperation between the UK and the EU after Brexit in many areas, cooperation between intelligence services is another obvious example, given the security challenges currently facing Europe? Moreover, there is no point in debating who needs the other more. Both Brussels and London stand to gain from a partnership. First of all, this will send a strong signal to the other global powers, such as Russia and China that in intelligence matters even after Brexit there still is one Europe, which is in the interest of all European states. Secondly, the UK will also benefit, because it retains an important asset in its own trans-Atlantic 'special relationship' with the US. And thirdly, the EU member states will benefit because if the UK remains fully involved in the CSDP, they need not fear the emergence of new parallel circuits that would bypass the EU".[9]

On 29 March 2017, former British Prime Minister Theresa May triggered article 50 of the Lisbon Treaty. A letter invoking Article-50 of the Lisbon Treaty was hand-delivered to the President of the EU, Mr. Donald Tusk by the UK Ambassador to the European Union, but experts warned that the UK withdrawal from the project, the future of NATO can also become under threat. Intelligence cooperation within the EU was of greater importance in fighting the threat of terrorism and radicalization, but the EU intelligence analysis centre (INTCEN) had nothing to offer as majority of member states intelligence agencies were competing for resources and attention from policy makers. Moreover, INTCEN had no formal mandate to collect intelligence as traditionally understood, because the centre mostly depended on open-source intelligence (OSINT). In 2012,

INTCEN tried to improve its intelligence analysis capabilities and focus on analysis with two divisions; analysis division, and general and external relations divisions, but the case still remains weak. The issue of electronic intelligence generated numerous controversies within the member states. Privacy international and other organizations deeply criticized the way EU member states spy on their citizens. Christine Andreeva has highlighted lack of confidence between partners that affect cross border and cross agency lack of cooperation. (The evolution of information-sharing in EU counter-terrorism post-2015: a paradigm shift? To cite this article: Christine Andreeva (2021):

"Before 2015 international terrorism had little effect on EU intelligence cooperation, because "[w]hile the EU has responsibilities for some strategic decision-making, it does not play any significant operational or tactical role" (Müller-Wille, 2008, p. 69). This institutional design flaw resulted in the identity crisis of Europol and the "chicken–egg" dilemma of its added value (Bures, 2013). Europol was intended as a hub for information collection and sharing, however, MS repeatedly resisted delegating such responsibilities to it, including in the aftermath of the 9/11 attacks, and 2004 Madrid bombings (Fägersten, 2010, pp. 506–507). At a time of heightened threat perception and calls for increased cooperation, MS unambiguously signalled their disinterest in an increased Europol role: they set up instead the Counter-Terrorism Group (CTG) a sub-grouping of the intergovernmental cooperation channel Club de Berne, where the majority of intelligence exchange occurs (Fägersten, 2010). One element of the problem is that "national agencies are both the main providers of intelligence to Europol and its main customers", thus intelligence often "perceive information-sharing through Europol as an extra burden" and a duplication of their efforts, giving them no incentive to share (Bures, 2013, p. 85; Fägersten, 2010; Müller-Wille, 2004, p. 26). Another flaw of the EU CT apparatus was that databases were non-interoperable, and not cross-border accessible (Müller-Wille, 2008)".[10] During the last 8 years, there were some legal developments in the United Kingdom dealing with terrorism and radicalization. Intelligence sharing and cooperation on law enforcement level among EU member states is crucial to stability and peace. As movements of EU citizens across borders and volatile regions increased, and groups like Islamic State, domestic radicalized organization and lone wolves had taken roots, trans-border intelligence sharing could prevent any possible terrorist attack.

Intelligence agencies of the European Union were playing an important role in protecting national security and national critical infrastructure. Terrorist attacks in Germany, France and Brussels forced several members of European Union to introduce intelligence and security sector reforms. By law, all EU Member States regulated the organisation of their country's intelligence services. The EUINTCEN is now a professional organization that had established its roots in European Security and Defence Policy in what was then called the Joint Situation Centre. In 2002, the Joint Situation Centre started to be a forum for exchange of sensitive information between the external intelligence services of France, Germany, Italy, the Netherlands, Spain, Sweden and the United Kingdom. Experts and analysts, Theodore Christakis, Kenneth Propp in their paper (How Europe's Intelligence Services Aim to Avoid the EU's Highest Court—and What It Means for the United States-March 8, 2021) highlighted legal developments and human rights in Europe:

"It is revealing that EU member states such as France—which are intent on entirely excluding the national security activities of their intelligence agencies from the scope of EU law—are less concerned by the fact that these activities will remain subject to ECHR law. This reflects that ECtHR surveillance jurisprudence is far from comprehensive. For example, there is not a single ECtHR judgment concerning international surveillance such as interceptions taking place outside the territory of a member state. And when a surveillance law is challenged, it often takes several years for the ECtHR to issue a judgment, allowing the intelligence agency in question to function without obstacles during this period. For instance, challenges to the French Intelligence Act of 24 July 2015 are still pending before the ECtHR six years later. Finally, when the ECtHR finally publishes its judgments in such cases, it often allows governments, particularly democratic ones, a "margin of appreciation" (a measure of discretion) in implementation in the national security area that is much broader than the one recognized by the CJEU. France also recently has taken a unilateral additional action in order to escape the data retention case law of the CJEU: It asked the country's highest administrative court—the Council of State—to ignore the CJEU ruling in the LQDN case. French government lawyers contend that the CJEU acted outside its scope (ultra vires) by usurping for the EU an important "sovereign" competence—national security and protection of public order—that member states had never transferred to it".[11]

Majority of European Union states introduced strict surveillance measures to collect data by legal and illegal means. Some foreign and domestic intelligence agencies became out of control and some started sharing data with American NSA. German Foreign Intelligence, BND also shared huge data with the US intelligence agencies. The German Court ruled that surveillance of communications between non-German citizens abroad carried out by the Federal Intelligence Service attracted widespread public attention in Germany. This caused wide-ranging debate in Europe that German intelligence was violating intelligence law. Analysts and experts, Kilian Vieth-Ditlmann and Thorsten Wetzling, (Caught in the Act? An analysis of Germany's new SIGINT reform. Research Report-25 November 2021. The Stiftung Neue Verantwortung) in their research paper highlighted amendment of BND Act and foreign intelligence reforms in Germany:

The BND Act, as amended in March 2021, now substantially changes and expands the surveillance powers of Germany's foreign intelligence agency, (BND). It also establishes a wide range of new safeguards and oversight structures….More specifically, Germany's foreign intelligence reform came at a time when the practice and legal bases for bulk collection and other forms of (automated) government access to personal data received renewed attention across Europe…. The central norm that regulates the BND's mandate to collect foreign communications in bulk is paragraph 19 of the BND Act (see the annex for an unofficial translation). It lists the aims which the government must pursue when seeking the authorization for strategic foreign telecommunications collection (Strategische Ausland-Fernmeldeaufklärung). Whereas paragraph 19 applies to foreign communications only, it does not mean that the collection of foreign communications under this provision is limited to non-German territory. Rather, if the communications of foreign entities or individuals are processed by providers within Germany, the BND can compel them to provide access to this data (§ 25 BND Act). Moreover, the BND Act now also includes an explicit regulation for the covert intrusion of communications systems if it is necessary for the implementation of bulk interception measures (§ 19 (6) BND Act). Accordingly, the BND may use technical means to secretly infiltrate the IT systems of a communications service provider abroad. Authorizing an intelligence agency to break into the computer systems of a foreign entity in a foreign country will, most likely, come into conflict with the law there. What is more, there is no requirement, as is the case in some other democracies, 18 for the ex-ante authorization involving independent oversight bodies nor is the duration and the volume of the data collection in pursuit of suitability tests subject to (effective) limitations. In general, data that has been collected in pursuit of the suitability test must be processed only for either purpose (listed above). This rule does not apply, however, when factual indications point to a grave threat to individuals or the security of either the Federal Republic of Germany or institutions of either the European Union or its Member States".[12]

# Chapter 5

# Surveillance Blankets, in Estonia, Bulgaria and Sweden, Challenges of Intelligence Cooperation and Human Rights

There are voluminous and billowing material in case of books, journals, and newspaper and research papers on European intelligence surveillance, available in libraries and markets that highlight violation of privacy and private life of citizens of all EU member states. In Internet, we can find important research papers on the decisions of EU Court of Human Rights against the human right violations in blanket surveillance. The EU has been accused of contributing to the development of 'surveillance' capacities in third countries without considering fundamental rights. Mr. Ioannis Kouvakas, legal officer and acting General Counsel at Privacy International warned corroborating respect for human rights in EU external relations: "EU bodies must equally ensure respect for human rights in their external relations, by, for example, assessing the risks that their actions pose to human rights. What our research suggests, however, is that these assessments are lacking when transferring surveillance capabilities outside the EU".[1] No doubt intelligence and surveillance play an important role in protecting national security and helping law enforcement to uphold the rule of law. European Union Agency for Fundamental Rights in its research paper (Surveillance by intelligence services: fundamental rights safeguards and remedies in the EU Volume II: field perspectives and legal update. European Union Agency for Fundamental Rights, 2017) has highlighted the issue with different perspectives:

"The specificities of international intelligence sharing require Member States to establish safeguards that are tailored to these processes. These include – but are not limited to – prior approval of any agreement or pattern of cooperation by the executive, the implementation of fundamental rights risk assessments, strong guarantees for protection of sources and personal information, data reliability assessments and the obligation to keep records. As identified by Born, Leigh and Wills, "requirements of this kind have a number of benefits. They establish a clear framework for approval of cooperation activities. They can help to ensure that cooperation is aligned with the government's foreign policy, defence, security, and diplomatic objectives and does not unwittingly undermine or contradict these. They ensure that political overseers have an understanding of the arrangements that the state's services have with partners. They allow for scrutiny to take place of any risks of particular partnerships at an appropriate political and managerial level." Prior approval may be required before the establishment of the agreement and/or before the exchange of data. In almost all Member States, intelligence services must obtain the approval of the executive before concluding an international agreement. Only in Slovenia is international intelligence cooperation at the discretion of the head of the service."[2]

European intelligence surveillance and its way of operation have deeply violated human rights of its citizens. From Google to Twitter and YouTube, all electronic organizations help European states in blanket surveillance to violate rights. Experts and analysts, Theodore Christakis, and Kenneth Propp in their analysis (How Europe's Intelligence Services Aim to Avoid the EU's Highest Court—and What It Means for the United States. Lawfare. March 8, 2021) of Court of Justice of the European Union against the foreign surveillance that forced the United States to consider changes to its foreign surveillance law and practices in order to re-establish a stable basis for transatlantic transfers of personal data:

"In the fall of 2020, the court softened that bitter pill when, for the first time, it also imposed limits on EU member states' intelligence services' own data collection and retention activities. But now the member state governments have struck back against the Luxembourg-based court, quietly slipping into their version of the EU's e-Privacy legislative reform proposal a provision that would put these contested national security activities beyond the court's reach. The U.S. government is already on record as objecting to what it perceives as a laxer data protection standard being applied by European courts to their own national intelligence services. This latest move in Brussels has only accentuated the sense of a disparity in treatment....In October 2020, the CJEU for the first time tackled the question of whether, and to what extent, EU fundamental rights relating to data protection should limit European intelligence services' data collection and retention programs. Nine member states, including the United Kingdom (an EU member at the time of argument) and France, intervened in the two linked cases, brought by nongovernmental organizations, most notably Privacy International and La Quadrature du Net (LQDN). In general, the EU exercises competences—such as data protection—granted by its member states, but only to the extent that member states have effectively transferred these powers to the EU. These member states contended that the cases fell under the general national security exception of Article 4(2) of the Treaty on European Union, according to which "national security remains the sole responsibility of each Member State."[3]

In Bulgaria, European court of Human Rights warned the Bulgarian government that its blanket surveillance system was violating the rights of citizens. "The European Court of Human Rights held, unanimously, that there had been a violation of Article 8 (right to respect for private life and correspondence) of the European Convention on Human Rights," it said in a statement. The court found that there was a lack of proper judicial oversight over decisions to issue warrants for surveillance in Bulgaria. The court ruled that Bulgarian government's special surveillance law permits violation of citizens' rights. Analyst and experts, Pearl Cohen Zedek Latzer Baratz in their article (European Court Finds Bulgarian Gov't Electronic Surveillance Violates Human Rights. European Union January 30, 2022) have noted ruling of the court against the rights of Bulgarian people: "Bulgaria's surveillance act, along with several articles of the Bulgarian Code of Criminal Procedure, authorize the government to surveil citizens (visually or otherwise) and to intercept citizens' telephonic and electronic communications on the grounds set out in the act. The petitioners asserted that the act violates the European human rights convention because the surveillance system is not appropriately supervised and the legislation does not provide sufficient safeguards against arbitrary or abusive use of or access to the information collected. In addition, the petitioners alleged that although the legislation ostensibly allows citizens to demand information about the surveillance to which they have been subjected, in practice, the authorities do not provide satisfactory responses to such requests."[4]

The European Union's common and security policy is in trouble and faces major security threats from in and outside of the project. Its external challenges are revolving with shifting US and China's foreign and military policy, internally the project facing domestic governance issues in several Central-Eastern European Member States. Home-Grown extremism and radicalization, racism and discrimination are more serious threats that the EU needed to address these challenges professionally. Until 2019, the Estonian government's EU policy have been strongly based domestic political consensus, while from 2019 to 2022, new government Eurosceptic populist party, which brought visible cracks to this consensus. The Estonian foreign intelligence service in its recent report (International Security and Estonia-2022) has highlighted interference of foreign intelligence agencies in the country. Director General of the Estonian Foreign Intelligence Service, Mikk Marran, (31 January 2022) in his front matter has noted military confrontation in Ukraine, and the hybrid attacks of Belarussian government NATO Eastern Border as a serious threat to the country's security:

"For the Foreign Intelligence Service, the keywords of 2021 were the Russian military exercise Zapad and escalation in the direction of Ukraine, as well as the hybrid attack staged by the Belarusian regime on NATO's eastern border. As of the beginning of 2022, our focus remains on the Kremlin's aggression against Ukraine, which has led to the sharpest confrontation with the West in decades and could also lead to Russia exerting pressure elsewhere in the coming months. Although a direct military offensive against Estonia and the other Baltic states is unlikely this year, various types of hybrid crises are probable. We might also see a renewed attempt to weaponized refugees. The presence of Russian forces in Belarus is worthy of particular attention. Once again, we also focus on China. The unprecedented Chinese reprisal against Lithuania in 2021 points to China's increasingly aggressive foreign policy in our region. In cooperation with the governments and security services of other democratic nations, we must make sure to have a comprehensive assessment of Beijing's ambitions".[5] The Estonian intelligence collecting information on Estonia's external security threats, and its information is of significant importance for national defence and security policy. The country faces precarious threat from Russian GRU that collects information for Russia's political and military leadership on countries and alliances of countries that Russia considers its adversaries or likely adversaries. Expert Jana Wrange has noted in his paper (Internal and external perceptions of small state security: the case of Estonia- 18 September 2019) security perception of small states:

"While perceived to be in a relatively secure situation (more secure than ever before, according to Expert EE1), Estonia still faces several threats to its security. The main threat is indisputably seen as coming from the eastern neighbour (Defence Minister; Expert EE1, EE2). However, the nature of threats has over time expanded from military aspects to a broader spectrum, as reflected for instance in discussions of hybrid threats, encompassing elements such as propaganda and disinformation, strategic use of natural resources, and cyber-attacks. With that in mind, the internal respondents identified several threats coming from Russia, including military, economic, cyber, hybrid warfare and political factors (Defence Minister; Expert EE1). Interestingly enough, the perception of threat from the Russian-speaking minorities in Estonia is not mentioned internally; on the contrary, the Prime Minister believes that the differentiation has decreased and that even Russian-speaking minorities in Estonia are patriotic and defence-oriented. In addition to the threats originating from Russia, terrorism is mentioned as a threat, given the general increase of terror attacks in Europe and the assaults that have occurred in states in close proximity to Estonia, such as Denmark and Sweden, but is not deemed a drastic threat to the state's existence (Defence Minister; Expert EE1). Of subordinate nature, Expert EE1 also mentions environmental challenges in the context of threats to Estonian security".[6]

The power of national security intelligence in the west was increased after the 9/11 terrorist attacks in the United States, and after the Snowden revelation in 2013 about the UK and UK surveillance mechanism. The intelligence communities and associated oversight frameworks in Australia, Canada, New Zealand, the United Kingdom and the United States evolved in different aspects to outline a strong security and intelligence cooperation in Europe, Asia and Middle East. These oversight bodies also came to concordance to establish a Five Eyes Intelligence Oversight and review council in 2016. Countries suchlike Australia, Canada, New Zealand, the United Kingdom and the United States have managed parliamentary and judicial oversights in their own states. The Canadian government passed a law to create parliamentarian's committee to review policy administration and operational mechanism of it intelligence infrastructure. The New Zealand's Intelligence and Security Act 2017 replaces the four acts that previously applied to the two intelligence and security agencies and their oversight bodies. A question raised about the operations of MI5 and Special Branch surveillance of the left, lack of parliamentary scrutiny, and a continuing veil of secrecy. The Lord Denning report described that not everything is going on right direction.

Five Eyes Intelligence Oversight and Review Council (FIORC) was established comprised of Australia, Canada, New Zealand, the United Kingdom, and the United States with the following oversight bodies: The Office of the Inspector-General of Intelligence and Security of Australia, the National Security and Intelligence Review Agency of Canada, the Office of the Intelligence Commissioner of Canada, the Commissioner of

Intelligence Warrants and the Office of the Inspector-General of Intelligence and Security of New Zealand, the Investigatory Powers Commissioner's Office of the United Kingdom and the Office of the Inspector General of the Intelligence Community of the United States. The council members discussed matter of their mutual interests. Professor and expert of intelligence, Daniel W. B. Lomas in his research paper ((Party politics and intelligence: the Labour Party, British intelligence and oversight, 1979-1994-2021, intelligence and security-Volume 36, 2021 - Issue 3) highlighted some aspects of intelligence oversight bodies in Australia, Canada, New Zealand, the United Kingdom, and the United States:

"Labour's drive for oversight of Britain's intelligence community took place against the backdrop of the Watergate scandal and 'year of intelligence' that shed the spotlight on the US intelligence community's alleged dirty tricks at home and around the world. Investigations by the US Senate Select Committee to 'Study Governmental Operations with Respect to Intelligence Activities', chaired by Senator Frank Church, and House of Representatives counterpart, the Pike Committee, revealed sensational claims about domestic surveillance, the assassination of foreign leaders and other excesses, rocking Washington and ushering in a new period of agency oversight. In Britain, both press commentators and those on the Labour left often viewed the activities of Britain's intelligence and security agencies through the prism of American abuses. Stories of MI5's surveillance of the left and claims that the Security Service had worked against Wilson's government did little to dampen concerns. Sensationally such claims came from Wilson himself who, following his resignation as Prime Minister in April 1976, approached BBC journalists Barrie Penrose and Roger Courtiour (or 'Pencourt') with the claim that right-wing elements of MI5, supported by the CIA and South African spies, had started a smear campaign against Labour. 'I am not certain that for the last eighteen months when I was Prime Minister', Wilson said, 'I knew what was happening, fully, in security'. Parts of MI5 were 'very right-wing' and believed, he told the journalists, that 'Socialist leaders were another form of Communist', including, Director General Sir Michael Hanley had reportedly told Wilson, a 'disaffected faction with extreme right-wing views'. The allegations, sensationalised in The Observer in 1977, and published as The Pencourt File a year later, although dismissed by Wilson as 'cock and bull', did little to dampen suspicion on Labour's backbenches that MI5 had gone rogue".[7]

In colleges and universities, students ask about the effectiveness of intelligence services and its functions. The 9/11 commission indicated that terrorist attacks the result of intelligence failure. Whenever a terrorist attack happens, intelligence becomes a major cause. The principal debate among EU and UK intelligence experts starts with the assumption that counter-terrorist decision making is influenced by intelligence analysis. One thing is certain though, boundaries of secrecy and classified data will consistently be challenged particularly when the public became acutely aware of surveillance. In Denmark, intelligence community has been in hot water since a decade as foreign espionage is making thing worse. Notwithstanding the different types of parliamentary and judicial oversight in the country, infiltration of intelligence and their exponentially growing networks have now become a bigger challenge. Experts, Sune J. Andersen, Martin Ejnar Hansen & Philip H. J. Davies in their research paper (Oversight and governance of the Danish intelligence community Sune J. Andersen, Martin Ejnar Hansen & Philip H. J. Davies (2022): Oversight and governance of the Danish intelligence community, Intelligence and National Security) have highlighted functions of intelligence, operation and oversight techniques:

"With the end of the Cold War, the Western intelligence agencies saw a change in priorities. Denmark was no different. With the demise of the USSR there was a gradual change in the requirements from decision-makers and the agencies were targeted for downsizing. That being said, FE made the transition into the post-Cold War with greater success than PET. Foreign and defence intelligence quickly acquired a renewed significance with FE tasked with to operational intelligence support to successive Danish deployments abroad during UN interventions into the Balkan brush-wars of the 1990s, and then the NATO-led campaign in Afghanistan after 9/11. PET, which had always faced persistent doubt and distrust in wider civil society, found the post-Cold War domestic political climate ever less amenable. Absent the ideological threat of Communism and on the wake of widespread demographic changes across Western Europe, PET increasingly appeared out of place in the New World Order of the 1990s. The result of this scrutiny was the establishment of the PET commission in 1998, much to the chagrin of the intelligence community. Despite arguing for 'a growing need to identify and understand the conflicts arising from ideological, religious, social and ethnic reasons both international and domestic', PET found itself scathingly described by one CIA officer as an agency 'almost completely devoid of minorities' and a country whose historical development had resulted in 'an ethnically and culturally homogenous society". Amidst the public debates and disputes around the role and work of Denmark's intelligence agencies, two commissions were established dealing with intelligence matters. The Parliamentary PET Commission was established in 1999 after media reports allegations about historical transgressions by PET, shortly before the Ministry of Justice had convened its own inquiry in the form of the Wendler Pedersen Commission in 1998. Each was mandated to review to review different aspects of the Danish intelligence community. The Danish system of intelligence oversight, therefore, evolved in a series of fits and starts, and in a fundamentally ad hoc fashion. This disjointed, discontinuous process results from the fact, despite the parallels with Great Britain, the Danish case shares far more in common with the experience of the United States".[8]

On 18 March 2022, Russian Foreign Minister Sergey Lavrov discussed Russia's standoff with the US and other Western nations in an interview with RT, and outlined the direction in which Moscow was moving. He said the West had encouraged Ukraine to turn into an "anti-Russia," and now its leader is trying to goad US President Joe Biden into going to war for Kiev. Foreign Minister Lavrov argued that Moscow was being subjected to "info-terrorism" by its opponents, who dropped all pretence of adhering to the values they preach. Tensions will calm down, but Russia will no longer be under any illusion that it would be welcomed as an equal in the West, he told RT. The United States, and its EU allies, imposed sanctions on Moscow, to target Russia's banking and energy sectors, but failed to get satisfactory results. There were different perceptions in the west about Russian interference in the EU; some states saw Russia as a friendly partner, and some viewed it as a hostile power, but, the majority of states wanted to maintain friendly relations with Russia, These factors matter, and relations with Russia certainly differed. Geir Hagen Karlsen in his research paper outlined Russian influence in Europe, and its relationship with different states. He has quoted several reports and experts on ethnic composition and in the EU:

"Russian influence activities are, at least partially, conducted by covert means, which makes it difficult to observe and analyse them. It is the task of Western secret services to unveil covert activity, and using data from intelligence reports gives access to information that is often not available elsewhere or that may supplement other sources. This study examines the perceptions of Western secret services regarding Russian influence activities, and is conducted through an analysis of about 40 annual reports from 15 security services of 11 Western countries: Czech Republic,

Denmark, Estonia, Finland, Germany, Latvia, Lithuania, Netherlands, Norway, Sweden, and the U.S. Annual reports were selected as they give an overview of each service's perspectives, and thus deemed suitable for this study. There is a wealth of other material available, including from parliamentary hearings, inquiries, media coverage, websites, public statements, legal documents, and so on. Using these as reference material, however, would require substantial search and translation resources in many languages, but they certainly provide a basis for future in-depth study. The Baltic States paint a particularly grim picture, possibly because of their unique history, geography and ethnic composition. The Estonian view is that the Russian regime will remain aggressive, conducting hostile influence operations and consistently cultivating tension and undermining trust in democratically elected governments (EISS, 2016: pp. 2–5; EIB, 2017:p.7). Russian influence activities in the information domain are seen as the main threat, having a detrimental effect on Latvia's national security, and subverting democratic processes (DP, 2017: p. 5). Russia's imperial ambitions and aggressive foreign policy is causing a tense security situation, and Russia is discrediting Lithuania, influencing political, social and economic processes and dividing the Lithuanian society (SSD, 2017a: pp. 7–8)".[9]

In newspapers and electronic media, concern about the Home Office web-spying powers caused torment. On 11 March 2021, BBC reported two UK internet providers help the Home Office and National Crime Agency tracking the websites visited by customers. However, on 12 March 2021, Brian Higgins reported that UK Law enforcement agencies and other authorities have long been able to legally request Communications Data from service providers. The Investigatory Powers Act allows the UK government and ISPs to violate the privacy of internet users through extremely invasive bulk data collection. Espionage in the UK has increased either by foreign espionage networks or by our own intelligence agencies. Digital spying is product of the cold war, but state are still using this technique. Experts and researchers, Joe Devanny, Ciaran Martin & Tim Stevens (To cite this article: Joe Devanny, Ciaran Martin & Tim Stevens (2021) On the strategic consequences of digital espionage, Journal of Cyber Policy) in their papers have highlighted some aspects of digital espionage:

"States spy on each other. Human intelligence (HUMINT), in which intelligence is gathered through human agency and interaction, was professionalised in the twentieth century but has a much longer and richer history (Hitz 2004; Scott 2013). This history includes many instances in which states have uncovered and remediated penetration cases involving human agents. Standard responses include the expulsion of intelligence officers from embassies and the incarceration of foreign spies. The Cold War also saw the growth of 'spy swaps', in which reciprocal exchanges were coordinated as a calibrated means of managing bilateral tensions and improving stability. These still occasionally take place, such as shortly after the arrest of ten Russian 'illegals' in the United States in June 2010 (Lefebvre and Porteous 2011). In HUMINT situations, therefore, costs are imposed through reputational damage and operational friction, as in declaring embassy staff *personae non gratae* and expelling them from one's jurisdiction. These actions tend to be proportionate–often strictly so – and provisional, as when numbers of embassy intelligence officers are permitted to rise once the initial furore has abated. In some cases, there is tension and uncertainty about the potential strategic ramifications of specific HUMINT operations, which may not attract approval, or for which regret is expressed retrospectively. For example, the head of East German intelligence reportedly came to regard the penetration of West German Chancellor Willy Brandt's private office as a strategic error (Wolf 1997, 171–172). Its exposure led to foreseeable adverse domestic-political consequences (resignation) for Brandt. This was a negative development for East Germany and the Soviet Union, who considered Brandt a more palatable head of government than his actual (or any likely) successor".[10]

Launched in October 2016, the UK National Cyber Security Centre on its website comment elucidated that 'the 2021 NCSC Annual Review that ransomware has now become the most significant cyber threat facing the UK, with the impact of an attack on critical national infrastructure stated in the UK National Cyber Strategy 2022 as potentially as harmful as state-sponsored espionage'. As we have experienced in yesteryears that the NCSC's performance has been excellent in protecting financial market and national critical infrastructure in the UK. The centre have identifies different instruments of threats. Experts and researchers, Joe Devanny, Ciaran Martin & Tim Stevens (To cite this article: Joe Devanny, Ciaran Martin & Tim Stevens (2021) on the strategic consequences of digital espionage, Journal of Cyber Policy) in their papers have highlighted strategic consequences digital espionage: "The strategic consequences of digital espionage depend, therefore, to a large extent on the response of the victim state. As proposed initially, the specific context of bilateral relations between the victim state and the spying state will shape the chosen response. As with non-cyber issues, asymmetries of power constrain the range of options from which victim states feel able to choose. The state of broader diplomatic relations, and leader-to-leader relations, are relevant, but so too is the existence of an effective conduit for bilateral intelligence diplomacy. This is an important element in the effort to maintain equilibrium and to avoid cross-domain escalation. Effective digital intelligence diplomacy, running parallel to conventional cyber diplomacy, is therefore instrumental for the vitality and prospects of multilateral efforts to foster responsible state behaviour in cyberspace".[11]

As I have authenticated by my deep research efforts that foreign espionage in the UK has been a bigger challenge since 2001. Intelligence agencies of South Asian States, spying power of their embassies in London have been reporting by newspapers since years but successive government have been helpless to counter their subversive campaign. Pakistani and Indian intelligence agencies are using targeted killers to eliminate their opponents and critics. In 2022, a London based British Pakistani terrorist Gaohar Khan was sentenced to life in prison. The Nation weekly reported that a 31-year-old British Pakistani man Muhammad Gaohar Khan was charged for conspiring to kill Netherlands-based journalist and blogger, Ahmad Waqass Goraya.[12] Terrorist Gaohar Khan will serve a prison term of 13 years, inclusive of the days already served in custody and only after that he will be eligible for parole. Mr. Gohir Khan was charged in June in 2021 with conspiracy to murder Goraya. During the trial, the prosecution maintained that Khan was hired by Pakistani ISI to carry out the killing of a journalist Goraya. Moreover, BBC (28 January 2022) reported that a British "hitman" was found guilty of conspiring to kill a Pakistani dissident in the Netherlands. Mr. Waqass Goraya, told the BBC he was sure the Pakistani intelligence services (ISI) was ultimately behind the plot. Mr. Waqass Goraya, is a prominent social media activist and critic of the Pakistani military and government, living in Rotterdam in the Netherlands. He was abducted and tortured whilst visiting Pakistan in January 2017 by suspected members of the intelligence services, and told the BBC he was convinced they had now attempted to have him killed in Europe.[13]

Research Scholar, Dr, Ayesha Siddiqa is an academic who has written extensively about the Pakistani military business received a visit and letter from police in Britain warning of "credible information" that her life was in danger if she travelled back to Pakistan. Three other Pakistanis living in the UK confirmed to the BBC they had contact with the police over the possibility of them being targeted in Britain. One of them, Fazal Khan, is a lawyer whose 14 year-old son Sahibzada Umer Khan was amongst the victims of a massacre at a school in Peshawar. A man brought to justice following an investigation by the Met's Counter Terror Command has been jailed for life for conspiracy to murder. Officers uncovered more than 2,000 WhatsApp messages between Muhammad Gohir Khan and his co-conspirator where they discussed and agreed to the contract killing of a Rotterdam-based Pakistani blogger and activist. Daily Dawn reported Mohammad Gaohar Khan, a 31-year-old British man convicted of conspiring to murder Netherlands-based dissident Pakistani blogger Ahmad Waqass Goraya was sentenced to life in prison at the Kingston-upon-Thames court. The UK intelligence agencies have failed to talk to Pakistani government and High Commission of Pakistan in London about its espionage activities and vandalism in the UK. Police and intelligence agencies are helpless to protect British Asian. They are shamelessly inform them by phone to manage their own security. The Gaohar Khan case is an ugly blot on the face of British police and intelligence agencies.

The Denmark intelligence agencies have recently warned that increased threat from foreign intelligence against Denmark, Greenland and Faroe Islands is matter of great concern for the government and law enforcement agencies. On 14 January 2022, the Danish Security and Intelligence Service in its report that warned there had been numerous examples of attempted spying on Denmark. "The threat from foreign intelligence activities against Denmark, Greenland, and the Faroe Islands have increased in recent years,"[14] Anders Henriksen, head of counterintelligence at the Danish Security and Intelligence Service warned. The report also warned that foreign espionage networks of China, Russia and Iran were trying to make contact with students and academics. The Islamic Republic of Iran categorically denied any involvement in the alleged activities construed falsely and distortedly as a threat against Denmark. "It is worth noting that Iran, relying on its indigenous capabilities and highly educated human resources, has registered tremendous progress in scientific achievements in the past couple of decades, thereby, contributing substantially to global scientific knowledge. The Iranian scientific and academic community has maintained excellent and healthy partnerships with prestigious universities and scientific institutions around the world. The Embassy of the Islamic Republic of Iran in Copenhagen reiterates its continued support for cooperation between Iranian and Danish scientific and academic circles. Iranian Embassy in Denmark clarified.

Anders Henriksen, Head of Counterintelligence Danish Security and Intelligence Service in his front matter of the report warned: "As a result, PET intensified its counter-intelligence efforts within the last couple of years. Our efforts seek to prevent, investigate and counter-intelligence activities carried out by foreign states in Denmark as well as intelligence activities targeting Danish interests abroad. As part of our intensified efforts, we now for the first time publish an overall assessment of the current threat to Denmark. Foreign states primarily use their intelligence activities to strengthen their political, military and economic position, and Denmark is an attractive target for foreign intelligence activities because of our active role on the international stage and membership of international organizations such as the EU, NATO and the UN. Furthermore, within certain areas Danish technology and research are world-leading and thus attractive targets of some foreign states". Mr. Anders Henriksen noted.[15]

## Chapter 6

# The Crisis of Danish Intelligence, Iran and China's Espionage Networks in Denmark, The PET Report, State Surveillance and Human Rights

The Danish intelligence report (PET Report) uncovered espionage networks of Iran, China, and Russia in Denmark to recruit people from different segments of society. The PET report also warned: "threat from foreign state intelligence activities targeting Denmark and Danish interests abroad presents our society with a number of significant political, security-related and economic challenges. In recent years, PET has uncovered several cases that illustrated how a number of foreign states were actively carrying out intelligence activities against Denmark. The authorities in other western countries had also uncovered cases of foreign espionage indicating the presence of a threat to their societies. PET assesses that the threat from foreign state intelligence activities in Denmark was specific and persistent. The activities include espionage, influence operations, harassment, attempts to illegally procure products, technology and knowledge and, in exceptional cases, outright assassination attempts. In practice, methods and targets vary according to the state actor behind the activities. While the threat primarily emanates from Russia, China and Iran, other states also carry out intelligence activities in Denmark. If foreign states gain access to sensitive information, it may prove detrimental to Denmark's security and scope to act. If it involves information concerning Denmark's relations with other countries, it could potentially be used not only against Denmark but also the countries with which we cooperate".[1]

Denmark military intelligence Chief was jailed for sharing sensitive intelligence information with foreign intelligence agencies. On 12 January 2022, analyst Charles Szumski (Danish military intelligence chief jailed for espionage-EURACTIV.com) reported that Military intelligence chief

Lars Findsen was jailed for a month for leaking classified documents to Danish media. "I plead not guilty," the head of the Danish military intelligence admitted before the judge rendered his verdict.[2] On 9 December, the Danish authorities announced, without revealing their identity, the arrest of four former or current members of the kingdom's two intelligence services. They were accused, among other things, of disclosing "highly confidential information from the intelligence services without authorisation". According to the local press, the case involves leaks of classified information to the Danish media. Several journalists have been interviewed by investigators. At the end of December, intelligence services warned journalists against publishing classified information. The warning was strongly condemned by the European Federation of Journalists which represents over 320,000 media workers in Europe. Mads Brandstrup, Chief Executive Officer of the Danish Media Association, said the intelligence services should be subject to public scrutiny, the same as any other part of the government. Expert Nikita Belukhin (The Scandal in Denmark's Military Intelligence: Too Much Transparency? Modern Diplomacy, 25 March 2022) has highlighted issue of espionage in Denmark:

"The delay in the key five military projects under the 2018–2023 defence agreement, including the full manning of the heavy mechanized 1st brigade in the amount of 4000 people, known as the "fist of the army" (Dan. hærens knytnæve), and especially, the scandal permeating the Military Intelligence Service of Denmark (Dan. Forsvarets Efterretningstjeneste, FE), which allegedly carried out espionage against German, Dutch, French, Swedish and Norwegian colleagues in favor of the U.S. National Security Agency, have not improved Denmark's standing in the alliance either. But it is the troubles within the FE, namely the so-called FE scandal, which has undoubtedly grabbed most of the public and mass media's attention. The highlights of this lengthy scandal were the arrest of four former and current surveillance officers of both the Danish Security and Intelligence Service (Dan. Politiets Efterretningstjeneste, PET) and the FE including the former FE-chief Lars Findsen on December 8, 2021 who was later released from custody on February 17, 2022 after successfully appealing his case and the former minister of defence Claus Hjort Frederiksen being officially suspected on December 20, 2021 for breaching the same paragraph as Lars Findsen of the Danish Criminal Code (Dan. Straffeloven), namely the extremely rarely used paragraph 109 known as «treason paragraph» related to revealing confidential data concerning national security or significant national economic interests abroad which has not been used by the courts since 1979. Both cases continue to be investigated behind closed doors and the precise wording of charges apart from the mentioned paragraph 109 is still unknown. Moreover, rather paradoxically, despite being suspected for the de-facto treason on national scale Claus Hjort-Frederiksen continues to participate in the Foreign Policy Committee of the Danish Parliament".[3]

The challenge of intelligence cooperation between the European Union and Britain is a complicated process. The lack of trust and attitude of both the British government and EU officials' irresponsible statements, further complicated intelligence sharing process. British intelligence infrastructure is so arrogant that its intelligence information is being collected by professional spies, so why authenticated information should be shared with the EU member state. The fact of the matter is their intelligence lacks public confidence, and professional security approach. All the UK intelligence agencies have accordingly failed to counter foreign intelligence networks. Intelligence agencies of South Asian states, Africa, China and Russia are openly dancing with impunity. Institutionally, intelligence cooperation relates to the intelligence interaction between the agencies respectively. The UK military failure in Afghanistan and Ukraine raised several questions. The failure of the state response means that an unreformed state and its intelligence infrastructure cannot manage a crisis with old strategies.

Expert and analyst, Christiaan Menkveld (Understanding the complexity of intelligence problems) in his research paper noted that effective intelligence and security services need to take the complexity of an intelligence problem into account when determining the aims of their investigation, the strategy of intelligence collection and its analytic approach: "The complexity of an intelligence problem (required intelligence assessment on a certain subject) determines to a great extent the certainty that intelligence and security services can provide on such an assessment. Even though this claim sounds almost obvious, its implications are significant, because it means that the public value of an intelligence service can vary depending on the complexity of an intelligence problem. This ranges from providing 'actionable' intelligence that can lead to interventions (legal, military, interruption operations, etc.), to providing insights that can be used as input for policymakers, and as context for interventions. Therefore, to be effective, intelligence and security services need to take the complexity of an intelligence problem into account when determining the aims of their investigation, the strategy of intelligence collection and its analytic approach. This also means that intelligence clients and oversight officials and legislators should take the complexity of intelligence problems into account when directing and appraising the performance of services."[4]

These challenges have debilitated the voice of Britain on international forums, and incapacitated its enforcement capabilities to energetically respond to the waves of foreign espionage, and extremism. External interference damaged the state's fundamental institutions. There have been several types of interference in the UK that further complicated security of citizens. To control society and political opponents, the government is using technology and their abusive powers that threaten our freedom. The introduction of Mass Surveillance programs by the British authorities prompted nationwide debate on the rights of civilians to be protected from illegitimate or warrantless intelligence information collection, and analysis of their data and metadata. The Home Office Web-Spying Powers and its collaboration with Internet Providers is a matter of great concern. No doubt, our privacy is under threat from all corners. On 11 March, 2021, BBC reported (Home Office tests web-spying powers with help of UK internet firms) uneasiness of privacy rights organisations on web-spying business of Home Office.

Privacy International (December, 2021) in its report noted strict surveillance measures of Britain and the EU to control population and maintain law and order, but this is not a rational panacea. Surveillance and secretly watching the civilian population and violating privacy cannot help maintain security. Privacy International in its report noted: "In the UK, we have experienced different types of watchdogs, spy networks and private intelligence and intelligence agencies collecting information and data by illegal means".[5] Privacy and human rights organizations filed numerous cases against the state surveillance swords, and tried to convince stakeholders that this way of privacy interference can alienate citizens from the state. If we look into the pool of cyber security strategy (2022-2030), we can find controversies and misunderstandings. We can spotlight the failure of the government to professionally respond to the cyber-attacks of Russia, China and private information warriors. In March 2021, anti-protest measures, or highly controversial covert human intelligence act became law in the UK, while the government proposed a police, crime, sentencing and court bill that contains new powers to clamp down on the right to protest. Statewatch, monitoring the state and civil liberties in Europe (11 March 2021) in its report noted the covert human intelligence sources (Criminal Conduct Act). Covert Human Intelligence agents might be secret police officers, informers and state agents. They will be instructed from police departments and intelligence offices. One of the most controversial aspects of the law, Statewatch noted is the fact that it contains no human rights safeguards of its own, and instead refers to the Human Rights Act 1988:

"With the CHIS Act on the books, the government has now published the Police, Crime, Sentencing and Courts Bill. This contains a whole host of measures, some of which may have positive effects, such as further laws on child abuse. However, it also plans stricter sentencing rules, new stop and search powers, and provisions that would criminalise trespass (currently a civil offence), which appears to be primarily targeted at gypsy and traveller groups but could also have serious negative effects for protesters, ramblers, wild swimmers and many others. The campaign group Friends, Families and Travellers (FFT) notes that: "Whilst the majority of over 26,000 responses to the Government's consultation did not support the proposals, the Government announced that it planned to still go ahead with plans to strengthen police powers against roadside camps. Under the Government's plans, a new criminal offence will be introduced for people living on roadside camps which could result in people being imprisoned, fined or having their home removed from them." Existing powers will also be extended -despite even the police stating that they don't need new powers to deal with unauthorised encampments, FFT underscores. The Bill also contains specific measures to crack down on protest. The government says these new powers will keep people safe and "ensure that they can get on with their daily lives peacefully and without unnecessary interference."[6]

Recent report of Contemporary Social Science-2021 has spotlighted limitations in the levelling up strategy that prioritize political agenda and centralization of powers rather than public policy. Lack of trust also exists to evolve powers to local leaders. As a multi-national and multi-ethnic state, the UK has been a failing country since 2001. Differences between poor regions and rich regions are crystal clear, and so is the case of poverty, unemployment and health. Different indicators in different fields present different stories of spatial disparities. We know National Security Secretariat is the bridge between intelligence and security, and the joint intelligence is an independent source of assessment of foreign policy and national security, and supporting the national security council in its analysis and assessment, but why national security council failed in many important strategic issues such like the case of Iraq, collapse of Afghan government in August 2021, and its professional response to the Covid-19 in 2020.

In May 2021, government announced a new unit to deal with the risk of foreign espionage and intelligence war in the UK, it means our agencies failed to tackle foreign espionage, noted the Russian interference report. In my previous papers and articles, I have already stressed the need for security sector reforms to make intelligence fit to the fight against intelligence war in the country. The reason that persistent intelligence approach to this issue is contradictory and weak. The Security Service (MI5) screeched and brawled about the Chinese female 'engaged in political interference activities on behalf of China, and warned that anyone contacted by the woman should be mindful of her affiliation and its remit to advance the CCP's agenda'. In February 2021, three Chinese spies were expelled who were potentially associated with China's Ministry of State Security.[7] President Putin raised the same question of foreign intelligence interference in Russia in the 1990s. He called for greater efforts to undermine foreign spy war on his soil. In 2017, President Putin communicated the threat of foreign intelligence interference in Russia, and said his country needed to stop the work of 52 foreign intelligence agencies.

We all know, how the UK intelligence works and how it counters foreign espionage? This is an important question. When we read in research reports, the fundamental function and operation of MI5 and MI6, we confuse and scrupulously analyse what's going on in our streets and towns. Some recent information elucidated that in No-10, National Security Secretariat provides coordination on security and intelligence issues of strategic importance across government, and Joint Intelligence Organisation produces independent all-source assessments on issues of national security and foreign policy importance. If this is the case, why our intelligence agencies have failed to counter foreign espionage networks, and why the National Security Council failed to update parliamentarians, intelligence agencies, and policy makers on Covid-19, Iraq, Ukraine and Afghanistan. The National Security Secretariat is providing policy advice to the National Security Council, where Ministers discuss national security issues at a strategic level, and coordinating policy, ethical and legal issues across the intelligence community, so why the performance of NSC has been underwhelming sine years. Expert and analyst, Sophia Hoffmann in her paper (Circulation, not cooperation: towards a new understanding of intelligence agencies as transnationally constituted knowledge providers-2021) noted demonstration of German Intelligence when it was sued an organization of journalist in May 2020:

"Thus, in May 2020, the German Supreme Court ruled that German intelligence's foreign relations required new controls, as the status quo violated the constitution. The ruling came after journalist organizations had sued, arguing that the way German intelligence was sharing knowledge with foreign counterparts could endanger journalists working in countries lacking press freedom and a prevailing climate of political oppression. Since the Supreme Court's ruling, German lawmakers have struggled to develop a new intelligence law that is adequate, amid controversial public debate. In Britain, the country's departure from the EU has shredded many transnational, institutional ties, yet research shows that UK intelligence relations with the EU remain fluid and durable, a matter which raises the question of how far international intelligence relations constitute an autonomous, transnational realm. The gap in scholarly attention to international intelligence relations begs important questions: do intelligence agencies develop autonomous power that they exercise internationally? What makes an intelligence agency powerful within the international intelligence realm? How does the international power of an intelligence agency relate to the power of its home state? Do intelligence agencies influence each other and, if so, how? How important are different factors, such as individuals, institutions, technology and information, in these relations? Studying only specific instances of intelligence alliances, as the current literature mainly does, is of little help here. What is needed instead is better general theory. In this article, I advance two main theoretical arguments: firstly, I argue that international intelligence relations can be better understood via the concept of knowledge circulation. Secondly, I argue that, considered via the prism of knowledge circulation, modern intelligence agencies emerge as fundamentally transnational actors, who have always been constituted via foreign relations".[8]

Intelligence agencies across Europe and the UK maintain a very poor record of professional approach when they comes to countering foreign espionage networks and activities of foreign embassies. In 2020, the UK government published a comprehensive report of Russian interference in the country, in which the main thing has been spotlighted was underestimation of the threat. On 21 July 2020, Intelligence and Security Committee published a Russian report and warned government to take immediate action to effectively counter Russian espionage. The committee said Russian influence in the UK was a top intelligence target. The ISC member, Stewart Hosie, said: "the government took its eye off the ball, because of its focus on counterterrorism, adding that the government had badly underestimated the response required to the Russian threat". The report criticised British intelligence agencies for failing to effectively respond to the espionage activities of Russian intelligence. The committee noted: "Had the relevant parts of the intelligence community conducted a similar threat assessment prior to the [EU] referendum, it is inconceivable that they would not have reached the same conclusion as to Russian intent, which might then have led them to take action to protect the process."[9] The report also noted that social media companies "hold the key and yet are failing to play their part", adding that the government should "name and shame those which fail to act."[10] In his DW analysis, Rob Mudge (From Russia with love: How damaging is the 'Russia Report' for the UK?-DW, July 21, 2020) noted some aspects of the report:

"At the core of a 50-page report compiled by the UK's Parliamentary Intelligence and Security Committee (ISC) over a year ago is the question of to what extent Russian influence held sway over UK political events, such as the 2016 Brexit referendum, and whether senior Conservatives were open to such advances. The report was unveiled on Tuesday, six months later than originally planned. That release date was scuppered by Prime Minister Boris Johnson's decision to dissolve parliament after calling a snap election, thus delaying its publication. The crux of the matter is that the report could not be made public while the ISC was in limbo. Indeed, the committee hadn't met since December's election—an anomaly in itself—due to Downing Street's failure to approve a list of MPs and peers nominated for membership. In a quirk of British politics, the ISC—which scrutinizes the activities of security and intelligence agencies—reports not to parliament but to the prime minister, who must clear its reports for publication. The delay has raised all sorts of questions and fuelled theories as to what kind of a smoking gun may be buried in the report. Details of the content remain scant as the ISC meets almost entirely behind closed doors. "The government kind of downplayed [the report] in the last few months that there won't be some great reveal. What we know is that [the ISC] decided quite early in the 2017 parliament to look at Russian interference in British public life, British elections. And they said they did that on the back of the US inquiry into Russian activities in the [2016] US presidential election. They also said they were concerned about Russian influence in the EU referendum," says Andrew Defty, associate professor of politics at the University of Lincoln and co-author of "Watching the Watchers: Parliament and the Intelligence Services."[11]

Russia's Foreign Ministry spokeswoman, called the report 'fake, but Financial Times, (George Parker and Helen Warrell in London and Henry Foy in Moscow-21 July 2020) reported that British Ministers were accused of turning a blind eye to possible interference by Moscow in the 2016 Brexit referendum. Kevan Jones said: "The outrage is not that there was interference. The outrage is that no one wanted to know if there was interference." However, "The report concluded that while there were many publicly available reports of Russian attempts to influence the 2014 Scottish independence referendum and the EU referendum two years later—and a known Russian hack during the last US Presidential Election—the UK government failed to order a proper inquiry into the issue. Britain's security services also appeared reluctant to take the initiative; the ISC said the issue of Russian interference in elections was seen as "a hot potato", with no organisation appearing to be in the lead. Elsewhere, the committee issued stark warnings about the extent of Moscow's operations in the UK, suggesting that Russian influence was the "new normal" with senior figures linked to the Kremlin enjoying access to top business and political leaders. Financial Times reported.[12]

Moreover, the Foreign, Commonwealth & Development Office and Elizabeth Truss warned that the UK, together with the US and other allies, exposed historic malign cyber activity of Russia's Federal Security Service (FSB). In its commentary on 24 March 2022, FCO noted: "KGB's successor agency, the Federal Security Service (FSB), was behind a historic global campaign targeting critical national infrastructure, and long list of cyber operations included UK energy sector, US aviation and a Russian dissident in the UK targeted using sophisticated hacking and spear-phishing..... Russia's targeting of critical national infrastructure was calculated and dangerous. It showed Putin was prepared to risk lives to sow division and confusion among allies. These sanctions followed a further 65 oligarchs and banks targeted by the Foreign Secretary, bringing the UK's sanctions on those who enabled Putin's war to more than £500 billion worth of bank assets and £150 billion in personal net worth."[13]

The current war of interests in Ukraine causing many problems between Russia and the UK. Britain, which is one of the guarantors of the territorial integrity of Ukraine, is being heavily criticised for its flawed approach to the expanding flare-ups along Europe's borders. In the Euro-committee of the House of Lords, the Cameron administration was deeply criticised for a 'catastrophic misreading' of the mood in Russia. As recent growing political tension in Ukraine changed the parameters of Russian and US priorities, intelligence war in the UK and the US also appeared with its evolving face. Being a US ally, the UK is facing the challenge of foreign intelligence networks on its soil, while the Federal Security Service of the Russian Federation (FSB) is becoming more aggressive with the intensification of its cyber terrorism against our state institutions.

Intelligence experts in London say that Russian intelligence war has returned to the Cold War era levels as the FSB is treating Britain with an aggressive mood. In fact, intelligence relations between the UK and Russia have deteriorated since 2006, following the murder of the former KGB agent, Alexander Litvinenko, in London. Alexander Litvinenko was a former FSB officer who arrived in the UK fearing court prosecution. He supported a wanted Russian businessman, Boris Berezovsky, in his media campaign. In 2006, Mr Litvinenko was poisoned in a hotel and died. Russian intelligence and espionage networks in the UK have been successfully collecting sensitive information from different state and government institutions by different means since years. The MI6 have often warned government of damaging activities of Russian intelligence, but successive governments never concentrated sincerely. British intelligence also failed to counter GRU and FSB in the streets of London. Hardly few people wrote articles in order to spotlight weaknesses of British intelligence and National Security Council to update policymakers. Analyst and expert, Precious Chatterje-Doody (The Evolution of Russian Hybrid Warfare: United Kingdom-29 January 2021) explained Russia's strategic priorities in the UK:

"The increased use of so-called hack-and-leak operations during international election campaigns has been a significant development over the past five or six years. These involve obtaining information and documentation sensitive to political parties via unsanctioned access, then leaking and amplifying them online. The U.K. government concluded that Russia-linked actors almost certainly attempted to interfere in the U.K.'s 2019 general election in this way, but their impact (if any) remains unclear pending an ongoing criminal investigation. Leaked content generally undermines both social values and the legitimacy of establishment institutions, which may be exacerbated by the strategic insertion of counterfeit documents. As in the case of the 2016 U.S. presidential election, the amplification of hacked content tends to take place via complex networks. Some of these (e.g., partisan online message boards) may have no connection to the Russian state and are pursuing their own interests in amplifying such stories. Others (e.g., bot and troll activity) may be the subject of clandestine state coordination, but be limited in their effectiveness by financially motivated mutual amplification. Some actors, like RT and Sputnik, have direct and open links to the Russian state. Their activities have been described in a general sense as "sowing doubt in Western media reporting (including information available to policy-makers)." The amplification of hacked content is one means to attempt this. A recent U.K. example concerns a 2018 cyberattack on the Integrity Initiative counter-disinformation program of the U.K.-based Institute for Statecraft. Funding and participant data (genuine and falsified) were released, then reported on by political bloggers, including some regularly featured on Russia's international broadcasters. RT and Sputnik presented the initiative as a U.K. government-funded "anti-Russia crusade" and an "information warfare effort run by British military intelligence specialists."[14]

As documented earlier, foreign intelligence networks in Britain received underwhelming attention from Westminster and intelligence infrastructure. South Asian intelligence agencies under diplomatic cover are making things worse. Indian and Pakistani agencies tackle their own opponents and critics in the UK, while ISI is tackling its critics, and the British intelligence enjoys their fight against Indian British and Pakistani British citizens. Recently, a British Pakistan national was tasked to kill another Pakistani dissident wanted by the Inter-Services Intelligence (ISI) in the Netherlands. A London Court heard Muhammad Gaohar Khan was offered £100,000 (about $134,000) by the ISI to kill Waqas Goraya in Rotterdam, but he failed to track his target down, and was arrested by Scotland Yard police on his return to the UK. The jury gave a unanimous guilty verdict of conspiracy to murder. Mr. Waqass Goraya, told BBC that "Pakistani intelligence services (ISI) were ultimately behind the plot and that it forms part of a wider crackdown on dissenting voices both inside and outside Pakistan".[15]

After this incidence, experts and politicians expressed deep concerns about the silence of British intelligence on Pakistan's illegal intelligence operation on UK soil. The country's intelligence agencies are openly hiring target-killers to kill their opponents and critics, but MI6 and MI5 never reacted professionally. The British intelligence agencies shamelessly warned dissident Pakistanis living in exile that their lives were in danger, but never took the issue on a diplomatic level with Pakistan. Mark Lyall Grant, a former UK High Commissioner to Pakistan, warned that the British government would take the matter seriously if the Pakistani military threatened persons from Pakistan in exile. He said, "If there is illegal pressure, in particular on journalists in the UK, then I would expect the law enforcement agencies and the British government to take notice of that and to make an appropriate legal and/or diplomatic response." Grant further said the British security agencies would not ignore evidence of intimidation on the behest of Pakistan's Inter-Services Intelligence (ISI). These warnings and concerns can be found only in newspaper pages, while practical actions has never been taken against ISI and Pakistan High Commission in London.

Now the question is why the UK government has announced a new unit to deal with the risk of foreign espionage? On 26 May 2021, Eanna Kelly reported to Science business News that "the UK government announced the formation of a new unit that will offer confidential security advice to researchers before entering international collaborations, in a drive to protect research assets from "hostile actors" in China and other countries. The creation of the team followed warnings from security experts about universities pursuing risky partnerships with Chinese companies and research labs. In February, it was reported that special agents were leading an investigation into more than a dozen UK universities for potential breach of export controls. "The threats to science and research in particular–primarily the theft, misuse or exploitation of intellectual property by hostile actors–are growing, evolving and increasingly complex," said the Department for Business, Energy and Industrial Strategy, which will manage the team. The unit, to be based in Manchester, will respond to requests from UK academics who have identified potential risks within current projects or proposals. Advisers will also proactively approach research labs and support them to implement advice and guidance already on offer".[16]

## Chapter 7

# The Home Office Web-Spying Powers, the French and German Intelligence Reforms, Intelligence Diversity and Foreign Intelligence Networks in the United Kingdom

When one talks about security and terrorism in the UK, he comes across many ideas, hypothesis and reports about the government and its agencies' failure to tackle violent extremism, international terrorism and espionage. There are thousands of research papers, essays, speeches and lectures available on the websites of think tanks, newspapers, journals and libraries that address crisis of national security with different approaches, but lack of professional approach and coordination in these research materials makes the case worse. As we have already tested the arrival of new surveillance technologies and their controversial use in our society. Snooper Charter Surveillance, and Facial Recognition Technologies by the police have made lives of citizens the hell. These weapons have badly failed to intercept jihadists joining the ranks of the Islamic State of Iraq and Syria (ISIS) and other groups in the Middle East and South Asia. We also understand that with the introduction of modern communication systems, surveillance and espionage networks have become a global phenomenon. The capturing, tracing and processing of personal data of citizens has become a controversial issue worldwide. Every state has promulgated its own communication and surveillance law that allows interception of communication, stops email trafficking and monitors Facebook, Twitter and YouTube. While we discuss these law enforcement related issues, many new things come to mind that force us to think that surveillance is not the only solution to our social problems. Yes, we know that modern state machinery in the UK ultimately depends on surveillance data but the way surveillance is used against the privacy of citizens has prompted deep frustration and social alienation.

The bureau of investigative journalism in the UK filed a case with the European Court of Human Rights in Strasbourg, challenging the current UK legislation on mass surveillance and its threat to journalism. On August 29, 2014, the UK's former Prime Minister warned that his country faced the "greatest and deepest" terror threat in history. Mr. David Cameron said that the risk posed by ISIS could last for "decades" and raised the prospect of an expanding terrorist nation "on the shores of the Mediterranean". Privacy and human rights groups complained that these day-to-day changing surveillance mechanisms might possibly alienate citizens from the state. The government and its security infrastructure are also worked up over the exacerbation of prevailing fear of online extremism across the country. We are living in a country where corruption and extremism have terminally damaged the smooth function of the state. The UK's local governments are under severe criticism due to a growing criminal and bureaucratic culture in borough (district) councils. The weakness and the growing unpopularity of local government, coupled with a decline in confidence and trust on the part of the communities, have received considerable attention from the print and electronic media.

Trust in local governments is at an all-time low where political influence, power and self-gratification are the drivers behind corruption. Officers of Councils often demonstrate racism and discrimination. Moreover, the issue of the Home Office spying programme on website visits received countrywide criticism. "The Home Office Web-Spying Powers and its collaboration with Internet Providers who helped its networks and National Crime Agency in tracking websites-visits is a matter of great concern. No doubt, our privacy is under threat. It also involved providers creating Internet connection records to show who visited this and that websites". On 11 March, 2021, BBC reported (Home Office tests web-spying powers with help of UK internet firms) uneasiness of privacy rights organisations on web-spying business of Home Office: "The power to spy on the websites people visit comes from the Investigatory Powers Act, which critics called it a "snoopers' charter" on account of widespread concerns about its scope. The act gives the secretary of state the power, with a judge's approval, to order internet providers to keep their records for up to a year. Unescorted strategies and measures couldn't help the government in maintaining security and stability unless practical steps are taken on different fronts".[1]

The issue of intelligence diversity was very important to me when the Intelligence and Security Committee of Parliament in its report (2018), emphasized the need of security sector reforms. I had already published several articles on this issue in different newspapers, in which I pointed to the fact that without security sector reforms, the UK law enforcement would not be able to address national security threats. In February 2021, the Times of London reported that Britain's foreign intelligence agency, the Secret Intelligence Service (SIS or MI6), was relaxing rules to allow applicants with dual UK nationality. Chief of the SIS Richard Moore apologised for the historical treatment of LGBT (Lesbian, Gay, Bisexual and Transgender) officials and the bar to gay men and women serving in SIS. There have been significant efforts to change the internal culture and promote change, the Big-3 having well established networks for women–SIS (DEUCE) and MI5 (GENIE)–and BAME groups- SIS (EMBRACE), MI5 (My5), GCHQ (REACH). LGBT and disability networks was also formed. For GCHQ, the REACH network led to increased engagement across the organisation, a change in approach to recruitment and traction with BAME communities across the country.

The issue of foreign espionage once more reverberated in British newspapers when British domestic intelligence agency (MI5) abruptly warned that Chinese intelligence agents were making things worse when they were introduced to parliamentarians. The MI5 said a female Chinese national was engaged in political interference activities on behalf of Beijing. But didn't explain why the agency didn't arrest her if she was a foreign agent. On 13 January 2022, Al Jazeera reported MI5's yell against the Chinese woman, and alleged that she was working on behalf of the Chinese Communist Party. MI5's own interference alert, which was circulated to parliamentarians, said anyone contacted by the woman should be "mindful of her affiliation" and its "remit to advance the CCP's agenda". "British spies said China and Russia have each sought to steal commercially sensitive data and intellectual property, as well as to interfere in domestic politics and sow misinformation". Al Jazeera reported.[2] The fact of the matter is that we never heard about the arrest of any Chinese spy on UK soil. Analyst and expert, Duncan Bartlett in his recent article (UK Intelligence Agency Targets China's United Front: Spymasters in the U.K. and other countries are going public in their push against CCP influence. The Diplomat January 22, 2022) noted the yell of British intelligence against China:

"The warning about Christine Ching Kui Lee, a solicitor who runs a law firm in London, was accompanied by her photograph, which ensured that her face appeared prominently across websites and social media, even though she was not arrested nor charged with any crime. Excited journalists jumped in to add new twists to the story. The next day the papers were filled with a great deal of comment and analysis – alongside plenty of hearsay and speculation. A key allegation is that Lee donated 420,000 British pounds ($572,000) to a senior Labour member of parliament, Barry Gardiner, who employed her son, Daniel Wilkes, as a member of his parliamentary staff. MI5 warned that anyone contacted by Lee "should be mindful of her affiliation with the Chinese state and remit to advance the CCP's agenda in UK politics." The warning was issued in the form of an alert which was sent by MI5 to the speaker of the House of Commons, Lindsay Hoyle, who chose to forward it to all MPs – ensuring immediate press attention. In his memo, Hoyle said: "I am writing now to draw your attention to the attached Interference Alert issued by the Security Service, MI5, about the activities of an individual, Christine Lee, who has been engaged in political inference activity on behalf of the Chinese Communist Party, engaging with members of parliament and associated political entities, including the former APPG (All Party Parliament Group) Chinese In Britain." Hoyle said Lee's donations were made in a covert way in order to mask the origins of the payments. "This is clearly unacceptable behaviour and steps are being taken to ensure it ceases," he added. The Chinese embassy in London said in a statement that China did not interfere in the internal affairs of other countries. In Beijing, foreign ministry spokesman Wang Wenbin said China has "no need" to engage in "so-called interference activities." "Perhaps, some people, after seeing too many James Bond movies, are imagining links where there is none".[3]

The Chief of the MI6 warned that China and Russia were racing to master artificial intelligence in a way that could revolutionise geopolitics over the next ten years. Richard Moore also argued that MI6 needed to adapt to new technology to survive. BBC correspondent, Frank Gardner (BBC-30 November 2021) reported Mr. Moore's public speech envisaging adaptation of artificial intelligence quantum computing and digital technology to completely transform the way human intelligence gathered by spies, presenting MI6 with major challenges in the digital age.[4] The UK's intelligence agency MI5, and GCHQ warned that the recruitment to UK universities of students from China, particularly postgraduates, was raising the risk of China stealing research and intellectual property from universities and of university computer systems being compromised. The agencies launched a campaign to warn of the dangers to national security of universities relying on Chinese money and students, particularly postgraduates. On 14 January, 2022, BBC reported MI5 accusations against a lawyer of trying to influence politicians on behalf of China. Home Secretary Priti Patel said it was "deeply concerning" that someone "who has knowingly engaged in political interference activities on behalf of the Chinese Communist Party has targeted parliamentarians". But she said the UK had measures in place "to identify foreign interference". The Chinese embassy in London said in a statement that: "China has always adhered to the principle of non-interference in the internal affairs of other countries. We have no need and never want to 'buy influence' in any foreign parliament. We strongly oppose the use of intimidation and defamation to malign the Chinese community in the UK."[5]

On 31 March 2022, Director General of GCHQ, Sir Jeremy Fleming in his public speech warned: "Believe it or not, it's only 36 days since Vladimir Putin launched an unprovoked and premeditated attack on Ukraine. It's been shocking in every sense of the word. But it wasn't surprising. We've seen this strategy before. We saw the intelligence picture building. And we're now seeing Putin trying to follow through on his plan. But it is failing. And his Plan B has been more barbarity against civilians and cities".[6] The British intelligence agencies and their sarcastic statements in newspapers and public forums mollycoddled the country's relationship with the EU and China. When intelligence agencies perform duties of politicians, then they are viewed as political organizations. Institutionally, intelligence leads policy makers in the right direction. They don't involve themselves in a blame game. Analyst and expert, Kyle S. Cunliffe (Hard target espionage in the information era: new challenges for the second oldest profession) highlighted the operation of Chinese and Western spies beyond borders:

"The relaxing of Russian and Chinese borders in the post-Cold War world brought about greater opportunities for Western intelligence officers. Tourists and businessmen could travel to their major cities with relative ease, with a larger footprint of international travellers putting new strains on surveillance while offering more wiggle room for foreign operatives. However, today the advantages offered by these more open societies must be weighed against emerging technological threats. In recent years, technological developments have created new challenges to intelligence officers' cover (the fake identities they use to enter and socialise in foreign environments), potentially allowing surveillance to function with unprecedented speed and efficiency. As argued by the former head of SIS, Alex Younger, today's intelligence officers face an 'existential threat' brought about by the information age. These technological challenges have already been documented to some extent by scholars and former practitioners, including former CIA case officer David Gioe and former deputy head of SIS, Nigel Inkster, but have not received sustained examination in the context of specific hard targets. This paper thus attempts to examine the state of street surveillance in contemporary Russia and China, alongside the solutions that intelligence agencies might adopt to address the problems it presents. It aims to show that the West faces a new and fraught era of Moscow/Beijing Rules with no easy resolution and dire implications for the value of espionage".[7]

In the UK, France, Germany, Netherlands, Italy, Greece and Brussels, the new arrival of radicalised elements, and home-grown jihadists challenged authority of government and law enforcement agencies. In the UK, the watch list of MI5 has been increased to 43,000 individuals, but intelligence reforms are extremely mandatory to end the culture of political and bureaucratic stakeholders within all EU member states. The Nice, London and Munich attacks exposed the EU national security approach, where political parties and civil society pointed to the incompetency of law enforcement agencies. The issue of security sector reforms in France and Germany, and Eastern European States is often discussed in print and electronic media, but in reality, their zeal and resolve revolved around old mechanisms. In yesteryears, some intelligence reforms were introduced in France, Germany, Poland and Romania, but Romania and Germany are still struggling to bring their intelligence agencies under democratic control. After that initiative, in 2015, an intelligence act was adopted in France, but after the terror attacks in 2015 and 2016, the country's parliamentary investigation identified multiple failures within the French intelligence infrastructure. The investigation inquiry, later on, recommended a fusion of all six intelligence agencies. Socialist lawmaker Sebastian Pietrasanta told journalists that two intelligence chiefs admitted intelligence failure. Tobias Bunde and Sophie Eisentraut, (Munich Security Brief, July 2020) have noted some aspects of the EU security crisis, and their approach to conflict management:

"For about a decade, the EU has been in constant crisis mode. The financial and economic crisis put the architecture of the euro to the test and triggered enduring debates about national fiscal responsibility and European solidarity. The war in Syria demonstrated Europe's inability to put an end to a serious conflict at Europe's doorstep–a conflict that has killed hundreds of thousands of people and strained relations among European nations due to the arrival of increasing numbers of refugees in Europe. The war in Ukraine revealed that the use of military force was still an option on the European continent and exposed the poor state of European defence. It also highlighted the fact that, without the support of the United States,

Europeans would be unable to defend themselves against major military aggression. The United Kingdom's decision to leave the EU showed that European integration had ceased to be a one-way street towards ever-closer union. In most EU member states, nationalist and populist forces have entered parliaments and shifted the contours of political discourse. In some countries, where they have entered government, illiberal forces have eroded European core values and undermined the rule of law – and the EU has been struggling to respond".[8]

In Eastern European states, the former Communist culture of intelligence is yet so strongly rooted in society and resists all new efforts of bringing intelligence under democratic control. In Greece, Lithuania, Estonia, Ukraine, Romania, and Poland, private, political, and bureaucratic stakeholders have generated numerous problems. In the UK, MI5 and MI6 have been tied to Interior and Foreign Ministries that curtailed their operational mechanism. Recent terrorist attacks in Britain and in the EU (2020) were the most extensive and dangerous the continent ever seen due to massive increase in illegal immigrants. By law, all EU member states need to regulate organizations of their country's intelligence services and establish different units to divide responsibilities between military and civilian agencies. The failure of French intelligence agencies before the 14 July 2016 terrorist attacks in Nice was mainly due to the lack of their coordination with law enforcement's agencies to prevent the truck runner. The consecutive failure of German intelligence agencies to intercept the lone wolves and religiously motivated Muslim extremists before they translated their ferments and resentment into a violent action, raised important question that reforms within the operational mechanism of its secret agencies was mandatory.

British intelligence is still following the old streaks and failed to effectively address national security challenges due to their involvement in Afghanistan, Iraq, Syria and Libya. However, amidst this inconsistent collective engagement among EU states, German intelligence spied on France, British intelligence spied on Germany, Denmark military intelligence besmirched in corruption, and the BND power of surveillance has been curtailed. The Crisis of intelligence sharing still exists within the EU project where political and bureaucratic stakeholders protect their own interests. German Parliament, politicians, security experts and the Cabinet have discussed intelligence reforms package for more than a year to bring the BND under democratic control. The reform set new rules for intelligence information gathering and surveillance. It was a great victory for politicians and the security and intelligence establishment who addressed flaws of the operational mechanism of all intelligence infrastructures. They expanded the BND's digital powers despite careless disclosure of German and European strategic interests to the Five Eyes intelligence alliance by the country's intelligence.

The DW New report (15 May 2020) noted a revised bill on reform of the German domestic intelligence agency to boost liaison with regional authorities. Electronic Frontier Foundation (14 January 2020) in its comprehensive report noted legal developments on the evaluating of intelligence act that entrust BND wide-ranging surveillance authority: "In 2016, Germany's Bundestag passed intelligence reform that many argued did not go far enough. Under the post-2016 order, an independent panel oversees the BND and any foreign intelligence collected from international communications networks must be authorized by the chancellor. However, the new reform explicitly allowed surveillance to be conducted on EU states and institutions for the purpose of "foreign policy and security," and permitted the BND to collaborate with the NSA—both of which allow for the privacy of foreign individuals to be invaded. It is worth noting that part of what allows a case like this to move forward is the ability of German citizens to know more about the surveillance programs their nation operates. In the United States, our lawsuit against NSA mass surveillance is being held up by the government's argument that it cannot submit into evidence any of the requisite documents necessary to adjudicate the case. In Germany, both the BND Act and its sibling, the G10 Act, as well as their technological underpinnings, are both openly discussed making it easier to confront their legality".[9]

Relationship of Greece National Intelligence Services (NIS) with EU intelligence agencies helped it in maintaining a culture of professional operations intact. This relationship further strengthened resolve of the NIS management to adopt offensive mood of operation against lone wolves, extremist and jihadist groups. Recent reform and restructuring of the intelligence community in Greece further expanded the role of NIS to include both domestic and foreign intelligence operations, but most of the current intelligence problems within the country, whether they relate to questions of ethics and privacy, are old dilemmas. After the London, Madrid, Paris, Munich and Nice attacks, the NIS was facing internal threats of extremism and foreign espionage networks and their relationship with local religious and ethnic groups, but the agency successfully intercepted, undermined and identified these elements within immigrants before they carried out attacks against civilian and military installations.

Romania's new intelligence infrastructure and its stakeholders faced backbreaking and laborious resistance from its former communist precursors' who wanted to push the reform convoy of democratic forces to the brink. Democratization of secret services and the policing forces in Romania has been a complicated issue since the dissolution of the Soviet Union when the old communist intelligence infrastructure refused to allow democratic reforms. The agency was also accused in the press of illegally investigating journalists, media agencies, and politicians. Often, the political struggle between parties or within parties to obtain the leadership of ministries that control the spy agencies is acute. Poland and Balkan's States are facing the same challenges where the process of security sector reforms is in danger due to the intransigence of former stakeholders and networks. The National Security Strategy of the Republic of Poland was approved on 12 May 2020 by the President of the Republic, which spotlights and asserts the adoption of different restructuring strategies:

"Integrating national security management, including state defence management and building of adaptation capabilities, integrate the national security management system, including state defence management, enabling the unification of processes, procedures and working practices by merging the so-far existing systems, in particular, national security management, crisis management and cybersecurity. Provide the ability of swift adaptation to new challenges and threats as well as identification of opportunities. Create an interagency coordination mechanism for the management of national security through setting up a committee of the Council of Ministers, responsible, at the strategic level, for dealing with issues in the field of policies, strategies and programmes pertaining to national security management, in a manner ensuring their consistent and coherent implementation and linking the committee with the new role and competences of the Government Crisis Management Team and the Government Centre for Security".[10]

More recently, Greece has become home to Turkish intelligence networks and illegal immigrants who entered the country on fake papers with unknown background established takfiri jihadist networks to recruit young fighters. Greece has been an attractive transit point for jihadists travelling to and from Syria, Iraq, Afghanistan, and Libya but the number of these jihadists has not been well documented by the police and intelligence services of the country. In 2015 alone, more than 2,000 jihadists used

Greece as a transit point to Iraq and Syria. The CBS News in September 2019 reported clandestine human smuggling networks in Athens. The networks were transporting jihadists to Greece, and then to other European states. However, the EU inspection team of Greek sea and land borders (CNN, Telegraph, and Greek Reporter PBS Frontline, and CTC Sentinel) noted: "Serious deficiencies in the carrying out of external border control by Greece, in particular due to the lack of appropriate identification and registration of irregular migrants at the islands, of sufficient staff, and of sufficient equipment for verifying identity documents".[11] Moreover, Human Rights Watch on 01 March 2020 reported Greece's Government National Security Council (GGNSC) decision about the suspension of access for asylum seekers for a month:

"The EU has an opportunity to show it can respond with compassion to the arrival of people fleeing conflict and persecution by putting their dignity and humanity at the centre of its response," said Lotte Leicht, EU director at Human Rights Watch. To identify these sarcastic and anti-state elements, the government needed to retrieve modern surveillance technology, but after the 9/11 terrorist attacks, intelligence agencies retrieved uncontrollable strength by imposing wide ranging surveillance practices on society as well. This is a modern technological development that transformed Greek society into democratization, and institutional modernization. With the technological transformation process, intelligence infrastructure of the country also embarked its journey from militarized culture of intelligence to civilian and democratic culture of spying, in order to fortify its roots within political and social stratifications."[12]

The NIS changed its mood of operation because it faced the threat of illegal migration, terrorist networks, and illicit trade of weapons of mass destruction. The agency has also been playing a crucial role in fighting the challenge of national security with its professionally designed strategies and security measures since 9/11. Intelligence cooperation, security, stability and prosperity are fundamental goals of all states in contemporary world affairs, while in Greece; more importance has been given to intelligence sharing from European Union member states to expand the range of watchdog to all parts of the country. To achieve the goal of a strong and competent state, the existence of well-trained armed forces, a professional intelligence system, and economic power was a must. I personally found no single report of the NIS corruption in Greece, but there are numerous reports of corruption of EU intelligence agencies available in newspapers and journals. Due to the lack of security sector reforms, corruption, and international engagement, major private and state intelligence agencies in the EU failed to intercept and disrupt the exponentially growing networks of radicalised groups and lone wolf attacks; for that reason, increasing numbers of dangers across borders could not reflect in their policies and strategies. The current waves of lone wolves' attacks in the EU are the most extensive and dangerous the continent has ever seen due to massive increase in migrants that caused insecurity and political pressure in Greece as well. By law, all EU member states are regulating organisations of their country's intelligence services and establishing different units to divide responsibilities of military and civilian intelligence agencies in dealing with national security threats. After the poisonous attack of Russian intelligence against Sergei and Yulia Skripal in Salisbury in March 2018, the Government decided to introduce legislation to "harden our defences against all forms of hostile state activity", including a power to detain those suspected of it at the border. The Teresa May Government passed the Counter-Terrorism and Border Security Act 2019. Notwithstanding all these efforts of British successive governments, foreign espionage networks expanded, stretched and intensified. Networks of Chinese intelligence in London is an underwhelming saga. The MI5 warned in January 2022 that a Chinese spy infiltrated the UK Parliament while a female Chinese national 'engaged in political interference activities' on behalf of Beijing.[13]

## Chapter 8

# Dematerialization of Civilian Intelligence in Romania: War of Strength between Democratic and Communist Intelligence Stakeholders

Intelligence and security sector reform has been a critical element of bringing intelligence under democratic control. Intelligence agencies perform an important role in protecting national security, and national critical infrastructure. Growing threats of extremism, and radicalization has rendered more urgent their efforts to protect state security. But, in majority EU states, the lack of expertise in dealing with secrecy and with technical matters has been a disturbing issue since years. On EU law enforcement level, intelligence information is shared among security agencies to make internal and external security of the project consolidated and secure. Information sharing is now being facilitated by centralised databases and various formal and informal networks. Policing agencies often keep information of criminal cases, and keep their strategies secret, but intelligence agencies build their work and strategies upon secrecy. The Paris, London and Brussels terrorist attacks forced national governments to introduce security and intelligence reforms to make intelligence and policing forces competent in the war against terrorism and radicalization, but security regime of some Central European states still remains largely unreformed.

The Romanian revolution that saw the seeds of self-government in December 1989 was the main starting point of the country's independence from the former Soviet Union. Communist leader, Nicolai Ceausescu was executed and the National Salvation Front (FSN) took power to lead the nation towards the establishment of a new and modern democratic state. The new government managed economic reforms but also designed national security measures to end dictatorship and introduce democratic culture of governance. Political and security sector reforms were an irksome state due to the strong networks of former communist administration, internal opposition and bureaucratic stakeholderism. There was a political and bureaucratic stakeholder's culture that deeply influenced foreign and domestic policies of the state. These stakeholders didn't allow democratization and modernization of state institutions. New constitution was introduced in December 1991. After 9/11, Romania ultimately joined the US camp, and sent troops to Afghanistan for fighting war against terrorism, while in 2004, NATO gave full membership to Romania. The country after three years of negotiation, joined the EU project in 2007.

Romanian intelligence faced numerous challenges under Soviet rule after it was established under the Decree No. 221 on 30 August 1948, as one of the Directorates of the Ministry of Home Affairs (DMIA). In 1952, under the decree No 324, intelligence was separated from the Ministry of Interior to work independently and design its own operational strategies, gather intelligence information and lead policy makers in the right direction. Later, on 07 September 1953, the State Security Ministry was merged with the Internal Affairs Ministry, and on 10 July 1956, Home Ministry was reorganized into the Department of Interior and Department of Security to meet the challenges of domestic security. Romanian intelligence Services and its management still needed to reform the undemocratic way of intelligence operation as there has been a long fight among different stakeholders to control the command of the agency. Analyst Elena Dragomir has noted these and other flawed strategies in her report:

"One of the most important problems that Romania had to address once communism collapsed in 1989 was how to deal with the legacy of its infamous Securitate - the all-pervasive Department of State Security. Although much of that legacy has been dealt with since then, the discussion and debate over security sector reform in general continues today. While numerous politicians, journalists, scholars, Romanian and non-Romanian alike, stress that Romania would need to confront many obstacles in order to bring the reform of the secret services to the desired end, relevant legislation remains under consideration and no final solutions have been reached".[1]

There has been confusion about how to provide a safe environment to the Intelligence and Interior Ministry but it was a difficult time for stakeholders to adopt reformed strategies. The separation of intelligence networks from the Home Office and re-emerging times and again caused misunderstanding between the government and political stakeholders. There was a weak perception of intelligence operations within the government circles and bureaucratic stakeholders, but tenacious resistance from old intelligence and policing infrastructure blocked the door to modernization and reforms. On 19 April 1972, there were proposals that the emerging Council of State Security with the Home Office of the country can help law and order management and fight against anti-states elements, but later on, the intelligence council was reorganized into six directorates. Counterintelligence and counterespionage departments were of great importance in the whole process of reorganization, but these departments were also hijacked by different stakeholders. In March 1978, Mihai Pacepa, the former Chief of Foreign Intelligence service, defected to the United States with a huge pack of secrets. His defection caused turmoil within the intelligence infrastructure, which forced the management to expel several secret agents due to their irksome loyalties. Analyst Elena Dragomir in her research report, reviewed the evolutionary process of Romanian intelligence:

"On 26 December 1989, the National Salvation Front decided on the termination of the Securitate, and subordination of the Department of State Security to the Ministry of National Defense, where it remained until the end of 1990. On March 26 1990, Decree No-181 created the Romanian Intelligence Service (SRI; in Romanian, Serviciul Român de Informații), the main secret service in Romania today. Many feared that the SRI inherited the personnel, the methods and the faults of the former Securitate. Today, it is unlikely that few, if any officers from the Communist period remain there, however. According to the law, the secret service is responsible to the Romanian Parliament".[2]

In 1990, Communist intelligence infrastructure of Romania was again reorganized and transformed into the Foreign Intelligence Service. The General Directorate for Intelligence and Internal Protection was another strong and well-established agency-subordinated to the Home Ministry. The newly established secret agency was named in 1992 as a Special Telecommunications Service. The General Directorate of Defence Ministry was a military intelligence agency-specializing in gathering, processing, checking, intelligence and data related to internal and external security. There has been a long fight between print and electronic media and the intelligence agencies for a number of reasons. However, one reason the agencies were criticized was their political role in making political alliances and creating challenges for governments in power. Policing and intelligence agencies were supporting different political camps. Transfer and posting was totally on political bases. In December 2009, Vasile Blaga criticized the

DGIPI committee, and in April 2010, while became Minister, he criticised his precursor.

Florina Cristiana Matei in her research paper (Reconciling Intelligence Effectiveness and Transparency: The Case of Romania, Strategic Insights, Volume VI, Issue 3, May 2007) has highlighted some aspects of professionalization of intelligence and replacement of old cadres with young agents. She also noted some technological developments that helped intelligence professionals in collecting intelligence information. Florina Cristiana Matei also described Romanian National Intelligence Agency and the High National Security College (HNSC) where specialized training units and other intelligence agencies retrieve training:

"To finish with the Securitate legacy, Romania has been undertaking major efforts to professionalize the IC (to foster expertise, corporateness, and responsibility), to replace, thus, the old generations of intelligence agents with young open-minded intelligence professionals, with a true sense of responsibility to democracy. To do this, it has institutionalized a new personnel management system, with modern recruiting, promotion, education and training techniques. By 2007, the average age in the intelligence agencies came down to 35. These personnel graduated after 1989 and have no relation with Romania's past political police. As well, the personnel of the IC anti-terrorist units are professional, selected from champions of various NATO/PfP special operations exercises. It is also worth mentioning president Traian Basescu's commitment to promote young personnel and most important to curb political appointments. President Basescu appointed George Cristian Maior, a member of one of the opposition party, as head of SRI, in October 2006; Maior is a law graduate from the University Babes-Bolyai, Cluj-Napoca (1991), and the College of International and Comparative Law of George Washington University, in Washington D.C. He was deputy defence minister (2000-2004) and president of one of the Parliament intelligence oversight committees from 2004 to October 2006. The post-communist IC personnel have benefited from modern, democratic intelligence and security education and training, both in Romania and abroad, which contributed greatly to increasing the IC professionalism. At the national level, Romania has the National Intelligence Agency (ANI), the High National Security College (HNSC), as well as specialized training units within other intelligence agencies, whose programs rely heavily on NATO/Western curricula and teaching expertise, and reflect the new security features. The HNSC was established following the Citizen's Academy within the U.S. Federal Bureau of Investigations

(FBI), while the SPP agents train together with the U.S. Secret Service agents".[3]

Romania's new intelligence infrastructure and its stakeholders faced back-breaking and laborious resistance from its communist precursors' who wanted to push the reform convoy of democratic forces to the brink. The intelligence and security sector reforms received mixed messages from the international community. The persisting complications in Romanian intelligence are corruption, stakeholderism, and the operational mood of former Securitate agents. Democratization of secret services and the policing forces in Romania has been a complicated issue since the dissolution of the Soviet Union when old communist intelligence infrastructure refused to allow democratic reforms. The agency was also accused in the press of illegally investigating journalists, media agencies, and politicians. Often, the political struggle between parties or within parties to obtain the leadership of ministries that control the spy agencies is acute. Elena Dragomir has also noted cases of malpractices within the security system:

"In 2009, for instance, the Council identified 298 alleged former Securitate officers. Another mission of the Council is to verify if different persons holding or standing for different public offices had collaborated with the communist secret services. In 2009, the Council looked into the backgrounds of over 7,000 such persons, and identified 29 former Securitate officers as currently holding public officers....... The accusation of having collaborated with the Securitate is one of the most important political tools in electoral campaigns or within the political struggle for power in general. Even Romania's President, Traian Basescu, has come under the suspicion of having been a high-level Securitate officer during the communist regime, and of having maintained its mandate and political power with the direct support of the secret services".[4]

Reforming agencies was a difficult task for Romainan government and its secret agencies, media, and the international community. Corruption was in peak and internal divisions were also disturbing that were causing weaknesses of operational intelligence mechanism. Dr. Diva Patang Wardak in her research paper on Romanian intelligence (Democratization and the Intelligence Service: A Comparative Reflection on Afghanistan and Romania-2018) has highlighted security sector reforms, and corruption of intelligence agency of Romania:

"The recent move against the culture of corruption and anti-government political developments in Romania raised irksome questions about the fairness of the Security Sector Reforms process and democratic transformation. The issue of Security Sector Reforms and political transition in the country has been of great importance during the last two decades. Romania's problem with corruption became transparent while European Commission accepted its membership, but created natural selection, and oversight of Security Sector Reforms. On 18 January 2017, Intellinews reported the resignation of the deputy head of Romanian intelligence, Florian Coldea. Mr. Florian was forced to resign on 17 January 2017, while the head of anti-corruption came under pressure to explain his position about the revelations of businessman Sebastian Ghita who claimed that the security service was involved in shaping the DNA in partnership with the State Intelligence Agency (SRI) (Ernst, 2017). Security picture in Romania presents an entirely different shape. Romania is a peaceful state where the reforms process is underway in a smooth way, but currently, its secret agencies came under media scrutiny, and have been criticized for a number of reasons, though much remains unclear due to a lack of accurate information".[5]

Romanian National Defence Strategy 2015-2019 has also outlined its national security and defence perceptions with new zeal and resolve. This strategy links with Constitutional Provisions that assert Romania as a national, sovereign state. Constitutional Provisions of Romania No-473/2004 explain the country national defence strategy and defence planning, also stresses the need to multifacet national security strategy for stabilising the country. In chapter-2 paragraph 33 and 34, and 35, the National Defence Strategy explained international security environment:

"Romania's position on the Eastern flank of the North-Atlantic Alliance and of the European Union, as well as at the crossroads of some areas with a high security shows that defense and security surpass the area of responsibility of a single state. It is necessary to revisit some concepts and establish new measures to ensure predictability and consensus in handling national instruments both independently, as well as in allied and community context, OSCE being, in this regard, an important element within the European security system. The main warranty provider when it comes to Romania's security is The North Atlantic Alliance, the transatlantic relationship representing the strategic binder which awards coherence and consistency to NATO actions. The solidity of the transatlantic relationship depends on the United States' maintaining their commitment in Europe, as well as the way allies and European partners will allot financial assistance to develop their own defense capabilities. An important actor in the European and Euro Atlantic environment is the Russian Federation. Its actions in the Black Sea Region, infringing upon international law, questioning international order, preserving frozen conflicts and the annexation of Crimea have raised again the NATO awareness upon fulfilling its fundamental mission that is collective defense, as well as the validity of the security arrangements agreed upon with Russia at the end of the 20th century".[6]

Security and stability of the EU, as mentioned in Romanian National Defence Strategy for 2015-2019, is under threat from homegrown extremist and radicalized forces that recruit young fighters and participate in the ISIS wars in Iraq, Syria and Afghanistan. In Eastern Europe, when governments fail to stabilise their societies, they accuse Russia for its interference in their internal affairs. Normally, EU governments are worried about the consternating picture of changing national security threats. Analysts and researchers, Susi Dennison, Ulrike Esther Franke, & Paweł Zerka, (The European Council of Foreign Relations, July 2018) noted aspects of this fear of internal division and looming threat:

"The conventional wisdom is that the EU's internal divisions are particularly sharp on security and defence issues, with the east mainly concerned about Russia and the south predominantly worried about terrorism. But the results of ECFR's survey suggest that the picture is more complex than this. Divergences in European threat perceptions are less apparent than the prevailing narrative would suggest, with terrorism and migration having to some extent made the southern neighbourhood a pan-EU preoccupation, and with cyber-attacks and information warfare having increased concern about Russia in member states outside central and Eastern Europe. Nonetheless, disagreements over how to address threats could become the most significant obstacle to the creation of independent European defence capabilities.......Unsurprisingly; eastern and southern Europeans were particularly concerned about uncontrolled migration into their countries. Indeed, Slovenia, Austria, Hungary, Bulgaria, Greece, Malta, and Italy saw this as the most significant threat they face. Concern about international crime is a southern story, with Greece, Malta, Spain, and Portugal (but also Slovakia and Austria) considering it a high-priority threat. Fear of terrorism is particularly evident in larger countries and those that have recently experienced terrorist attacks (the UK, France, Spain, Germany, Denmark, and Belgium). Concern about Russia is strongest in the east

(Estonia, Romania, Lithuania, Poland, and Finland), although Germany and the UK also perceive it as a major threat. Estonia and Lithuania are especially worried about Russian meddling in domestic politics".[7]

There are clefts, political and strategic differences within the EU while every state is following its own national agenda. They do not wholeheartedly share intelligence information on law enforcement level with each other. Some states are not interested in the EU international war against terrorism and their interference in Afghanistan, Libya, Iraq and Syria. These differences have painted an ambiguous picture of their intelligence and military cooperation. Analysts and researchers, Susi Dennison, Ulrike Esther Franke, & Paweł Zerka (The European Council of Foreign Relations, July 2018) have noted aspects of weaknesses, divisions and narratives of the EU member states: "These divisions initially appear to confirm the narrative on a divided EU. But there are few actual contradictions among Europeans even when their top priorities diverge: threats that are a top priority for some EU countries are generally a significant threat for the rest, while issues that many view as benign are at most "somehow a threat" for others. Such broad alignments will ease the search for common responses. There are only two exceptions to this rule. The first is Turkey, which ten countries consider to be no threat but two others (Greece and Cyprus) see as their top threat. The most problematic division is in European states' perceptions of Russia, which seven countries regard as the most important to their security and six others as a significant threat, but which five, predominantly southern, countries (Greece, Italy, Portugal, Hungary, and Cyprus) view as no threat at all".[8]

Figuring out security and intelligence sector reforms in newly independent Eastern and Central European countries have been complicated issues due to their weak response to conflicting security paradigms. Prominent scholar and intelligence expert Larry L. Watts, a former Rand consultant and adviser on military reform to the Romanian Defense Ministry, in his well-written paper (Intelligence Reform in Europe's Emerging Democracy, Studies in Intelligence, Vol 48, No 1) has highlighted the crisis of democratization, post-communist transition in Central and Eastern Europe, and institutional reforms after NATO opened its doors to new members in 1993:

"Intelligence reform is a critical element of democratization, but it is frequently relegated to the back burner in the early days of post-authoritarian regime transitions. This is due, in part, to a reflexive aversion to what was commonly the most brutal legacy of the former regimes.

Transition populations tend to favour the destruction of intelligence apparatuses, not their reform. In the post-communist transitions in central and Eastern Europe, competing priorities also distracted attention from intelligence reform as political, economic, and other security institutions simultaneously underwent changes. Given recurrent intelligence and "political policing" problems in the transition states, it was inevitable that reform in those domains would eventually become a western priority, particularly after NATO opened its doors to new members in 1993. Unbridled political competition within the post-communist states, where the rules of the game were still in contention and abuses of executive power common, heightened concerns regarding the impact of partly reformed or unreformed intelligence services on an enlarged western alliance. Unfortunately, the West's attempts to evaluate the intelligence reform process in the various states of the region were handicapped by the differences among the new democracies, which limited comparative analysis; by the inappropriateness of western models developed under different political, social, and economic circumstances; and by the failure of western analysts to recognize that the post-Cold War revolution in intelligence affairs conflicts in many respects with the classic model of intelligence reform".[9]

Chapter 9

# The Key to Intelligence Reform in Germany: Strengthening the G10-Commission's Role to Authorise Strategic Surveillance

## *Dr. Thorsten Wetzling*

### Executive Summary

Many European countries have recently adopted new intelligence laws or are currently reviewing them. Germany is about to follow suit. Unlike their European colleagues, legislators in Berlin will have to align and defend their particular reform proposals against the substantial shortcomings that the Bundestag's in-depth investigation into signals intelligence cooperation between the Bundesnachrichtendienst (BND) and its intelligence partners (particularly NSA and GCHQ) unearthed. It is against this backdrop that this paper first reviews the main deficits of the current oversight system for signals intelligence (SIGINT) and then provides recommendations on how to improve and modernize its authorisation, oversight and transparency. Within the current system of intelligence oversight in Germany, the G10-Commission is responsible for examining and authorising governmental requests to allow the federal intelligence services to intercept private communications. Unlike other parliamentary control bodies, it holds the important power to order an immediate end to surveillance measures it deems unlawful or unnecessary. However, due to grave institutional deficits and significant gaps in the current intelligence law, the G10-Commission cannot properly perform its important democratic control function. For example, the core business of the BND's SIGINT activities – i.e. the acquisition and collection of foreign-foreign communication data (data

132

that has both its origin and destination outside of Germany) – does not fall within the mandate of the G10-Commission.

Currently, this important practice is not subject to democratic control, let alone sufficiently regulated by the intelligence law. The G 10-Commission also lacks the resources and the technical know-how to conduct meaningful judicial review over the data processing by the federal intelligence services. A significant reform of the current SIGINT authorisation and control process is required to overcome the current democratic deficits and to ensure that surveillance legislation and practice conform to international human rights standards and the German Basic Law. The following reform measures are particularly important and ought to be addressed by Germany's pending intelligence reform.

- The G 10-Commission must be able to review the legality and necessity of foreign telecommunications surveillance. A new intelligence law ought to address the entire spectrum of possible infringements of the right to private communication.

- A civil liberties advocate should be embedded in the process of authorizing communication surveillance in Germany. He/she would represent the interest of those directly affected by SIGINT measures who currently play no part in Germany's unique quasi-judicial "substitute procedure" (German Constitutional Court). The civil liberties advocate would delineate how an envisaged surveillance measure would conflict with the right to private communication and could make the case for a less intrusive but perhaps equally insightful SIGINT operation.

- The G 10-Commission needs substantial empowerment. More important than the amount of individual commissioners is an efficient secretariat. This requires financial and human resources to enable them to pre-examine interception warrants in light of the extended mandate of the G 10-Commission.

## Introduction

The work of the "NSA Inquiry Committee" set up by the German Parliament (Bundestag) provided a first opportunity for the public to learn about the country's Foreign Intelligence Service (Bundesnachrichtendienst, BND) bulk collection of foreign-foreign communication data. This pertains to the collection, processing and use of millions of communication data originating and ending outside of Germany.[1] The BND refers to this practice as "routine surveillance", a practice which is estimated to amount to ninety percent of all BND SIGINT activities. (Löffelmann 2015: 2). This practice runs counter to the European Convention on Human Rights, the International Covenant on Civil and Political Rights and the German Basic Law. These guarantee the privacy of correspondence, post and telecommunications as a "Right to protection (Abwehrrecht) against tapping, monitoring and recording of telecommunication contents [...] the analysis of their contents and the use of the data thus gained" (Drucksache 18/3709: 2). Article 10 of the Basic Law lists "subjective rights that primarily obligate the state to refrain from interfering with privacy. When tele-communications are monitored, a deep intrusion into the fundamental right to privacy takes place. The infringement is particularly severe given that the imperative secrecy of these measures means that the targeted individuals are excluded from the authorisation procedure" (Drucksache 17/8639: 2, personal translation). Prominent experts in constitutional law agree on the fact that the BND practice of collecting foreign communication data infringes upon the right to private communication guaranteed by Article 10 of the Basic Law.

This is right, so the widespread consensus protects not just German citizens but every person. The prevailing opinion is that neither the nationality of the communicating participants nor their countries of residence are decisive criteria for the protection of civil rights (Bäcker 2014: 19). More decisive is the fact that German public authorities are bound by the provisions of the Basic Law at all times. The intrusions of intelligence services into the constitutionally protected privacy of telecommunication are considered particularly severe (Epping 2012: 319). They may only be mandated on the basis of a law. Derogations from the course of law may take place only within strict conditions.[2] The Gesetz zur Beschränkung des Brief-, Post- und Fernmeldegeheimnis, commonly referred to as „Article 10 Law" in reference to Article 10 of the Basic Law which ascertains the right to privacy of communication, defines the cases, scope and conditions for the three federal intelligence services to engage in communication surveillance.

Yet, the authority of the BND in the field of strategic surveillance of foreign telecommunication data fails to be governed by that law. Neither the Article 10 Law nor the vague mandate of the foreign intelligence services in the BND law provides the necessary legal basis (Huber 2013; SPD-Bundestagsfraktion 2015). In the absence of a sufficient legal basis, the executive faces allegations of massive violations of the fundamental right to privacy. What is more, in this highly sensitive field of security policy and fundamental rights, the entire spectrum of executive conduct has been bypassing not only the general public but also the supervisory bodies of the Bundestag. There has been no independent assessment of the legal interpretations for the strategic surveillance of foreign telecommunication, not to mention the handling of collected data and their transfer to third parties. No Parliamentary Intelligence Oversight Panel (Parlamentarisches Kontrollgremium, PKGr), no G 10-Commission and no Data Protection Commissioner (Bundesbeauftragte für Datenschutz und die Informationsfreiheit, BfDI) ever had any say in this process.

Considering that these massive infringements of fundamental rights continue to lack legitimacy and considering the complete lack of separation of powers as regards the authorisation and execution of strategic surveillance of foreign telecommunications, it is urgent and necessary to discuss on a fundamental level how to ensure that the intrusion of intelligence services into telecommunication privacy complies with the rule of law and is subject to democratic control. This debate should not focus solely on expressing criticism but also formulate "concrete and viable reform proposals" (SPD-Bundestagsfraktion 2015:[3]). This policy brief aims at providing such a contribution and particularly examines the practice and the institutional framework of the G 10-Commission.

This hitherto rather unknown panel of the Bundestag is quasi-judicial in nature. Its function is to authorise the intrusion of intelligence services into the privacy of correspondence, post and telecommunication and it takes on a crucial role for the protection of fundamental rights in cases of state surveillance. The G 10-Commission is the sole body in the German oversight system that is qualified to assess whether intrusions of the intelligence services into telecommunication privacy are necessary and lawful. Unlike the Parliamentary Intelligence Oversight Body (PKGr), the G 10-Commission may demand that measures considered unlawful be stopped immediately. It can thus ensure an effective protection of fundamental rights. At present however, the G 10-Commission is not capable of fulfilling this role. These brief first points out the severe deficits of the actual G 10 procedure before generating clear recommendations for action to remedy the considerable constitutional unbalance without putting national security at risk.

## A Critique of the Present System

This section first summarises the wide scope of deficits as regards the democratic control of SIGINT in Germany. These include the quality of the relevant intelligence service legislation as well as the mandate of the G

10-Commission. In a further step, it will outline decisive shortcomings of the present system as regards the institutional and practical implementation.

## Foreign-Foreign telecommunication surveillance: a source of illegitimate infringements of fundamental rights and unconstitutionality

At the international level, the Article 10 law has been enjoying a good reputation for years. Countries willing to democratize their security sector often refer to the German legislation for guidance.[3] Just recently, in its report on the democratic control of SIGINT, the renowned Venice Commission of the Council of Europe highlighted Germany and Sweden as two states with laws that "present definite advantages" in international comparison (Venice Commission 2015: para 27). Germany cannot, however, rest on its international laurels any longer. Article 10 Law may contain progressive elements but it solely regulates the interception and surveillance of domestic communication or communications that originate or end in Germany. Once one knows that the "core business" (Huber 2013) of German SIGINT is beyond the reach of the German oversight system, the exemplarity of Germany's law and practice wanes. Without the option to pronounce on the lawfulness and necessity of the quantitatively much more significant foreign telecommunication surveillance, the G 10-Commission would remain, even in the opinion of one of its members, a "fair-weather commission" (Expert interview -1).

## Static body of intelligence law and secret interpretations

Compared to German police law, the federal legislation on intelligence services presents a much lower density (Löffelmann 2015: 2). Clear and determined provisions, however are of especially great significance for the legislation on intelligence services. After all, "[t]he secret nature of specific surveillance powers brings with it a greater risk of arbitrary exercise of discretion which, in turn, demands greater precision in the rule governing the exercise of discretion, and additional oversight" (OHCHR 2014: para. 29). Further, the intelligence law is too static. The structures required for the continuous assessment and adjustment of this body of laws are missing.[4] While the police law is characterised by dense case law, the German intelligence legislation, by virtue of the frequent exclusions of legal proceedings, rarely benefits from the important contributions that judges, lawyers and prosecutors can make to the definition and clarification of norms. This explains why the surprising and much criticised legal interpretation and practices of the executive as regards the territorial restriction of Ar-ticle 10 of the Basic Law could remain unchallenged for years.[5]

Secret interpretations of the intelligence law have expanded the latitude of the executive far beyond the core area of executive responsibility attributed to it by the German Constitutional Court. The fact that the government was able to do entirely without the democratic legitimation of the Bundestag shows how severely disrupted the separation of powers is in this important field of security politics. By contrast, consider the normal practice: Parliament passes a law and the executive branch applies it. Its interpretation can then be subjected to judicial review and the entire process is conducted under the watch of academia and the public. "Secret provisions and secret interpretations – even secret judicial interpretations – do not comply with the criteria of a 'law,'" the former UN High Commissioner for Human Rights states with concern in her report on the right to privacy (OHCHR 2014: para. 29).

The duty of each State is rather to ensure „that every intrusion into the right to privacy, family, home or correspondence is authorized by laws that a) are publicly accessible, b) contain provisions that ensure that collection of, access to and use of communications data are tailored to specific legitimate aims; c) are sufficiently precise and specify in detail the precise circumstances in which any such interference may be permitted, the procedures for authorization, the categories of persons who may be placed under surveillance, the limit on the duration of surveillance; procedures for the use and storage of data collected; and d) provide for effective safeguards against abuse." (OHCHR 2014: para 28).

## The Role of the Executive Is not sufficiently accounted for in the law

The Federal Ministry of the Interior (Bundesinnenministerium, BMI) plays a decisive role in the authorization of communications surveillance by the federal intelligence services. Bertold Huber, Vice Chairman of the G 10-Commission, recently described the procedure for authorizing the telecommunication surveillance measures stipulated in the Article 10 Law in those terms: "The service in question [Federal Intelligence Service, Federal Office for the Protection of the Constitution or the Military Counter Intelligence Agency (MAD), note by the author] submits a request to the BMI. The ministry carefully examines the request and when it considers it to be justified, it authorises the request and issues the corresponding warrant which generally however may not be executed before the G 10-Commission has given its approval" (Huber 2014: 43).

Irrespective of the fact that foreign-foreign communications control is excluded from these procedures, the executive control also seems woefully ineffective: concrete verifiable information on the authorisation procedure of strategic surveillance of foreign-foreign communication, a procedure settled and agreed on solely by the executive, is missing. In the case of foreign communication surveillance, the BMI does not issue any warrants (Expert interview-2)–the BND presumably conducts its key business based entirely on its own competence and without any control. Unlike the procedures provided for in the Article 10 Law regarding interferences of intelligence services with the privacy of communication, the BND is apparently not required to submit requests to the BMI in order to conduct what it calls "routine surveillance". It thus remains unclear whether and how the Federal Government actually exercises any executive control over foreign communications surveillance: Does the BND have to formally justify the geographic and temporal dimension of interception measures? In how far are the necessity criteria for the justification of intrusions in the affected communication and data transmission observed?

It also remains open to question whether the handling of the intercepted data originating from sole foreign surveillance is examined to verify that the otherwise mandatory procedural provisions are respected (examination, labelling and deletion requirements, release of information and principle of purpose). Equally doubtful is whether the BMI is presently assessing whether "those occurrences in foreign countries that the BND would like to collect data on present any direct connection to the concrete assignment profile (Auftragsprofil, APB) defined by the federal government for the BND or are related to the protection of the lives of German and allied forces deployed in crisis areas ("Force Protection")" (SPD-Bundestagsfraktion 2015: 10). One may thus suspect that the BND monitors communications starting and ending in foreign countries without being subjected to any external control by the Federal Government, the Bundestag or the Data Protection Authority.

Practically No Independent Control of the BND Data Processing the Article 10 Law specifies that the remit of the G 10-Commission covers the entire collection, processing and use of the personal data that the Federal Intelligence Service gathers under this law. Setting aside the fact that the BND also collects personal data in a manner that is not regulated by the Article 10 Law, the wording here is emblematic. The law does not talk of control obligations or of control responsibilities. Rather, the honorary members of the commission are free, if they wish to and have the time, to also control the manner in which the BND handles the collected data. Hence, it amounts to an open invitation to conduct more work in addition to the required examinations of admissibility and necessity of surveillance under the Article 10 Law. As described earlier, the G 10-Commission is the only body in the German intelligence oversight system that is able to effectively protect fundamental rights and safeguard privacy of telecommunications from interference by the three federal intelligence services. This "responsible task" (Drucksache 18/3709: 4) has so far been performed by four persons holding part-time, honorary positions and a rather vague formal competence to look into data handling. This is hardly sufficient. The G 10-Commission members "are to be given access to any documentation, especially stored data and the data processing software connected to the surveillance measure" (§15 Para. 5. No. 3 Article 10 Law).

What may sound progressive at first - and is to be commended as regards the unrestricted access – does, on closer inspection, not result in de facto independent control of intelligence data processing. The G 10-Commission is not subject to any information required as regards its work. The relevant ministries, not the G 10-Commission, inform the Parliamentary Intelligence Oversight Body (PKGr) which in turn informs the Bundestag on a yearly basis on the "execution as well as type and scope" of the surveillance measures. The latest publicly accessible information given by the PKGr solely states the following on the matter: "Further, the members of the [G 10] Commission and the staff of the [PD-5] secretary [of the Bundestag administration] conducted information and control visits to the services and gathered information on the concrete implementation of the concerned measures and on compliance with statutory provisions" (Drucksache 18/3709: 4).

It is worth remarking that the members of the G 10-Commission will generally travel from the whole of Germany to Berlin once a month in order to decide on the admissibility and necessity of intelligence communication surveillance activities, not only of the BND but also of BfV and MAD. Realistically, this leaves little time to conduct examinations in the field of data protection. Open to question is also whether all members possess the required juridical and technical expertise or acquire this knowledge in the course of their mandate. While the G 10-Commission members may provide the "Data Protection Commissioner with opportunities to comment on data protection issues" (§15 Para. 5 Article 10 Law) and while the BfDI is theoretically also entitled to perform controls "in so far as the intelligence services are gathering or processing personal data", this does not however apply to personal data collected on the basis of the Art. 10 law.

This fall under the exclusive control competence of the G 10-Commission: (Drucksache 18/59: 5). Thus if, as this has been implied by the former Data Protection Commissioner in the case of strategic surveillance of foreign telecommunications, no G 10 regulation is available and the government does not provide any information to the BfDI (Bundestagstextarchiv 2015; Krempl 2015), then a severe control vacuum exists. Considering the lack of capacity and of reporting obligations of the G 10-Commission and in light of the fact that neither G 10-Commission nor BfDI exert independent control over the strategic surveillance of foreign telecommunications, it has so far remained in the hands of the authority that is gathering the data to also heed legal standards for data processing.[6] Clearly, Germany does therefore not meet the standards for independent control of data processing that the Venice Commission has recently emphasized anew (Venice Commission 2015: para 121).[7]

## The Authorization Procedure is insufficient and not immune to Abuse by the Executive

Considering the gravity of the fundamental right infringements and the complexity of SIGINT, it is important to thoroughly clarify the questions of the extent of the restriction measures submitted for approval as well as their legality and necessity. The secretariat of the G 10-Commission is currently responsible for the preparation of the monthly sessions. Notably, the commission members receive information on the BMI warrants only on the day of their monthly meeting. It is thus questionable whether the commission members are amply prepared to challenge the position that the executive has taken. Understandably, the honorary members of the commission who travelled from outside of Berlin wish to take a train home in the evening. What happens, however when their deliberations require more time and a series of warrants have yet to be discussed towards the end of their meeting? Will they be resubmitted to the commission the following month or does the work of the commission inevitably become less thorough towards the end? In that case, it is far more likely that fundamental rights rather than security concerns fall victim to a rushed assessment of the warrants.[8]

It is precisely in situations like this that there is a risk to see important questions related to the legality and necessity of specific surveillance measures being neglected in practice. Thus, a catalogue of minimal requirements should be available that would automatically be applied in those cases where a thorough assessment is not feasible. In a statement to the NSA Inquiry Committee, Hans De With, chairman of the G 10-Commission until January 2014, pointed out a further severe deficit of the present authorisation procedure: It is prone to abuse by the executive. Frank Hofman (current member of the G 10-Commission) took this up again in an interview: "The government consciously deceived the G 10-Commission on the true purpose of the surveillance measures in Frankfurt. [...] One expected that the BND wanted to get permission from the Commission for the wiretapping of German citizens outside of Germany. In fact, the intelligence service used the approval in order to massively tap into transit traffic. [...] The G 10-Commission is abused as a Trojan Horse." (Strozyk 2015).

## Anachronistic 20 Percent Rule for the Collection of "International Telecommunications"

At present, the Article 10 Law allows the Intelligence Service to "automatically collect, record and exploit telecommunications that take place from Germany to a foreign country (in specific States/ areas) or from there to Germany." (Drucksache 18/59: 4). To do so, "the BND may screen up to 20 percent of all telecommunications handled over a specific hub according to predefined criteria" (Ibid). The 20 percent limit however does not refer to the data quantity sent through an internet cable but to the capacity of the wire through which the transport takes place (Bundestagstextarchiv 2015b). Klaus Landefeld, Chairman for Infrastructure and Networks at the Association of the Internet Industry (eco) e.V. as well as council member of the DE-CIX Management GmbH, put this into more concrete terms for the NSA Inquiry Committee: "The capacity is always only partially used so that the BND may collect far more than 20 percent of the data that flows through a cable. This is not what one has in mind when one pictures restrictions of the surveillance of telecommunication" (Bundestagstextarchiv 2015b).

## Insufficient selection criteria and lack of transparency

According to the Article 10 law, the chairman of the G 10-Commission is the only member who has to be qualified to hold the position of a judge. The other commission members are not submitted to any selection criteria. The commission members receive no training or any other preparation for the honorary position when they first take on their office. Thus for many, the start is a bit of a "plunge" (Expert interview 2). This becomes particularly apparent in situations where the Federal Ministry mandates communication surveillances according to § 3 or § 5 of the Article 10 Law and the commission members cannot adequately estimate whether to trust the argumentation of the BMI or the statements of single sources. "Precisely because we do not sit together with the BMI officers, it is from time to time difficult to evaluate whether to follow the reasoning for a mandated restriction measure" (Expert interview 1). The commission members thus often fumble in the dark and detailed assessments are the result of the interest or avocation of single commission members rather than an expression of systemic procedures. The lack of any reporting requirements for the G 10-Commission has already been emphasised. Its secretariat (PD-5) keeps the minutes of its decisions. These however do not include the assessments of the commission members (Expert interview 3). It also remains unclear whether the members of the G 10-Commission are allowed to pass information onto the members of the Parliamentary Intelligence Oversight Body, and if so, which. The following table summarises the deficits as regards the existing system of SIGINT control in Germany:

- Core business of the BND's SIGINT activities (i.e. the surveillance of communication originating and ending outside of Germany) is presently exempt from democratic control and not based on a legal footing

- Lack of technical, expert and staff capacity in the secretariat of the G 10-Commission

- Role of the executive insufficiently accounted for in the intelligence law

- Executive control over BND's core SIGINT activities is dysfunctional

- Existing G 10 authorisation procedure prone to executive abuse

- Inadequate control of data processing by the G 10-Commission and exclusion of the BfDI in cases of G 10 procedures and core business

- Selection criteria for G 10-Commission members and honorary positions inadequate for this important control function

- No contradictory procedure embedded in the authorisation procedure

- De facto circumventions of the existing 20 percent rule that restricts the collection of domestic-foreign communication

- No reporting requirements for the G 10-Commission

## Reform Proposals

Considering the previously delineated problems affecting the protection of fundamental rights and the imbalanced separation of powers, it is high time to lead a broad discussion on how to provide legal and democratic control over the whole of SIGINT activities by the BND in future. Recently, the German Social Democratic Party (SPD) deplored the lack of "concrete and viable proposals for a reform of the pertinent SIGINT law and practice that has become a constitutional necessity" (SPD-Bundestagsfraktion 2015: 3). The deficits previously described may not be dispelled simply by extending the legal scope of the Article 10 Law to the bulk collection of foreign telecommunication data. Rather, a clear catalogue of criteria should be compiled giving due consideration to security interests, other available options for the collection of information and the intrusion intensity of the measure. Such a catalogue should be developed with the participation of civil liberty experts and define the process and decision criteria for a new authorisation procedure. This would not only apply to the necessary assessments of legality and necessity of the single measures but also to the further handling of the data collected as part of the measures and to the question of how to take reasonable account of the guarantees provided by law in this area. The necessary reform of democratic control over SIGINT should pay consideration to the following aspects:

- Authorisation procedure

- The subsequent handling of the collected data

- The right to effective remedy (Art. 19 Para. 4 Basic Law).

The following section considers policy recommendations. They were developed on the basis of a series of background talks and expert interviews and emphasise the aspects that a reform should most urgently address.

- The Entire Range of SIGINT Activities should be regulated.

- The Bundestag should adopt a new Article 10 law that unequivocally and bindingly regulates all intrusions into the privacy of correspondence, post and telecommunications by the federal intelligence services. As Article 10 of the Basic Law does not solely apply to German citizens, it is also valid for natural persons in foreign countries. Hence, at the very least, non-German communication data must also benefit from some form of basic protection. Surveillance measures conducted purely on data from outside Germany must in future also fall under the remit of the G 10-Commission. This, however, by no means implies that the quality of data protection offered by the Basic Law should be identical for German citizens, EU citizens and the rest of the world. In order to shake off its reputation as an "irrelevant fair-weather commission" (Expert-interview-1), and to prevent future abuse as Trojan Horse, the new Article 10 Law, by analogy with § 3 and § 5 of the present law, should provide a sufficiently detailed list of the conditions required for a lawful authorization of foreign telecommunications data surveillance.

This law must respect the minimal requirements as concerns the clarity and precision of provisions in national security legislation. As regards the requirements for the surveillance of foreign telecommunications, the general guidelines laid out by the SPD paper contain good individual suggestions: The paper e.g. demands that "processes taking place outside of Germany for which the BND wishes to collect information must be directly related to the concrete assignment profile (APB) of the Federal Government for the BND or be connected with the protection of the lives of German and allied forces deployed in crisis areas ("Force Protection")". (SPD-Bundestagsfraktion 2015: 10). In this case however, not only the „Federal Chancellery should be legally required to pass on the BND assignment profile in an appropriate form to the G 10-Commission" (Ibid). The assignment profile must also be underpinned by democratic legitimacy, which would require at the very least a fundamental discussion on the essential issues of the APB to take place in the plenary of the Bundestag. The core issues of the APB must subsequently be recapitulated in the BND law.

## Time for the "Super G 10-Commission" and closer co-ordination with the Federal Commissioner for Data Protection

In addition to the extension of the authorisation procedure onto foreign telecommunications surveillance, it is necessary to decisively improve the controlling capacity and options of the G 10-Commission as regards the authorized measures. The required amendment of the Article 10 Law would otherwise prove futile, as the G 10-Commission could not guarantee an effective protection of fundamental rights. After all, the "control of foreign telecommunication surveillance by intelligence services is not an activity that can take place "on the side" but rather requires a high level of legal and technical expertise and a great deal of personal dedication" (Löffelmann 2015: 3). Should the G 10-Commission be responsible for the authorisation of all BND telecommunication surveillance in future, this significant supervisory body then requires massive reinforcement? In this respect, a secretariat able to work effectively seems much more decisive than the number of members. It should conduct preliminary examinations of the warrants in line with and on behalf of the G 10-Commission. After specialists conducted a comprehensive prelimi-nary examination, they could present the G 10-Commission with a decision proposal comprising the main issues. This requires significantly more "material resources and qualified support staff of the Bundestag administration" with "juristic, technical and intelligence expertise" (SPD-Bundestagsfraktion 2015: 8) to be invested into the Secretariat PD 5 of the Bundestag as is presently the case. What is more, it is time to replace the honorary character of the G 10-Commission membership with employed status. Instead of presently four honorary members (and their deputies), the G 10-Commission should consist in future of at least just as many employed members who meet on several days every month if need be.

The authority to be informed and assess in detail the feeding-in of selectors into the collection system of the BND also bears great significance for the effectiveness of the G 10-Commission. The SPD general guidelines formulates an important demand: "The G 10-Commission must be entitled at all times to review all search terms used for the selection of the information gathered and verify whether these serve the purpose of fulfilling the task and do not contravene German interests. All rights resulting from § 15 Para. 5 of the Article 10 Law must extend to the control of the entire strategic surveillance of telecommunications by the BND" (SPD-Bundestagsfraktion 2015: 13). In this matter, experts such as Klaus Landefeld draw attention to the fact that selectors cannot be controlled statically. They change on an hourly basis.

Thus not only is an increase in the staff of the G 10-Commission necessary but also an ongoing, permanent control of the surveillance measures. This would be the only way to counter massive data collection with a proper, independent control. The future G 10-Commission should also be commissioned to critically assess the cable selection for the strategic surveillance of foreign telecommunications. The following questions play a central role: What justifies the cable selection? Could another, less intrusive measure be sufficient to gain the same knowledge? As with the requirements of the warrants under the Article 10 Law, in the case of foreign-foreign communication surveillance the option must be available for the Commission to have the executive cancel without delay a warrant "which the commission declares to be illegal or unnecessary" (§ 6 Sentence 3 Article 10 Law).

Further, the G 10-Commission should assess, in close co-ordination with the Federal Data Protection Agency, whether the BND's collection, processing and exchange of data as well as deletion of no longer useful data is conducted in accordance with the legal data protection requirements. In order to do so, and as with the present provisions of the Article 10 Law (in particular §§ 4, 6, 7, 7a, 11), similar provisions pertinent to the strategic surveillance of foreign telecommunications must be included into the law. It would also be conceivable to set up a new unit for security audits at the BfDI which would be sufficiently staffed and equipped with adequate expertise and technology. A close connection with the G 10-Commission could be promoted by setting up the new BfDI unit geographically close to the Bundestag. This would thus partly counter the risk of fragmentation of the controlling bodies.

## Introduce a Contradictory Procedure within the G-10 Authorisation Process

A fundamental principle of the Rechtsstaat consists in "[…] the freedom from state control and surveillance measures so long as no ground exists for a criminal procedure" (Drucksache 18/5453: 3). A further principle, the so-called Richtervorbehalt, states that intrusions of a severe or potentially abusive nature into essential rights of individuals must be conditional on judicial order or authorisation. The groundless and massive collection of communication data in the absence of any suspicion by the Federal Intelligence Services conflicts with the first principle. Furthermore, the German control system over infringements of the fundamental right deriving from Art. 10 Basic Law has been referred to as a "substitute procedure" (2BvF 1/69) by the Bundesverfassungsgericht given that no exhaustive judicial control is intended prior to the implementation of such surveillance measures.[9] The situation is different in the case of e.g. police preparatory investigation. Due to the lack of transparency in the use of undercover investigators, the Bundestag saw grounds to "make provisions for prior judicial control. Both the code of criminal procedure and the police law provide for […] a judicial decision on the permissibility of the use of an undercover investigator" (Roggan 2006: 191). In contrast, the

Federal Constitutional Court considers the „G 10-Commission to be a controlling body of its own kind beyond judicial power that serves as a substitute precisely for judicial review" (NVwZ 1994: 367).

The party Die Linke recently called for the complete termination of intelligence intrusions into the privacy of correspondence, post and telecommunications and presented a "legislative proposal for the termination of the Article 10 Law" (Drucksache 18/5453). This proposal rightly points to the great discrepancy between the low encroachment threshold (i.e. the required preconditions for the surveillance measures) that applies to the intelligence services on one side and the significantly higher intrusion barrier that applies to the authorities for public risk prevention and criminal prosecution on the other. Considering the trend towards increasing overlaps of the three areas of constitutional relevance "intelligence service activity, preventive police measures and criminal prosecution", members of the Government Commission for the Review of Security Legislation (Regierungskommission zur Überprüfung der Sicherheitsgesetzgebung) also recommend to "assess whether and in how far overlapping areas may be reduced" and in doing so "reduce [...] prima facie the competence of the intelligence services" (Regierungskommission 2013: 164).

Some in security circles conceded that a lot of what the intelligence services undertake as part of the technical surveillance inside Germany should be conducted by the Federal Criminal Police Officer and other police agencies (Expert interview 4). Thus it is inherently right and important to consider how to raise the encroachment threshold of intelligence services in future. This does not imply that intelligence service intrusions into the privacy of telecommunications be entirely abolished. Further, these considerations must include the critique that has been repeatedly expressed as regards the practicalities of the Richtervorbehalt.[10] Finally, the most constructive approach at present seems to be to hold on to the construct of the G 10-Commission. Besides an increase in personnel and the extension of controlling authority, a further decisive change is however urgently required: the integration of a civil liberty advocate into its authorisation process. This would significantly raise the practical encroachment threshold for the implementation of surveillance measures by intelligence services. The new Article 10 Law should for its part stipulate that, besides the BMI representatives who explain the various warrants to the G 10-Commission, one person should be present who represents the interests of the persons targeted by the surveillance measures who "have no opportunity to play a part in this substitute procedure".

The role of the civil liberty advocate is to justify to the commission members in how far the warrant contradicts the right to privacy and which measures with a lower intrusive intensity would serve a similar purpose. Within the G 10 procedure, the civil liberty advocate should be allotted the competence to notify the Parliamentary Intelligence Oversight Body of decisions of a specific significance and of relevance to fundamental rights, such as decisions that justify new methods or goals of operation. One should also take into consideration the option to provide this person with the competence to file a law suit against the surveillance measures that he/she considers to be contradicting fundamental rights. The implementation of this recommendation would put Germany on the footsteps of the very promising reform efforts undertaken by Sweden and the USA.[11]

## Best Practices in Tackling the "Discrimination Problem"

Over the course of the past decades, democratic states have created a series of protection and control mechanisms to protect the privacy of their own citizens from intrusions by their own intelligence services. Edward Snowden's disclosures on the extent and the practice of worldwide internet and communication surveillance by western intelligence services, however, provided impressive proof of how defenceless these citizens are in the face of surveillance by foreign intelligence services. Further, it became evident in the NSA inquiry committee of the Bundestag that the Federal Intelligence Services pays just as little attention to the protection of the rights and data of non-German citizens as the NSA to the rights and data of non-US citizens. The indignation of the Federal Government over the spying among friends presents little credibility considering its own practice. More so: Now that Austria, the Netherlands, Belgium, Switzerland and Luxembourg have started investigating on the collection, processing and transmission of data from the transit traffic of European wires, the Federal Government must consider the European dimension of the "BND/NSA scandal". This sensitive problem of international relations can be addressed at least in part with an exemplary reform of the democratic control over intelligence services. Implementing international best practices related to the "discrimination problem" would make an important contribution to a better protection of the data of German citizens from the intelligence services of allied or befriended states.

Instead of venturing on a „non-binding ‚No-Spy'agreement", Germany could start by creating good constitutional protection mechanisms that offer significantly better protection for the data of foreigners. This standard would then be actively demanded by others so as to eventually become a common standard. "The more our partners resolve to adopt comparable standards, the less our citizens have to fear an intrusion on their privacy by the services of befriended countries" (SPD-Bundestagsfraktion 2015: 8). This goal is not easy to implement in practice. Would the collected data of all non-EU citizens receive the same protection as the data of German citizens (including prior authorisation of data collection, requirements for data processing and identification, regulations for the deletion and transmission of data, notification requirements, legal protection guarantees), then these changes would put the constitutional obligation of the intelligence service into question. Hence the following specifications appear moderate: First, no distinction should be made between the data of German residents and EU-citizens. The same data protection provisions and right to effective remedy that are currently only granted to German citizens as regards intrusions by the intelligence service into their telecommunication privacy should be extended and equally apply to EU-citizens. This will result in an additional burden for the controlling bodies. The state must however establish and maintain the necessary infrastructure for the assertion of these comprehensive citizens' fundamental rights. The fact that the administrations would face a great challenge is not a convincing argument against the assertion of rights and legal claims.

Second, it is true that the quasi-judicial prior authorisation will be extended to all surveillance measures executed by intelligence services, i.e. also to those measures that solely aim at collecting data of non-EU citizens. Sufficient expertise and increased personnel in the G 10-Commission, including the involvement of a civil liberty advocate in the authorisation procedure and the use of a clear justification requirement (see below) for the newly created G 10-Commission, already create significantly higher barriers for intelligence service intrusions into the telecommunication privacy of upright non-German citizens. Third, as regards the specific procedures of data collection and data processing, Germany should at least not rank behind the standard laid out in US Presidential Policy Directive 28. This directive states that domestic and foreign data should as much as possible be governed by the same standards to the extent that is compatible with national security.[12]

Fourth, and tempering the previous a little, an essential distinction must be made when it comes to the extension of the right to effective remedy to Non-Germans. Here it may be permissible to reserve the right to notification (§ 12 Article 10 Law) and the right to effective remedy (Art. 19IV Basic Law) only to Germans and EU-citizens. Based on the existing jurisprudence of the Federal Constitutional Court, such an interpretation of the obligation to provide for an effective protection of basic rights appears possible.[13]

## More Transparency with a Justification Requirement and the Publication of G10 Commission Decisions

The separation of powers does not function well when the public is entirely excluded. Respecting internationally proven standards is not the only decisive aspect in order to bring about an improved performance of the executive, judicial and parliamentary control of secret services; a minimum of transparency plays an equally important role, too. Thus the G 10-Commission should in future be subject to a requirement to justify its decisions. As is the case for court decisions, the individual decisions made by the G 10-Commission should be justified in detail. This justification should include such aspects as a clear identification of the specific constitutional issues that require a decision and notes on how these issues were resolved using which interpretation of the law.

The justification should also indicate whether and in how far the G 10 decision differs from previous decisions or guiding principles of the decision making process.[14] The G 10 secretariat should keep minutes of the whole of the G 10 decisions and hand these for review to the parliamentary control committee. The US-American practice should basically serve as an example: The Director of National Intelligence publishes individual decisions of the FISA courts[15] based on the recommendations of the President's Review Group on Intelligence and Communications Technologies in order to inform the public of the arguments used to approve or reject instructed restriction measures. For reasons of confidentiality, individual G 10 decisions would similarly have to be blackened.

## Conclusion

The federal intelligence services have thus far been able to conduct foreign telecommunication data surveillance without much interference from the executive, the legislative or the judiciary. Apparently, they have been apprehensive of a "moratorium of G 10 collection and [...] a parliamentary consideration of the subject with unpredictable consequences" (Strozyk

2015). Our democracy should welcome a proper "parliamentary consideration" of this important security practice. In fact, the Bundestag could in future better protect the intelligence services from unethical or unwise instructions of the executive. In addition, the intelligence services ought to provide convincing arguments to make the case for why the surveillance of telecommunications is and should remain an important instrument of the German security policy. Regardless of the important issues addressed in this study as regards the legal basis and the constitutionality of the authorisation procedure, there is so far no convincing evidence that the massive surveillance of communications offers an efficient mean to gain information that are of significance for the German foreign and security policy.[16] Many of the deficits described in this study have been known for more than two years now.

No serious measures have been taken so far to overcome this constitutionally unacceptable situation. This is particularly surprising considering that in autumn 2013 Germany had already pleaded at the United Nations for the extension of the protection of privacy in the digital age. The resolution adopted by the General Assembly calls on all member states to protect the right to privacy and to "review their procedures, practices and legislation regarding the surveillance of communications, their interception and the collection of personal data, including mass surveillance, interception and collection," as well as "To establish or maintain existing independent, effective, adequately resourced and impartial judicial, administrative and/ or parliamentary domestic oversight mechanisms capable of ensuring transparency, as appropriate, and accountability for State surveillance of communications, their interception and the collection of personal data, including metadata" (United Nations 2015: para. 4c and 4d).

The NSA Inquiry Committee of the Bundestag, set up in March 2014, is also tasked with clarifying whether "legal and technical changes [are] required to the German system of foreign surveillance carried out by the intelligence services in order to ensure that German authorities comply fully with fundamental and human rights, and if so, which? In addition, the inquiry committee is expected to recommend ways to ensure that the executive, parliamentary, judicial and independent data-protection oversight of the federal security authorities [can] be ensured fully and effectively." (Drucksache 18/843: 5). The German system of democratic intelligence oversight presently lacks concrete and verifiable provisions that would allow Parliament or an independent expert body to rein in on the bulk of the BND's SIGINT activities. To date, these activities of the state are solely administered in closely-knit executive circles. This concerns both the authorisation procedure, the data processing and the exchange of data with foreign intelligence partners. If one wants to avoid political damage in future, as well as support effective intelligence services in their critically important work while pursuing a credible international foreign and security policy, then the many deficits outlined in this study may no longer be ignored. It is high time for a comprehensive reform of the legislation, management and control practice pertaining to SIGINT in Germany. The strengthening and extension of the G 10-Commission represents a particularly important step in this respect. The credibility of German foreign and security policy, Germany's respectful contribution to the implementation of the very UN Resolution that she has tabled and numerous lawsuits that have already been filed require a prompt reaction on the part of both the Bundestag and the Federal Government.[17]

*About the author: Dr. Thorsten Wetzling leads the privacy project at the stiftung neue verantwortung. The project engages policy makers, civil society and experts in the development of reform proposals to improve the democratization and professionalization of intelligence governance in Germany. Thorsten holds a doctorate degree in political science from the Graduate Institute of International and Development Studies in Geneva. About snv: The stiftung neue verantwortung is a non-profit think tank in Berlin that brings together expertise from government, research institutions, NGOs and companies to develop, discuss, and disseminate proposals on current political issues. The goal of stiftung neue verantwortung is to assist stakeholders, both in and outside of politics, in making effective decisions that benefit the common good by using a combination of content-based expertise, practical political experience and cross-sectoral cooperation. Impressum stiftung neue verantwortung e. V. Beisheim Center Berliner Freiheit 2 10785 Berlin T. +49 30 81 45 03 78 80 F. +49 30 81 45 03 78 97 www.stiftung- nv.de info@stiftung- nv.de Twitter: @snv_Berlin. This Policy Brief is subject to a Creative Commons license (CC BY-SA). The redistribution, publication, transformation or translation of publications of the stiftung neue verantwortung which are marked with the license "CC BY-SA", including any derivative products, is permitted under the conditions "Attribution" and "Share Alike". More details on the licensing terms can be found here: http:// creativecommons.org/licenses/by-sa/4.0/ Policy Brief The key to intelligence reform in Germany: Strengthening the G 10-Commission's role to authorise strategic surveillance. Many excellent research institutes and think tanks already contribute to the fields of foreign policy, economic policy or environmental policy in Germany. Issues related to new technologies, however lack comparable expert organisations that focus on current politics and social debates. The Stiftung Neue Verantwortung (SNV) wants to fill this gap in the landscape of German institutes and think tanks. This think tank seeks to provide a focal point for all people whose work covers current political and social questions of the cross-sectional issue of digitalization. We compile and publish analyses, develop recommendations for action for policymakers, conduct expert workshops, invite experts to engage in publicly accessible policy debates, and explain contexts and backgrounds in the media. Topics and focus of the work of Stiftung Neue Verantwortung: Many technology-intensive issues of politics are cross-sectional issues that change at a rapid pace. When it comes to developing working proposals in this area, expertise from many different disciplines is often needed. The combination of different knowledge, continuous testing of ideas and speed thus forms the core of the organisation. Therefore, our organisation does not focus on a specific field such as defence, economic or foreign policy, but rather brings together the expertise needed to solve a specific problem. One example is our work in the field of IT security policy: here our experts deal with the global supply chains of IT manufacturers, with experiences from consumer protection, the strategies of online criminals, the developments of technology markets or with standardisation bodies at the European level.*

*Our activities are affected by social developments and are constantly changing. Currently, we are dealing with the following questions, among others: Data Economy: The introduction of big data architectures in companies and the associated methods of artificial intelligence (including machine learning) are changing traditional value chains, competitive dynamics and consumer behaviour in markets. How can economic policy react? Digital Rights, Surveillance and Democracy: How can government monitoring in a networked society be effectively controlled, reasonably limited, and sufficiently documented? Technology and Geopolitics: What is Europe's position within global semiconductor supply chains and what relevance and potential impact does this have on industrial competitiveness, technological dependency on foreign countries and national security? International Cybersecurity Policy: Cybersecurity and cyber defense are new areas for German policy. What can we learn from the global developments and strategies of other states? Artificial Intelligence: Developments in the field of artificial intelligence are forcing new dependencies in the global economy and changing the military power relations between states. What does this mean for German foreign policy? Strengthening the Digital Public Sphere: Strengthening the digital public sphere: Digital platforms open up new communication spaces for individuals and societies, but they also entail risks. What measures and reforms are appropriate to address not only symptoms, but structural challenges of digital platforms and information spaces? Data Science Unit: With the SNV Data Science Unit, we are expanding our think tank work to include quantitative, data-driven methods. SNV's Working Method: Many technology-intensive issues of politics are cross-sectional issues that change at a rapid pace. The combination of different knowledge, of continuous testing of ideas and of speed thus forms the core of the organisation. That is why Stiftung Neue Verantwortung works differently than conventional research institutes and think tanks. Collaboration: SNV systematically involves and co-operates with experts in the fields of politics, economy, NGOs and research institutes and this already at an early stage in the process to rapidly test and improve policy proposals. This collaborative working method allows for different perspectives to participate in the process, inoperative proposals to be discarded early and ideas to be made practicable. Although SNV's experts are themselves specialists in their field, they always work closely together in a network of other experts or professionals.*

# Chapter 10

# Caught in the Act? An analysis of Germany's new SIGINT reform

## Kilian Vieth-Ditlmann and Thorsten Wetzling

When the German parliament amended the legal framework for Germany's foreign intelligence service in March 2021, it had a unique chance to set the pace among liberal democracies for better legal standards on proportionate government access to data and the protection of fundamental rights. Recent European jurisprudence such as the Schrems II ruling by the Court of Justice of the European Union and the Big Brother Watch and Centrum för Rättvisa decisions by the European Court of Human Rights brought additional momentum to the international quest for better standards in legislation and oversight practice. Unfortunately, the Bundestag did not seize the moment. Despite laudable progress in some areas, there is a pressing need for future legislative work to align the German legal framework on foreign intelligence collection with international standards and to better meet the German Constitutional Court's minimal requirements. This report thus calls for a comprehensive intelligence reform to improve the quality of the legal framework and to guarantee more robust fundamental rights protections and to overcome the undue fragmentation of oversight and authorization processes.

Regarding the quality of the legal framework, lawmakers should - establish a clear and consolidated legal framework for investigatory powers across the German intelligence and security sector. This should include a single judicial authorization mechanism that eliminates inefficient duplications. - regulate bulk data access more transparently, including provisions on commercial data purchases, suitability tests, and interception of machine-to-machine communications. Regarding fundamental rights protection, lawmakers should - create an effective judicial remedy mechanism for ex post facto review of foreign surveillance, as required by European jurisprudence. - apply the same standards and safeguards that pertain to the collection of personal content data also to the collection of metadata. This is in line with the recent ECtHR Grand Chamber judgement which deemed both data types as equally worthy of protection.

Regarding the oversight and authorization process, lawmakers should- expand the independent approval powers to cover bulk data analysis (examination warrants), suitability tests (testing and training warrants), and commercial data buying (data acquisition warrants).-include systematic points of friction in the judicial authorization process by allowing for adversarial counsel in the assessment of bulk warrants, as well as by providing direct access for the oversight body to bearers of communications in order to verify adherence to warrant criteria, as is common practice in the Swedish foreign intelligence framework. That is; a) define a concrete ex-post control mandate that enables data-driven oversight of the BND's data handling, including the independent analysis of the selectors used; b) introduce binding enforcement powers for the independent oversight body, including the power to prohibit certain data collection and to require data destruction; and c) codify comprehensive public reporting obligations for the oversight body.

## Introduction

After a far-reaching judgement by the German Constitutional Court in May 2020, Angela Merkel's governing coalition of conservatives and social democrats found themselves, yet again, in the position to pass a foreign intelligence reform through the Bundestag.[2] This had become necessary after the Court settled the basic question whether the territorial reach of the right to private communication and press freedom as guaranteed under Article 10 and Article 5 of the German constitution extends beyond the German territory and protects not just German nationals and residents. Unlike the government, the Constitutional Court unequivocally affirmed that these fundamental rights are human rights and not citizen rights, and that they can therefore apply extraterritorially, when state authorities collect data of individuals abroad.[3] In turn, this required a wholesale amendment of both the legal framework for foreign intelligence and its judicial oversight. The BND Act, as amended in March 2021, now substantially changes and expands the surveillance powers of Germany's foreign intelligence agency, the Bundesnachrichtendienst (BND).[4] It also establishes a wide range of new safeguards and oversight structures.[5] This report introduces the new regulatory framework and offers an assessment of its merits and shortcomings. It does this in recognition of other recent legal and political developments at the international level. More specifically, Germany's foreign intelligence reform came at a time when the practice and legal bases for bulk collection and other forms of (automated) government access to personal data received renewed attention across Europe. Among these recent developments were:

- The Schrems II6 ruling by the Court of Justice of the European Union (CJEU) which saw inadequate safeguards against government access to personal data as the main reason to terminate the Privacy Shield agreement for data transfers from the EU to the US.

- The CJEU's ruling on the Quadrature du Net and the Privacy International cases which pronounced on some EU member states' laws on mandatory data retention in the private sector, and which prohibited general and indiscriminate data retention and established conditions for effective oversight of government access to this data.

- The European Court of Human Rights (ECtHR) recently observed that "seven Contracting States (being Finland, France, Germany, the Netherlands, Sweden, Switzerland and the United Kingdom) officially operate bulk interception regimes over cables and/ or the airways,"[7] and called for a more robust legal framework and restrictions to ensure data protection standards, effective oversight, and remedies in Centrum för Rättvisa v Sweden judgement, and requiring more in-depth and rigorous oversight in Big Brother Watch and others v UK.

- The Council of Europe promotes its modernised Convention 108 as the only legally binding international agreement on data processing and data protection that extends to the realm of national security and defence (Council of Europe 2018) but key representatives acknowledge publicly: "While Convention 108+ provides a robust international legal framework for the protection of personal data, it does not fully and explicitly address some of the challenges posed in our digital era by unprecedented surveillance capacities."[8]

- The Organisation for Economic Co-operation and Development (OECD) has initiated work towards adopting a high-level principles document to establish basic common standards for government access to personal data held by the private sector.[9]

Much like Germany's second attempt to reform the legal bases and oversight framework for the BND's foreign intelligence collection, many of these developments are tied to pressing political and legal questions regarding the de jure and de facto conditions, guarantees, and safeguards for bulk collection and oversight. Together, this might create a new momentum for a collective search for appropriate safeguards and effective oversight and redress mechanisms which the Snowden revelations had initially ignited. Hence, this report's deep dive into how Germany has just redesigned its legal framework for strategic bulk collection and computer network exploitation, it is hoped, might be of interest to non-German readers, too.[10]

## Reformed bulk surveillance powers

This section discusses the main changes of the BND Act after the comprehensive reform of 2021 in order to make them intelligible for non-German readers. Beginning with an overview of the central foreign surveillance powers exercised by the BND (2.1), the section then dissects three key bulk powers, namely strategic bulk interception (2.2), computer network exploitation (2.3) and transnational data sharing (2.4) based on detailed reference to the underlying reformed provisions. By comparing the new legal framework to the criteria provided by the German Constitutional Court ruling, the section provides context for the intricate regulations. Section 3 then deals with the new oversight structures. A subjective assessment of the reform's advantages and deficits as well as the remaining gaps in relation to international standards and case law follows in section 4.

### *Overview of key surveillance powers*

Before digging deeper into the individual data collection authorities and their respective requirements, a short general overview of key surveillance powers shall help readers to get a better grasp of Germany's foreign intelligence law. By way of introduction, an overview of the BND's key legal authorities to access data under the new BND Act. First, the BND wields a general mandate to collect communications for foreign intelligence purposes. It may compel actors from the private sector to provide communications data, such as data streams flowing through backbone fibre optic cables which are administered by telecommunications providers. Compelled access is typically directed at domestic communications providers which are subject to German jurisdiction. Due to Germany's geographical location in the heart of Europe, routing of foreign communications makes up a relevant fraction of overall telecommunication traffic, even in domestic communications networks.[11] Second, foreign communications networks, such as internet service providers (ISPs) or mobile phone network operators can also be directly targeted by the BND. On the one hand, it may infiltrate foreign providers covertly, interfering with the IT systems to enable data access (covert bulk data collection). On the other hand, the BND can request the assistance of foreign intelligence agencies to access data.

Assisted data collection entails sending relevant search terms to a foreign public body, which then sends relevant hits, for example for certain IP or MAC addresses, back to the BND. These two forms of data access are used if the company that holds or routes the data cannot be legally compelled by the BND. Importantly, there is also a general authority to conduct bulk collection suitability tests. The BND can tap into foreign and domestic communications networks in order to assess the usability of a specific provider or networks for strategic surveillance purposes and to check the relevance of search terms. Third, a legal authority to interfere with and exploit foreign computer systems has been enshrined in the new BND Act. This hacking authority may target IT systems abroad that the BND expects to yield relevant foreign intelligence data. Fourth, albeit not included in the illustration, the report will discuss transnational data-sharing as a separate important authority. The amended BND Act features new standards for international SIGINT data transfers and cooperation. The BND can share data with foreign agencies ad hoc and in bulk, even automated transmissions are possible. The agency can also transfer large amounts of data to the German military and other domestic actors.

*Strategic foreign communications collection (bulk interception)*

## Legal basis and scope

The central norm that regulates the BND's mandate to collect foreign communications in bulk is paragraph 19 of the BND Act (see the annex for an unofficial translation). It lists the aims which the government must pursue when seeking the authorization for strategic foreign telecommunications collection (Strategische Ausland-Fernmeldeaufklärung).[12] Whereas paragraph 19 applies to foreign communications only,[13] it does not mean that the collection of foreign communications under this provision is limited to non-German territory. Rather, if the communications of foreign entities or individuals are processed by providers within Germany, the BND can compel them to provide access to this data (§ 25 BND Act). Moreover, the BND Act now also includes an explicit regulation for the covert intrusion of communications systems if it is necessary for the implementation of bulk interception measures (§ 19 (6) BND Act). Accordingly, the BND may use technical means to secretly infiltrate the IT systems of a communications service provider abroad. Authorizing an intelligence agency to break into the computer systems of a foreign entity in a foreign country will, most likely, come into conflict with the law there.

The Federal Constitutional Court acknowledged this tension in its May 2020 judgement and noted that this may still be afforded: "In the interest of the Federal Republic of Germany's security and capacity to act, the intelligence that can be obtained must also include information that is deliberately withheld from Germany – possibly with negative intentions – and is kept secret within the other jurisdiction. Under the law of the state targeted by surveillance measures, such measures may also be illegal, or at least unwanted."[14] In response to this, the 2021 reform of the BND Act took this controversial practice of covert bulk interception out of the legal grey zone and established a specific legal basis for it. The general scope of paragraph 19 of the BND Act is limited to the collection of personal content data (personenbezogene Inhaltsdaten) in the context of strategic foreign communications collection. Consequently, a range of other data collection practices in the pursuit of, for example, human intelligence, the commercial acquisition of data, open source intelligence and social media intelligence are not covered by the comprehensive regulation and oversight regime that the 2021 reform of the BND Act established.[15]

These forms of foreign intelligence gathering were not part of the 2021 reform legislation and are subject to other, often less stringent, legal requirements. The BND Act distinguishes between different data categories: content data, metadata, traffic data and inventory data. One key distinction is the one between content data and metadata. Whereas paragraph 19 applies only to personal content data, the collection and processing of metadata, including traffic data, are subject to separate and far less stringent requirements (for example § 26 BND Act regarding domestic traffic data). Most importantly, the collection and processing of foreign metadata is exempt from most legal restrictions. The collection of inventory data is only explicitly referred to in the context of covert bulk interception (§ 19 (6) BND Act).

Suitability tests (Cold-starting capability) beyond the general authority to conduct bulk interception discussed above, the BND Act also allows for another form of bulk collection–albeit with far fewer safeguards and control requirements.

As an exception to the general rule that content data may only be collected in bulk on the basis of search terms (§ 19 (5) BND Act), the BND may perform so-called suitability tests (Eignungsprüfungen; § 24 BND Act) in order to either test the suitability of specific telecommunication networks for bulk collection purposes (purpose 1) or to generate new search terms or to assess the relevance of existing search terms (purpose 2). On the face of it, suitability testing is intended to ensure that bulk collection is targeted at the most relevant carriers, using the most appropriate search terms. Suitability tests in pursuit of purpose 1 (relevant networks) require a written order by the president of the BND or his or her designated deputy and may only be performed if factual indications exist that the selected telecommunications networks bear appropriate data for the purposes of strategic foreign surveillance as regulated in the BND Act. Suitability tests in pursuit of purpose 2 (relevant search terms), however, do not require such safeguards.

What is more, there is no requirement, as is the case in some other democracies,[18]for the ex-ante authorization involving independent oversight bodies nor is the duration and the volume of the data collection in pursuit of suitability tests subject to (effective) limitations.[19]In general, data that has been collected in pursuit of the suitability test must be processed only for either purpose (listed above). This rule does not apply, however, when factual indications point to a grave threat to individuals or the security of either the Federal Republic of Germany or institutions of either the European Union and its Member States, EFTA and NATO (§ 24 (7) sentence 1 BND Act). Another exception to this rule is the force protection of the German military and that of EU, NATO and EFTA Member States: If factual indications exist that data from suitability tests points to threats to either of them, it may also be processed. Finally, and importantly, the BND may also transmit data from suitability tests automatically (i.e., without further data minimization) to the German Armed Forces (§ 24 (7) sentence 3 BND Act) where the requirements govern the processing, transfers and deletion of such data are far less stringent and transparent. Moreover, it should be borne in mind that the new judicial and administrative oversight mechanisms created as part of the 2021 reform of the BND Act (see section 3.2) have no mandate to review the use of such data by the German Armed Forces.

## Requirements

### Lawful aims

The basic authority to conduct strategic foreign intelligence collection requires a prior written application that ought to state which lawful aim is being pursued. According to paragraph 19 this can only be one of the following two general cases: gathering information for the Federal Government of Germany (aim 1) and to detect threats of international relevance (aim 2). In general, the BND may conduct strategic surveillance based on orders of the Federal Chancellery in order to provide information for foreign and security political decision-making (§ 19 (3) BND Act). This general authority may not be used for economic espionage, which is defined as gaining competitive economic advantages (§ 19 (9) BND Act). Applications for strategic foreign communications collection to gather information for the Federal Government of Germany (aim 1) can only be issued if they serve the purpose to obtain information about foreign countries, are relevant for German foreign and security policy, and were ordered by the Federal Chancellery.

By contrast, applications for strategic foreign communications collection to detect threats of international relevance (aim 2) ought to satisfy the same criteria required for aim 1, and in addition they must meet the requirement that factual indications exist at the time of the application that such measure might produce insights into eight general threat areas such as crises abroad, national defense, and threats to critical infrastructure, or if they yield insights that allow to protect five legal interests, for example the security of the German state or of institutions of the European Union. The list of permissible aims demonstrates the BND's dual role as a foreign intelligence and a military intelligence agency. While being formally supervised by the Federal Chancellery, different parts of the government and their subordinated agencies, including the foreign ministry, the interior ministry and the domestic intelligence services as well as the defense ministry and the armed forces receive information from the BND's SIGINT operations and contribute to its national intelligence priority framework (Aufgabenprofil BND).

### Volume limitation

Besides requesting new and more detailed legal authorities for main operational aims discussed above, the Federal Constitutional Court's judgement also demanded that bulk interception of communications must not be unlimited and "sweeping,"[20] which prompted lawmakers to include a new data volume limitation. It limits the amount of data that the BND may collect to a maximum of 30 percent of the transmission capacity of all globally existing telecommunications networks (§ 19 (8) BND Act).[21] We will discuss the relevance of this legal boundary for bulk data collection in the analysis section below. It should be noted, also, that this volume limitation does not pertain to bulk collection in pursuit of the suitability tests. Specific protections and exceptions The BND Act also comprises a number of specific provisions that ought to protect the fundamental rights to privacy of correspondence, posts and telecommunications (Art. 10 of the Basic Law), press freedom (Art. 5 of the Basic Law), and the right to informational self-determination as well as confidentiality and integrity of IT systems (derived from Art. 2 (1) in connection with Art. 1 (1) of the Basic Law). Following the landmark decision by the Constitutional Court, the BND Act now includes additional rules that seek to better protect these rights in specific SIGINT governance contexts. By way of introduction and illustration, these protections are tied to the distinction into different data protection categories summarized below.

Most of the protections of data categories listed are constructed according to the same logic: the provision first prohibits the collection of certain communications in principle, and then lists exceptions from that basic rule. The discrimination of foreign and domestic data is the most basic distinction throughout the BND Act. While the collection of foreign data is the BND's mission, it must not, in principle, collect domestic data. Paragraph 19 section 7 prohibits the collection of data of any German citizen, even if they are located abroad, as well as any person located on German territory. It also bans the BND from intercepting the communications of companies and other legal bodies within Germany, because their communications are also protected by the right to private correspondence. That said, incidental collection of domestic data is inevitable if an intelligence agency collects bulk data in telecommunication networks. How the BND approaches the challenge to filter out domestic data is discussed below in the subsection on data processing. Put differently, unless one's communication data is protected by virtue of its professional characterization or by virtue of one's identity as a German citizen, German company or resident in Germany or the European Union, the new SIGINT framework in Germany offers little explicit protection, let alone redress options.

The BND ought to afford everyone the right to privacy under Art. 10 of the German Constitution, irrespective of citizenship or current geographical location. This basic legal premise, however, does not amount to equal treatment in practice. Rather, when it comes to the authorization procedure, non-EU communications are subject to far less stringent requirements and data subjects have virtually no options available to obtain effective remedy for misuse of their personal data. According to the Constitutional Court, a strengthened judicial and administrative oversight over the BND's treatment of non-national communications data was necessary in order to compensate "for the virtual absence of safeguards commonly guaranteed (to non-nationals) under the rule of law."[22]More specifically, it found that an amended BND Act "must compensate for the gap in legal protection that follows from the weak possibilities for individual legal protection in practice. Given that very limited information and notification requirements apply to the surveillance of foreign telecommunications in light of its need for secrecy, effective legal protection can hardly be obtained."[23]

Protected professional communications Following the Constitutional Court's demand that the surveillance of communication of professional groups such as journalists, lawyers or priests must be further restricted, the BND Act now offers increased protections to communications of certain professional groups (§ 21 BND Act).[24] The legal norm states that targeted collection of personal content data with search terms is illegal, if it relates to the communications of clerics, lawyers and journalists. The protection is limited to these three professional groups, because they have a right to confidential communications and a privilege to refuse to give evidence.[25] The professions listed in the German code of criminal procedure that enjoy similar confidentiality safeguards would also include members of parliament, social workers, tax consultants, physicians, psychologists, pharmacists, midwives and others,[26] but they are not included in the wording of paragraph 21 of the BND Act.[27] The second section of § 21 specifies the exceptions to the general protection of journalists, lawyers and clerical professions. When facts justify the assumption that a person from one of these three groups is the perpetrator or participant in certain criminal offenses,[28] so-called 'targeted' data collection (i.e., the use of search terms related to that person) is allowed.

The same is the case if the data collection is necessary to prevent serious threats to life, limb or freedom of a person and a number of other legal interests listed in section 2 of paragraph 21. The legal norm, thus, makes two basic weighting decisions necessary. First, the BND needs to assess whether a person belongs to one of the protected professional groups. Second, it must decide if there are facts that allow exceptional data collection. Regarding the first decision on classifying someone as a journalist, attorney or pastor, the policy makers acknowledge that such assessments require more detailed criteria, especially in the case of journalists, because this profession is not legally defined and not necessarily linked to an employer or organization. More detailed requirements regarding who counts as a journalist will, according to the explanatory statement, be subject to a secret executive decree (Dienstvorschrift).[29] Data related to the core of private life German law recognizes the "core of private life" (Kernbereich privater Lebensgestaltung) as another basic principle aimed at protecting the individual from government surveillance.

It was developed in case law and insulates the core of private life, for example communications of highly personal character such as soliloquy, expression of feelings, unconscious experience or sexuality from state surveillance. In so doing, the essence of privacy and intimacy shall be off-limits, and this applies also in the context of strategic foreign communications surveillance (§ 22 BND Act). Even interests of paramount importance cannot justify an intrusion in the core of private life.[30]Given that technical parameters and search terms are insufficient means to determine whether the core sphere of private life is affected, the BND is required to conduct manual assessments and must delete pertinent data immediately. In unclear cases, the Independent Control Council (see section 3) must scrutinize whether the data may be processed further (§ 22 (3) BND Act).

## Data processing

When pressed, the BND stated in the constitutional court proceedings that it collects about 270.000 human communications such as phone calls or chat messages per day of which "an average of 260 data transmissions are identified and forwarded to the relevant departments every day."[31] The processing of data – from the collection point to the final intelligence output – is consequently an important element in a legal framework for strategic surveillance operations.[32] The BND Act addresses the role of data filters in paragraph 19 section 7 and the handling of domestic metadata in paragraph 26.

## Filtering (data minimization)

According to paragraph 19, section 7, sentence 1 of the BND Act domestic content data that was collected in foreign SIGINT operations must be automatically filtered out and immediately deleted. Yet, the technical infrastructure of the internet makes incidental collection of domestic data inevitable. Despite the general prohibition, the legal framework includes an exception that allows processing incidentally collected domestic content data if the BND has reason to believe that the further processing of the illegally collected domestic data may help to prevent dangers to life or freedom of a person, national security or the security of an EU or NATO member state (§ 19 (7) sentence 6 BND Act). In practice, this rule might create an incentive to actually retain and process domestic data instead of immediately deleting it. The exception presupposes that domestic data has already been processed to some extent, because otherwise, no actual evidence with regard to the permissible exceptions could have been retrieved.

The Federal Constitutional Court, in principle, accepted that the BND deploys filter systems to process as little domestic content data as possible in foreign intelligence collection. Regarding the accuracy and sophistication of the filter technology, the judgement required that the "legislator must impose an obligation on the intelligence service to continually develop filtering methods and to keep them up to date with developments in science and technology."[33] The governing coalition, however, decided to introduce a less ambitious legal requirement that demands that the filter methods shall be continuously developed and must be kept up to date with the current state of the art (§ 19 (7) sentence 4 BND Act). This limits the development of the filter methods to minimization techniques that are already available and does not comply with the standard formulated by the Federal Constitutional Court. Search terms under the authority of a bulk interception warrant, the BND may collect and process content data only with the help of search terms (also called selectors). The processing of metadata does not require the use of search terms and is not covered by the requirements of paragraph 19 of the BND Act.[34] The BND Act states that it is not necessary to list individual search terms in the bulk interception warrants (§ 23 (6) sentence 2 BND Act), which in practice exempts most search terms from ex ante approval of lawfulness.

Only specific categories of search terms that target, for example, EU citizens or journalists, are subject to ex ante approval of the judicial control body (§ 42 BND Act). Other selectors that do not target one of the specifically protected categories such as confidential professional communications (see above), cannot be checked prior to their use. Search terms that are not approved on the basis of a warrant, can, however, be reviewed at random by the administrative control body.[35]During the Constitutional Court proceedings the BND revealed that it uses a "six digits" number of search terms in its SIGINT operations.[36] If between 100.000 and 999.000 selectors are used simultaneously to collect content data, manual random inspections appear largely ineffective. The BND Act, though, does not include requirements for more structured or automated oversight of the use of search terms. Only the transfer of search terms to foreign intelligence services must be subjected to automated checks.

## Assisted data collection

The BND may also ask a foreign intelligence service for permission to feed certain selectors into their operational systems. Prior to a foreign public body using BND search terms, the government ought to make sure that these terms meet the same requirements as those governing the BND's own use of search terms (§ 28 (3) BND Act): They must not lead to the processing of telecommunications traffic from German nationals, domestic legal entities or persons residing in Germany. Equally off limits are search terms to engage in industrial espionage. The surveillance of EU institutions, of public bodies of its member states or of EU citizens requires the same independent approval. In addition, search terms must respect the protection of confidentiality relationships, as well as the safeguards related to highly private content data.[37]

## Domestic metadata

Compared to the more detailed provisions on personal content data, the federal legislators shied away from writing specific requirements and safeguards into the law as regards metadata. Thus, most of the data protection categories specified in paragraphs 19 to 23 concern personal content data, despite the fact that most of the data collected and processed in SIGINT is metadata (including traffic data).[38] While paragraph 26 declares the processing of personal domestic traffic data, i.e. data related to German citizens, German legal bodies and all persons located on German territory, as illegal in principle, it also introduces two broad exceptions to this basic prohibition: First, the BND may collect metadata in the context of machine-to-machine communications. This is defined as automated technical data transmissions without the intervention of the user (§ 26 (3) sentence 2 number 1 BND Act). Examples for such automated communications could be back ups and other synchronizations with servers, automated online payments, log in exchanges between mobile phones and cell towers, or automatically logged location data. The legislators presume that such data flows should not be regarded as related to personal communications and should fall outside the scope of the constitutionally protected confidentiality of telecommunication (Article 10 of the Basic Law)[39] Second, it permits the processing of domestic traffic data without restriction if it is automatically made unreadable immediately after their collection (§ 26 (3) sentence 2 number 2 BND Act).

This masking of personal domestic traffic data shall be implemented by using hash functions that would allow a re-identification of the original data "only with disproportionate effort."[40] All traffic data that does not allow to identify participants in domestic communications, such as time stamps and other technical parameters, need not be hashed. The metadata of the foreign participants of the communication must also not be made unreadable with the hash function. This raises the question whether the hashing achieves the intended goal of anonymization of domestic data. If only one side of a communication is hashed, there could remain a possibility to re-identify the domestic persons based on correlations.[41] If the BND's operational systems fail to anonymize domestic data, the law requires that the respective data be hashed belatedly as soon as possible or deleted immediately. But this requirement is also subject to the exception that the BND may process the domestic traffic data if facts indicate that it might help to prevent significant dangers.[42]

Data retention sums up the different retention limits for personal data collected under the authorities for suitability tests and bulk interception. Notice, there is no definite retention limit for content in bulk interception. The previous BND Act included a maximum retention limit for content of ten years, which was replaced by a mandatory evaluation of whether data is still needed in intervals of seven years. Traffic data may be retained for up to six months, but longer storage is possible if the BND regards the data as necessary. Personal data collected in search term suitability tests can be stored for up to two weeks, network suitability tests can be retained for up to four weeks (§ 24 (6) BND Act). An exception applies to encrypted data, which can be retained for up to ten years. Authorization and Oversight The strategic foreign communications collection pursuant to paragraph 19 of the BND Act requires written bulk warrants (Anordnungen) which must be signed off by either the president of the BND or his or her deputy (§ 23 BND Act). These bulk warrants must include information on the purpose of the data collection, the relevant topic within the lawful aims of paragraph 19 sections 3 or 4, the geographical focus, the duration, and a justification. The law does not provide a period of validity for the warrants. The warrant's lawfulness must then be approved by the judicial control body of the Independent Control Council before its implementation (§ 23 (4) BND Act, see section 3.2 of this report). If the warrant is declared unlawful, the warrant expires. In cases of imminent danger, a preliminary approval can be obtained by one single member of the judicial control body (for details on oversight structures and ex ante approval powers, see section 4 of this report). Once the warrant has been approved by the judicial oversight body, the BND sends an order to each implicated communications provider, which must include the name of the compelled company, the duration of the measure, and the affected communications (§ 25 (2) BND Act).

*Computer network exploitation*

## Legal basis and scope

The amended BND Act now includes a (bulk) equipment interference authority (§ 34 BND Act). The provision allows the BND to compromise IT systems used by foreigners abroad and to collect communications as well as stored data on these systems.[43] The main reasons to hack into foreign IT systems are that a global expansion of encryption undermines the effectiveness of (bulk) interception and that the BND has no jurisdiction to order compelled access to data held by private parties abroad. This constraint has also been addressed under the general authority for strategic foreign communications surveillance. It states that if the BND cannot establish "cooperative access" (kooperativer Zugang), then it may use secret means to collect data and infiltrate the information systems of telecommunications providers to overcome security measures (§ 19 (6) BND Act, see above). The typical targets of the BND's computer network exploitation (CNE) are not individual smartphones, but rather computer systems used for business purposes or to operate IT infrastructure such as computer networks of military facilities or telecommunications providers.[44] Paragraph 34 and following, nonetheless, allow interfering with the personal devices of individuals abroad, too. It also permits collecting both stored data as well as ongoing communications. The use of computer network exploitation is now also explicitly permissible if it "inevitably" affects data of other individuals or systems (§ 34 (6) BND Act). According to the official explanatory statement that accompanies the new BND Act this would, for example, include a scenario in which the BND first needs to compromise the computer of a network administrator and intercept her password in order to, then, infiltrate the actual target system of the operation.[45]

# Requirements

## *Lawful aims*

The BND may deploy means of equipment interference for the same lawful aims that apply to the use of bulk interception (see section 2.2). These are either the (political) information of the German Federal Government (aim 1), or the early detection of imminent dangers of international significance (aim 2).[46] The only difference is that CNE requires "facts" rather than "factual indications" that the hacking operation conducted in pursuit of aim 2 will allow detecting threats of international importance (§ 34 (3) BND Act). This represents a higher legal threshold if CNE is used for threat detection instead of information gathering.

## *Specific protections and exceptions*

Only computers used by foreigners abroad may be targeted under this authority (§ 34 (1) BND Act). Thus, the BND is, pursuant to the BND Act, not allowed to hack into the devices of German citizens, domestic organizations and persons located on German territory.[47] In addition, the BND Act provides the same protections for confidential professional communications of lawyers, clerics and journalists that are also protected under the rules for strategic foreign communications surveillance (cf. discussion of § 21 in section 2.2 above). No hacking operations may thus be directed at members of said professions, if they communicated in confidential professional relationships. The same exceptions to this rule, however, also apply.[48] The legal norm requires the same case-by-case weighting decisions, in which the BND agents need to determine if the computer system in question belongs to one of the protected professional groups, secondly, whether there are legal exceptions that permit hacking the device. Equally, any data collection related to the core of private life, i.e. content that relates to the essence of an individual's privacy or intimacy, is off limits in the context of hacking operations. Paragraph 36 (parallel to § 22, see section 2.2.2 above) provides the same general prohibition and subsequent balancing considerations. The processing of highly private information is illegal, and if the BND is uncertain as to whether specific material touches this core sphere of private life, the independent oversight council needs to authorize further processing. On a technical level, the Act requires that the BND must ensure that modifications made to the targeted IT systems are necessary for data collection and that they are revoked automatically once the operation ends (§ 34 (4) number 1 BND Act). The software and hardware used to break into foreign computers and exfiltrate data must be protected against unauthorized use in accordance with up-to-date technical standards (§ 34 (4) number 2 BND Act).

## Data processing

The data processing rules included in the framework for CNE only relate to data retention, and do not touch upon data minimization rules or metadata processing, as is the case in bulk interception. The BND must immediately check whether personal data gathered in hacking operations is necessary for one of the permissible aims. The wording in § 34 (7) BND Act suggests that the data could also be deemed necessary for a different operational purpose than the one that was included in the initially signed CNE warrant.[49] If an immediate assessment of the data is not possible, for example if the data is encrypted, the data can be retained for up to three years. The Independent Control Council may approve longer retention periods than three years for encrypted devices or their images, such as copies of storage medium (§ 34 (9) BND Act).

## Authorization and Oversight

Parallel to bulk interception warrants, all CNE measures pursuant to paragraph 34 BND Act must first be signed off by either the president of the BND or his or her deputy and then approved in advance by the Independent Control Council, based on written warrants. The CNE warrant must include the following information:

1. Purpose of the hacking operation

2. Corresponding subject matter of the measure

3. Goal of the measure

4. Type, scope and duration of the hacking operation

5. Justification

6. If applicable the extended data analysis period.[50]

The warrants are limited to 12 months, with an (unlimited) renewal option for another 12 months at a time, if the necessary conditions are still met (§ 37 (3) BND Act). The warrants neither have to include specifications of the targeted system or person nor information about the tools used to infiltrate the system. This means that the oversight body will not be able to verify whether the technical means used in CNE measures complies with basic human rights standards.[51]The BND Act also remains silent as regards the management of vulnerabilities and exploits that the BND uses to conduct hacking operations. Retaining and exploiting the vulnerabilities for intelligence hacking operations – instead of patching them–may affect large numbers of users. Whether and how known and unknown vulnerabilities may be exploited and how the BND approaches the trade-offs of IT security and intelligence gathering, remain unregulated by the BND Act and are not subject to independent oversight.[52]

## *Transnational data transfer and cooperation*

## Legal basis and scope

As Germany's core signals intelligence agency, the BND maintains close connections with foreign intelligence services around the globe and shares data in large quantities with other agencies. It cooperates with about 450 intelligence services in over 160 countries,[53] and maintains close ties to institutions of the European Union and NATO. Between 50 and 60 percent of search terms used by the BND stem from intelligence services of allied states, such as the Five Eyes.[54] The role of the BND's transnational cooperation with so-called partner services was scrutinized closely by the Constitutional Court, in part because it had previously been subject of political contestation within the parliamentary inquiry committee.[55] The NSA inquiry committee in the Bundestag showed that previous intelligence legislation and oversight regimes were insufficient to prevent abuse and malfeasance in the context of international SIGINT cooperation. In the Constitutional Court proceedings, the judges frequently expressed their discontent with the previous oversight structure characterized (in part) by inadequate access, impenetrable secrecy and lack of resources and control instruments. While the court acknowledged the basic need to cooperate with foreign services as a means to fulfil the BND's mandate, it also held that "German state authority is responsible for the sharing of data and is bound by the fundamental rights when sharing data."[56]

Under German constitutional law, the judges argued, sharing data with other bodies constitutes a separate interference with fundamental rights and consequently requires independent statutory protections that must be necessary and proportionate. And this, the Court argued, was not sufficiently guaranteed in the 2016 reform, even though one of the main drivers for that reform had been to rein-in on intelligence cooperation malpractice. Notably, the CJEU argued in the same vein in its Schrems II decision, where it found "that the communication of personal data to a third party, such as a public authority, constitutes an interference with the fundamental rights enshrined in Articles 7 and 8 of the Charter, whatever the subsequent use of the information communicated. The same is true of the retention of personal data and access to that data with a view to its use by public authorities, irrespective of whether the information in question relating to private life is sensitive or whether the persons concerned have been inconvenienced in any way on account of that interference."[57]

The BND Act distinguishes between ad hoc transnational data transfer and data sharing and exchanges that are administered under written cooperation agreements, so-called Memorandums of Understanding (MoU). The transfer of personal SIGINT data to foreign and transnational bodies in the absence of a cooperation agreement is now governed by paragraph 30, which enables the BND to exchange data with foreign intelligence services and other foreign public bodies. If the data-sharing happens within a cooperation, for example with agencies from EU member states or NATO, the formation of this cooperation falls under the rules of paragraph 31 BND Act. It is important to note that the requirements discussed below only apply in the context of SIGINT and do not replace the general regulations on data transfers and joint databases included in paragraphs 11 to 18 of the BND Act.

Moreover, the BND Act includes a wide range of provisions governing the transfer of SIGINT data with domestic bodies, including other domestic intelligence agencies at the federal and state level and other public bodies of the German security sector, as well as private actors. These domestic data sharing processes, in the context of SIGINT, are for the most part regulated in paragraph 29 of the BND Act. In this section, the discussion focuses on the transnational dimension of intelligence sharing, discussing the requirements for cross-border data transfers, international SIGINT cooperation, and the enhanced data sharing between the BND and the German Federal Armed Forces, the Bundeswehr.

## Requirements

### Lawful aims

SIGINT data transfer

Personal data collected under the legal authorities for bulk interception or computer network exploitation may be transferred to foreign agencies and transnational bodies if this is necessary to fulfil the BND's mandate in the context of international political cooperation (§ 30 (1) and § 39 (1) BND Act). Beyond that, data may, for example, also be shared for law enforcement purposes (§ 30 (2) and § 39 (2) BND Act) and other aims such as prevention of significant dangers (§ 30 (3) and § 39 (3) BND Act). Data gathered for information purposes can exceptionally be shared outside of the context of international political cooperation, too, with the aim to prevent imminent dangers (§ 30 (5) BND Act). It is basically the BND's responsibility that the data transfer is lawful. It must inform the recipients about the applicable purpose restrictions and can inquire whether the data has been processed by them for permissible purposes only. The recipient must agree to a binding assurance to comply with the request to delete data. Transfers can no longer take place if factual indications exist that such a binding assurance is not being honoured by the recipient (§ 30 (8) BND Act). The legal norm further specifies cases in which data may not be transferred to foreign agencies: "A transmission does not take place if the BND recognizes that, by taking into account the type of personal data and its collection, the legitimate interests of the data subject exceed the general public interest in the transfer of data."[58]

The interests of an individual under surveillance that are "worthy of protection" (schutzwürdig) may prevail, if there are factual indications that the use of the shared data in the recipient country could lead to significant human rights violations or the violation of basic principles of the rule of law. This would be the case if the data is used for "political persecution or inhuman or degrading punishment or abuse" (§ 30 (6) sentence 2 BND Act, own translation). The law, thus, imposes a weighting of interests in borderline cases before the BND shares personal data in the SIGINT context. In cases of doubt, the BND has to take into account whether the recipient provides a binding assurance of adequate protection for the shared data, and whether there is evidence that such assurances will not be complied with. When the BND makes this assessment, it needs to factor in the type of information as well as the previous handling of shared data by the recipient (§ 30 (6) sentence 3 BND Act).

This "generalised assessment of the factual and legal situation in the receiving states"[59] was a requirement of the Federal Constitutional Court which requested that all data transfers must be balanced and justifiable according to minimum safeguards (Rechtsstaatlichkeitsvergewisserungpflicht). It leaves a significant scope of consideration to the BND and does not require proactive investigations to corroborate the rule of law assessment. It suffices that the BND "recognizes"[60] that the protection of the individual outweighs the interest in the data transfer. SIGINT cooperation agreements Bulk data sharing that goes beyond ad hoc transfers of information requires written agreements, so-called memorandums of understanding (Absichtserklärung) that specify the purposes of bulk data exchanges. Paragraph 31 section 3 outlines the three operational purposes for transnational cooperation with other intelligence services, which include the early detection of severe threats and the protection of foreign and security interests of the Federal Republic of Germany.

It also allows cooperation if the operations of the BND would otherwise be made very difficult or impossible. In practice, this means that the legislator mandates the BND to negotiate agreements with foreign services about the exchange of search terms for bulk interception, as well as automated transfer of unevaluated bulk data. For data collection based on search terms, the BND can receive and use search terms determined by foreign intelligence services to scan data traffic and to forward the relevant hits automatically to the foreign services. Conversely, the BND may also transmit its own search terms to foreign agencies, who then feed them in their operational data collection systems (assisted data collection pursuant § 28 BND Act). The MoUs with partner services from EU or NATO member states must be approved by the Federal Chancellery (§ 31 (7) BND Act). All other cooperation agreements must be approved by the head of the Federal Chancellery and the parliamentary oversight committee must be informed about the conclusion of new MoUs. If the MoU entails sharing unevaluated bulk data automatically, it requires the head of the BND to sign off (§ 33 (3) BND Act).

The eight binding assurances that the BND needs to negotiate with its partner services mostly include the same rules that the BND needs to comply with in its own bulk interception activities. For example, the Foreign Service needs to agree to delete data related to German citizens and organizations, protected groups and the core of private life. Next to the binding assurances listed in paragraph 31, section 4 of the BND Act, the law names eleven permissible cooperation purposes, which range from gathering information on early detection of threats, protection of armed forces, and organized crime, to "comparable cases" (§ 31 (5) number 11 BND Act). The permissible purposes are worded in broad terms, which leaves a significant scope of action for the BND.

## Expanded data sharing with the armed forces

The BND, and especially its SIGINT branch, serves also as a provider of military intelligence to the Federal Armed Forces (Bundeswehr). While the German military manages its own strategic surveillance capabilities,[61]the

BND Act provides for designated data sharing arrangements. Next to jointly administered databases between the BND and the armed forces (§ 12 BND Act), the BND may also transfer bulk data to agencies under the auspices of the defense ministry. Bulk data gathered as part of the SIGINT suitability tests can be shared in an automated way (§ 24 (7) BND Act). Such bulk collection measures for testing purposes serve to determine relevant search terms and relevant communications networks for future bulk interception measures. They are exempt from any ex ante oversight, and it is unclear which legal provisions regulate the data handling by the armed forces (see section 4 for details). Data collected for threat detection purposes based on search terms can also be transferred automatically to the German military under certain conditions. This applies to data collected in CNE operations, as well as bulk collection based on search terms.[62] The Federal Government included the provisions that allow automated data sharing with the Armed Forces, although the constitutional judgement did not include substantial considerations regarding (automated) sharing of data between the BND and the military.

**Data processing SIGINT data transfer**

The legal rules on transnational data sharing include that recipients may only process the shared data for a previously defined purpose. The BND must inform all recipients that such purpose limitations apply and that it may request information from them about how they have processed the shared data. To put this into practice, the BND is required to arrange corresponding access to information rights (Auskunftsrechte) with the body that receives the data. The recipient must also give a binding assurance to comply with a request for deletion by the BND. If there are factual indications that such an assurance by the recipient will not be complied with, no data collected in the context of strategic surveillance may be shared (§ 30 (8) BND Act). In addition, the foreign recipient must check whether the shared personal data is actually needed and delete the shared data if it is not necessary. It must not be deleted, though, if the data that was evaluated as non-essential is linked to other information and the separation of the data would create undue costs.[63] If the personal data that is supposed to be shared is linked or grouped together with additional personal data, for example of other individuals, then the data can still be shared as long as the legitimate interests of the third person do not "clearly prevail" (§ 29 (14) BND Act). Furthermore, if shared personal data is incomplete or incorrect, the BND must notify the recipient, unless the mistakes are inconsequential (§ 29 (15) BND Act).

## Selector-based bulk data

The search terms that foreign intelligence services feed into the BND's data collection systems are subject to the same filter requirements that apply to the use of the BND's own selectors.[64] The law requires an automated scan to check whether the search terms determined by foreign partners are compliant with the written cooperation agreement. Automated filters shall verify whether the data includes information on the core area of private life, domestic personal data (e.g., on German residents) or specially protected confidential relationships (e.g. journalists). It must also be checked in an automated way whether the transmission of the data collected would conflict with the national interests of the German state (§ 32 (3) and (4) BND Act). Regarding protected professional communications, the BND must maintain block lists of identifiers of journalists, lawyers and clerics whose communications are afforded special confidentiality protection in order to gradually improve the filter accuracy (§ 32 (5) BND Act). Creating such block lists for protected groups was an explicit requirement put forward by the Constitutional Court judgement.[65]

Subsequent to these automated scans, the selector-based data is transferred automatically to the partner service. The accuracy and veracity of the automated checks and filtering of search terms must be subject to random checks by internal BND staff. According to the BND, about 300 search terms are checked manually per month.[66] Despite frequent calls to the contrary, the current law does not foresee an active involvement of the Independent Control Council in the filter verification. The Chancellery must be informed every six months about the BND's manual random inspections of automated data sharing (§ 32 (7) BND Act). The BND is explicitly allowed to retain the search terms submitted by cooperation partners for two weeks in order to enable random checks. The shared search terms from partner services may also be probed by the BND to generate additional search terms for its own purposes (§ 32 (8)). After two weeks, the selectors are deleted automatically.

## Unevaluated bulk data

Beyond the collection and transfer of selector-based communications data, the BND now also has the legal mandate to process unevaluated data in the context of SIGINT cooperation (§ 33 BND Act). This includes the transfer of metadata and content in bulk to a foreign intelligence service. The constitutional court had explicitly demanded a separate statutory basis for this kind of exchange, because the BND ceases any control over how the partner service processes content.[67] The same rules that apply to automated transfer of selector-based data summarized above, apply here, too. Additionally, the law requires to determine a so-called "qualified intelligence need" (qualifizierter Aufklärungsbedarf) that justifies the sharing of bulk data. It lists the following six threats as lawful purposes (§ 33 (2) BND Act):

1. The preparation of an armed attack on Germany or EU and NATO member states, or the cooperating state

2. Preparing for terrorist attacks,

3. Proliferation of weapons of war on a specific route or with a specific destination

4. International criminal, terrorist or state attacks using malware on the confidentiality, integrity or availability of IT systems,

5. Investigation of disinformation campaigns targeted at Germany

6. Preparation of attacks that threaten Germany's security.

The "qualified intelligence need" must be declared in writing and assigned to a strategic bulk interception warrant for threat detection purposes.[68] The Independent Control Council must check the lawfulness of the declared intelligence need as a basis for the cooperation before the data is transferred. If the oversight body does not confirm the lawfulness of the proposal, the data must not be transferred (§ 33 (3) BND Act).

### *Authorization and Oversight SIGINT data transfer*

The Federal Government shied away from introducing a general independent approval power for transnational data sharing. It established, based on the guidelines of the Constitutional Court,[69] an ex ante approval power limited to data sharing related to communications of protected professions.[70] The BND may share personal data from communications of protected professions, for example by journalists, if the judicial control body approves the transfer: It must weigh the foreigners' interests in protected confidential communications against the legitimate operational aims of the BND in its lawfulness test before data is transferred. Such a transfer of a lawyer's personal data would be allowed if evidence justifies the suspicion that the person in question may be the perpetrator or participant of a crime or if the transfer is necessary to prevent dangers to certain legal interests.[71] In case of imminent danger, a preliminary approval by one member of the oversight body suffices to permit the data transfer. If the decision is later revoked, the BND shall request the deletion of the shared data (§ 29 (8) sentence 5 BND Act). The Independent Control Council must also review, ex post, the repurposing of data. This can be the case if data that was first collected for information purposes is then transferred for threat prevention purposes.[72] Future case law will tell whether this rule on purpose changes satisfies the courts requirements for data sharing, including that lawmakers must create safeguards to ensure that undue purpose changes are excluded in principle.[73]

## New oversight framework

Building on the description of the three codified bulk powers of the BND, this section elaborates on the new oversight structure that the BND Act also established. Section 3.1 provides an overview of the institutional set-up and the specific focus and features of the new oversight mechanisms; followed by an analysis of the overseers' respective new control mandates (3.2).

*Institutional set-up*

## Legal basis and scope

The constitutional court demanded that the amended legal framework must provide for two distinct types of oversight for the BND's SIGINT activities: judicial and administrative control.[74] It did not prescribe, however, whether these separate oversight functions should be performed by one or several bodies. The lawmakers decided to combine both tasks within just one new oversight institution, the Independent Control Council (Unabhängiger Kontrollrat).[75] The Federal Government and the majority in parliament saw a unitary oversight body for the BND's SIGINT department as a precondition for continued international cooperation. They warned that, if too many oversight or review agencies would be involved, say a separate court for judicial review and a separate administrative control body, which might have involved the Federal Commissioner for Data Protection, foreign intelligence agencies might shy away from sharing information because of a fear that their data might not remain confidential.[76] Foreign-domestic bulk interception measures, that is to say selector-based collection of communications that involve German citizens, residents or organizations, continue to be governed by a different legal framework and remain exempt from the mandate of the new ICC.[77] Despite this split legal framework and oversight regime for domestic and foreign collection of communications, according to the Federal Government, the new oversight The judicial control body of the ICC consists of six federal judges, of which one serves as president and one as vice president of the Independent Control Council as a whole.[79] The second branch, called the administrative control body, must be headed by a fully qualified lawyer and is subject to the directions of the president of the ICC (§ 50 BND Act). The new ICC replaces the previous oversight body for foreign intelligence collection created by the 2016 intelligence reform, a part-time body called the Independent Committee (Unabhängiges Gremium). The level of available personnel and resources for the new budget estimates show that the BND's budget will most likely continue to increase significantly in the coming years. In 2021, it surpassed the mark of one billion euros for the first time, after considerable annual budget increases over the past couple of years (doubling its budget since the Snowden revelations. The Federal Government estimates that the implementation of the BND Act will produce one-time costs of about 450 million euro, and consecutively, also increased annual operational costs. Notice, though, that these figures are estimates published in the context of a legislative process and that the actual costs for implementing the new law and the concrete allocation of funds will be part of the budgeting process for 2022.

### Requirements Independence

Much like the European Court of Human Rights in its recent Big Brother Watch and Centrum för Rättvisa decisions, the German Constitutional Court also placed significant emphasis on the independence of the new oversight body from the BND and the Federal Government. According to the amended BND Act, the ICC is not bound by instructions from the Federal Government (§ 41 (3) BND Act), and it can define its own internal rules and procedures as well as its own oversight priorities and resources. The judges that form the judicial control body are elected for a term of 12 years and no reelection is permitted (§ 45 BND Act). The candidates for the six seats that form the senate of the judicial control body must be experienced federal judges that are proposed by the Federal Court of Justice (Bundesgerichtshof) and the Federal Administrative Court (Bundesverwaltungsgericht) and are elected by the parliamentary control committee of the Bundestag (§ 43 BND Act). The same rules that apply to ensure the independence of judges in Germany also apply to members of the judicial control body.[83] In addition, the six members of the judicial control body make their decisions in chambers of three judges. The composition of the two chambers must be changed every two years (§ 49 (2) BND Act). The administrative oversight body, as the second branch of the ICC, works under the direction of the judicial oversight body and is led by a legally trained civil servant.

## Access to information

The oversight body will be based in Berlin and Pullach (Bavaria). There, the ICC enjoys comprehensive access to all BND premises and to all its IT systems as long as they are under the sole direction of the BND (§ 56 (3) BND Act). If the ICC requests access to data that is not under the BND's sole direction, the BND shall "take appropriate measures" to facilitate access (§ 56 (3) number 2 sentence 2 BND Act). However, the law does neither include specifications of what such "appropriate measures" shall be and nor does it entail a duty to proactively inform the ICC about all operational systems and jointly administered databases with foreign services.[84] Moreover, the BND is not obliged to provide a comprehensive overview over the complex systems used to collect and process foreign intelligence. It was a firm requirement by the Constitutional Court that the so-called "Third Party Rule" (also known as the originator control principle), the basic principle that intelligence services must not share any information they receive from foreign agencies with other – third – parties, may not undermine the effective and comprehensive oversight by the ICC. The judges pronounced that "the legislator must ensure that the Federal Intelligence Service cannot prevent oversight by invoking the third party rule."[85] Hence, there continues to be a risk that there will be "unknown unknowns" for the independent oversight body as regards operational systems and data processing:

The mandatory logging for audit purposes is required for a few selected cases of data deletion and purpose changes, but the law does not foresee the mandatory recording of comprehensive audit trails. Plus, the limited audit logs that are required–for example if the confidential communications of a journalist that were unlawfully collected in a hacking operation are deleted (§ 35 (3) BND Act) – appear to be only accessible for review by the internal data protection and compliance unit of the BND. The same is the case, for instance, if unevaluated bulk data is shared with a foreign intelligence service. The automated transfer must be logged, but only internal BND inspections may access these audit logs (§ 32 (6) and (7) BND Act).

## Reporting

The work of the ICC ought to remain strictly confidential (§ 54 BND Act) and the BND Act does not impose a public reporting obligation upon the ICC.[86] Instead, it must report to the parliamentary oversight committee every six months (§ 55 (1) BND Act), but the content of these reports is not specified in the law. While the ICC is, at least formally, exempt from the Third Party Rule, the Federal Government continues to regard the parliamentary oversight committee as a third party in the context of information sharing. This has consequences for the ICC's reporting to the parliamentary committee: Only information that is under the exclusive control of the BND may be included. The ICC must consult the Federal Chancellery before reporting to the parliamentary committee, to ensure that the report does not comprise third party information (§ 55 (2) BND Act).

*Oversight cooperation*

The ICC may exchange views and compare notes with other domestic oversight bodies, namely the Federal Commissioner for Data Protection, the G10 Commission and the parliamentary oversight committee about oversight-related matters. In doing so, it must comply with the respective obligations to protect secrecy. There is no analogue reference to international oversight cooperation, for example in the context of the European intelligence oversight working group.[87]

## Control Competences

*Judicial control body*

The new control council is only competent to review the lawfulness of foreign SIGINT activities. In German administrative law, this involves an assessment of the formal and substantial legality of a given action. The evaluation of the utility of the BND's surveillance measures remains a prerogative of the executive. In order to encircle the independent control mandate, the BND Act includes a very specific catalogue of control competences for the judicial control body (§ 42 BND Act). The lawmakers distinguished between ex ante approval and ex post review competences that the judges may exercise. The list of oversight competencies includes the approval of bulk interception and computer network exploitation based on the warrants submitted by the BND. As outlined above, the bulk warrants are authorized by the president of the BND and the lawfulness of this authorization is then assessed by one of the chambers of three members of the judicial control body. The warrants have to state explicitly if the respective SIGINT measures, such as selector-based bulk interception or hacking operations, target certain groups such as EU citizens, journalists, lawyers or clerics. In addition, the judges need to validate the justification for automated bulk data transfers and the sharing of personal data related to protected professional communications in advance. They also make weighting decisions about the processing of data related to the core of private life, if the BND is unsure whether the processing is proportionate.

The ICC's ex ante approval powers neither include the collection of foreign metadata nor the lawfulness of suitability tests. If the lawfulness of a bulk warrant is rejected by the judges of the judicial oversight body, the warrant expires (§ 23 (4) sentence 2 BND Act). Beyond that, the law does not prescribe concrete powers to deter unlawful warrants or to sanction noncompliance with legal safeguards. Also, if bulk warrants repeatedly feature the same boilerplate text or if BND staff do not cooperate adequately with the overseers, the judicial control body has no specified legal enforcement tools at its disposal which undermines their practice of effective review. In addition, the judicial control body is, ex post, responsible for reviewing the lawfulness of the processing of data related to protected professional communications, the repurposing of data that was initially only collected for information purposes, the BND's non-public internal regulations for data processing, as well as the complaints submitted by the administrative control body. The legal norms do not specify what the control of lawfulness (Rechtmäßigkeit) must include in concrete judicial oversight practice. Consider the balancing of interests between the protections for journalists and the BND's general aim to gather foreign intelligence information: What determines its assessment and does the oversight body have the adequate information to arrive at a well-founded decision? An informed balancing of legitimate aims and safeguards requires substantial context information. The law remains unclear as to whether the warrants will contain sufficient material to assess the form and content of a proposed collection measure and how oversight staff are trained to fulfil their review tasks.

*Warrants*

The table below summarizes the different warrant types included in the BND Act. Some of the warrants are very specific in their scope of application, for example if they refer to the communications of EU citizens, EU institutions, and public bodies in EU member states (§ 42 (1) number 2 BND Act). Other bulk warrants, such as the general foreign bulk collection warrant and the CNE warrant may be broader in their scope of application and may cover a "topic" related to a "geographical focus" for an unspecified period of time. Some warrants are also generally missing, but have been included in other SIGINT frameworks, such as examination warrants[88] and testing and training warrants.[89]

Next to the warrants listed in table 10, the judicial approval of bulk data transfers is a notable novelty in the amended Act. The lawful justification of a "qualified intelligence need" for automated transfer of unevaluated bulk data to a foreign intelligence agency is now subject to independent judicial approval.[90] With this approval power, the legislator implements, again, a specific requirement put forward by the Constitutional Court. It had declared that "the sharing of an entire set of traffic data cannot be authorised continually and merely on the basis of the purpose pursued but requires a qualified need for intelligence relating to specific indications that a specific danger may emerge."[91] The judicial oversight body has to make an assessment whether the need for intelligence is lawful, otherwise the raw bulk data may not be shared (§ 33 (3) BND Act).

### Search terms

It is not required to list individual search terms in the bulk interception warrants (§ 23 (6) sentence 2 BND Act), which in practice exempts most search terms from ex ante approval of legality. Only specific categories of search terms that target, for example, EU citizens or journalists, are subject to ex ante approval of the judicial control body (§ 42 BND Act). Other selectors that do not target one of the specifically protected categories such as confidential professional communications, cannot be checked prior to their use. Search terms that are not approved based on a warrant, can, however, be reviewed at random by the administrative control body. The explicit exclusion of most search terms from ex ante approval raises the question whether all the search terms used by the BND are stored and made accessible for independent oversight purposes. Some selectors might only be used for short periods of time, and the BND Act does not include a provision that requires their retention for ex post review. In this regard, the BND Act might be at odds with the jurisprudence of the European Court for Human Rights (ECtHR). In its first assessment of the Swedish bulk collection regime, the court acknowledged that applications for strategic surveillance measures "must specify not only the mission request in question and the need for the intelligence sought but also the signal carriers to which access is needed and the search terms – or at least the categories of search terms – that will be used."[92]

### Weighting decisions

What qualifies as protected communications, for example of an attorney who communicates with a client? And under what conditions might the BND still be allowed to monitor these communications? The

Constitutional Court requires "in any case [that] ex ante oversight resembling judicial review must in principle ensure that such relationships are protected."[93] Despite this clear demand, the BND Act does not provide for ex ante oversight of the classification decision on what is regarded as a confidentiality relationship and which individuals enjoy protection in the first place. This initial decision, which is the basic precondition, is not subject to the approval powers of the judicial control body and can only be reviewed ex-post by the administrative control body. There is, though, an ex-ante approval competence for decisions on exceptions to the protections of professional groups.[94] What is more, incidental collection of protected professional communications, for example if a journalist is communicating with the target of a surveillance operation about a topic without foreign intelligence relevance, can never be fully prevented.

The BND Act addresses this problem by clarifying that insofar as the collection of data from confidentiality relationships is only noticed during data analysis, the BND must check whether collection of this data would have been materially permissible according to the requirements illustrated in the section above. That means, further processing of the incidentally collected data is allowed if it serves to prevent serious crimes and dangers (listed in § 21 (2) BND Act). This decision is then subject to ex post reviews by the judicial control body.

## Administrative control body

Contrary to the specific control competences of the judicial control body, the BND Act bestows a vague mandate upon the administrative control body. Given that the constitutional court saw the need to establish a "continual legal oversight that allows for comprehensive access,"[95] the BND Act remains surprisingly silent on the actual remit, the process, the tools and the overall objective of the ICC's administrative control body. The Act merely states that the administrative control body shall support the work of the judicial control body and is responsible for auditing all SIGINT activities that are not explicit competences of the judicial control body (§ 51 (1) BND Act). Hierarchically, it is subordinated to the judicial branch of the ICC. Due to its vague mandate, it also remains unclear to what extent the control competences of the Federal Commissioner for Data Protection and the administrative control body overlap. The amended law also does not foresee any independent review of the data minimization systems (filters) used by the BND. This unspecific review mandate bears the risk that the administrative control body needs to constantly justify its oversight competence and oversight priorities. It could also be an advantage, though, if a review mandate is rather broad, if it allows for unannounced inspections and independent investigations. In the context of data sharing, the accuracy and veracity of the automated checks and filtering of search terms must be subject to random checks by internal BND staff, but not the administrative control body (§ 32 (7) BND Act). The independent overseers also do not have an explicit mandate to check the block lists that the BND needs to maintain to filter out protected professional communications before sharing data (§ 32 (5) BND Act).

Complaints The administrative control body has the legal standing to initiate a formal complaint procedure (Beanstandung) if it identifies unlawful conduct, such as non-compliance with certain legal protections in data processing (§ 52 BND Act). The administrative control body must first consult with the BND before it initiates a formal complaint. If the cause for complaint is not eliminated, it may bring the complaint to the attention of the Federal Chancellery. If the Chancellery does not rectify the cause of the complaint, the judicial control body gets to finally decide how to handle the complaint, but it is not specified in the law what the legal consequences of this final decision shall be.

## Discussion and assessment

Having primarily explained the key regulatory changes to German legislation on foreign intelligence in response to the Constitutional Court's landmark decision, the focus now turns to an assessment of those changes. For this, the text first elaborates on aspects the authors consider laudable improvements (4.1). Next, it accounts for missed opportunities and what the authors consider to be poor legislative practice (4.2). Each section features arguments that refer to the quality of the legal framework, the degree of fundamental rights protection and the authorization and oversight process. As indicated, the discussion draws on the authors' subjective reading of the reform. They very much encourage direct feedback and acknowledge upfront that their account does not claim to be exhaustive. They hope to contribute, however, to more inclusive debates in like-minded democracies on the evolving authorities, safeguards and governance processes for government surveillance including standards regarding transnational data transfers.

## Improvements of the status quo

*Quality of the legal framework*

## More comprehensive and transparent legal framework

When compared to previous intelligence reforms but also with a view to how other democracies have codified (or not) foreign intelligence collection in their respective laws, Germany has undoubtedly come a long way with the 2021 reform of the BND Act.[96] With this reform, it cements its position among the few democracies in the world that offer comprehensive legislation and key safeguards regarding the use of bulk powers for foreign intelligence collection[97] Not only did bulk collection receive a far more comprehensive legal footing, (bulk) computer network exploitation is now also explicitly recognised and codified as state practice. In addition, the BND Act now features probably one of the world's most detailed legal frameworks regarding the dos and don'ts when it comes to (automatic) international data transfers, with separate chapters devoted to their authorization, documentation and corresponding judicial and administrative oversight, including specific obligations on the part of the BND to restrict the subsequent use of shared data by partner services. The following two examples illustrate further why and how the legal framework for foreign intelligence collection has improved significantly. First, the BND Act now features new and more comprehensive rules on aspects that were previously dealt with in classified executive decrees (Dienstvorschriften).

This includes provisions on the exceptional processing of data of specially protected persons – which should have been deleted immediately but are used nevertheless – where the Constitutional Court called for a reformed set of regulations which needs to be subjected to parliamentary approval and receive proper statutory footing.[98] This gap has now been fixed. Likewise, whereas the previous quasi-judicial oversight body, the Independent Committee, did not have full access to the executive decree relating to data transfers to foreign partner services, this has now been changed and a number of the provisions from that executive decree have found their way into the BND Act. Second, the BND Act now includes detailed provisions with respect to standing SIGINT cooperation with foreign partner services, ad hoc data transfers and jointly administered databases with foreign partner services to name just a few dimensions. Each aspect now received a more comprehensive legal footing. Consider, for example, the fact that eight (!) binding assurances (on different data use aspects) now have to be included in written MoUs that the BND signs with foreign partners (§ 31 (4) number 3, littera a-h BND Act). Furthermore, as regards standing SIGINT cooperation agreements, the BND is now under the legal obligation to verify in an automated way whether the transmission of the data collected would conflict with the national interests of the German state (§ 32 (3) and (4) BND Act). Also, as regards protected professional communications and international SIGINT cooperation, the BND must maintain block lists of identifiers of journalists, lawyers or similar persons or groups whose communications are afforded special confidentiality protection in order to gradually improve the filter accuracy (§ 32 (5) BND Act).

### Fundamental rights protection

Extraterritorial reach of fundamental rights no longer disputed Probably the single most important bone of contention with previous reforms of foreign intelligence legislation was the hitherto open question, whether or not the territorial reach of the right to private communication and press freedom as guaranteed under Article 10 and Article 5 of the German constitution extends beyond German territory and beyond German nationals and residents. While the German government argued consistently up until May 2020 that it does not, the Constitutional Court unequivocally affirmed that these fundamental rights are human rights and not citizen rights. It held that the German state's obligation to protect these fundamental rights cannot be restricted to cover only certain groups of people or only some geographical regions. In turn, this required a wholesale amendment of both the legal framework and the remit of German intelligence oversight institutions. In practice, however, as argued further below, this does not mean that foreign nationals now enjoy the same de facto protection from electronic surveillance by the BND or that the pathway to effective remedy for a German citizen equals that of a non-national.

## Enhanced protection for journalists, lawyers and clerics

When compared to previous legislation, the amended BND Act now offers improved protections as regards the communications of foreign professionals who require greater confidentiality. Following the landmark judgement, the drafters of the reform had to accept the premise that foreign journalists, for example, have a special right to have their communication data exempt from bulk surveillance measures. By itself, this is an important step in the right direction, despite significant criticism that ought to be voiced as regards the implementation of this premise (see the discussion in section on the many exceptions and their room for improvement).

*Authorization process and oversight*

## Judicial oversight of foreign intelligence collection

Whereas the previous reform went the extra mile to prevent it, the 2021 reform had to finally establish a proper judicial review body – the Independent Control Council – in Germany. Unlike its predecessor, the Independent Committee, the ICC will have recourse to roughly sixty fulltime staffers and a much greater budget, at least according to the projections made in the explanatory statement of the new law.[99] Its judicial branch is responsible for a wide range of legality reviews, many of them ex ante (see the catalogue in § 41) and will consist of six federal judges to be appointed for twelve years – both important preconditions for the ICC's independence.[100]

## Improved oversight access and logging requirements

At least de jure, the amended BND Act also establishes a much improved access for the judicial oversight body to the IT systems and operational databases of the BND. Whether this is sufficient to allow for data-driven intelligence oversight using new supervisory technology needed for 21st century audits will be discussed further below. Fact is, however, that concerns about the Third Party Rule can no longer prevent the independent judicial oversight body from accessing such information. In addition, the various provisions that now require logging (e.g., to protect the core area of private life or the protected communications of certain professions) combined with an obligation to promptly delete such data gives further substance to the remit of the administrative branch of the ICC. In sum, the 2021 reform of the BND Act improves the democratic legitimacy, the transparency and the legal certainty of foreign intelligence collection. Other parliaments might find it insightful, it is hoped, to consider in particular the comprehensive catalogue of data transfer requirements and the robust institutional independence of the ICC.

*Missed opportunities and the need for further reform*

The German government, it ought to be remembered, has tried hard to prevent many aspects of the 2021 reforms which only came into being as the result of strategic litigation. Unsurprisingly, then, it could have gone much further to rectify the many grave deficits that became apparent in the litigation process. The next section aims to show why the 2021 reform, taken together, did not establish a model legal framework for foreign intelligence collection.

*Quality of the legal framework*

## Fragmented legal framework

Unlike other democracies, such as the UK or Canada, Germany sports far too many individual pieces of intelligence legislation.[101] German lawmakers tend to focus primarily on the individual security service at hand and have thus far shied away from a more functional approach that focuses instead on the general nature of investigatory powers that the state may use to obtain access to different types of data – irrespective of which agency then deploys them. Given that more and more powers and software converge across the security sector, the Bundestag's approach to intelligence reform has done very little to improve legal clarity. Instead, new reforms add to the sheer complexity of the subject matter by inserting various new cross-references to similar yet still different provisions in other laws. It is also increasingly questionable whether this approach–which requires the establishment of (too many) separate oversight mandates for (too many) oversight bodies–is compatible with important international obligations. As observed recently by the Dutch intelligence oversight bodies CTIVD and TIB in their memo on the Council of Europe's modernised Convention 108, "when appointing the oversight body/supervisory authority (i.e. Article 11.3, 15, and 16(2) of the Convention), it must be clear that the entire national security domain falls under the responsibility of the oversight body or bodies to be appointed."[102]

This is certainly not the case in Germany where very different oversight entities work with very different resources, tools and mandates to ensure different types of government accountability for the military, intelligence and police forces' use of investigatory powers. More specifically, not only is the pursuit of bulk collection and computer network exploitation by the German armed forces subject to different oversight bodies (and control densities), even the BND's own bulk collection is still overseen by two separate judicial bodies. More specifically, the G10- Commission's remit under the Article 10 Act covers foreign-domestic bulk collection, whereas the ICC's mandate under the BND Act is to review the legality of the bulk collection of foreign traffic. While the Federal Government sees no problem with this at present,[103] consider how the new Canadian oversight body NSIRA reports on its "additional and novel mandate to review any activity in the federal government that relates to national security or intelligence. [...]

190

This allows NSIRA to break down the previously compartmentalized approach to review and accountability, and replace it with horizontal, in-depth interagency review."[104] Against this backdrop and knowing that the Constitutional Court's judgement pointed only to minimal standards that had to be implemented in order for Germany to have a constitutional framework for foreign intelligence, the reform could and should have aimed for more. Arguably, the drafters of this reform did not seize the unique and timely chance to pursue a more ambitious reform consolidated and clear legal framework on Germany's investigatory powers. Instead, it added to the complexity of German intelligence law which leaves it to the 20th Bundestag, for example, to extend the mandate of the ICC to other investigatory powers and – at the very least – to codify the BND's bulk collection powers in one single piece of legislation and to work against undue duplications both in the authorization and oversight process.

## Disconnect with recent European jurisprudence

Those who amended the BND Act in March 2021 should have paid more attention to the October 2020 jurisprudence of the European Court of Justice (CJEU) on security and intelligence legislation in the United Kingdom and France. What is more, relevant insights on opportunities for future reforms can now also be gleaned from the European Court of Human Rights (ECtHR) Grand Chamber judgements on surveillance legislation in the United Kingdom and Sweden that were delivered in May 2021.

First, the discussion draws on pertinent insights from the CJEU's Privacy International v. Secretary of State[105] and La Quadrature du Net and Others v. Premier Ministre and Others case.[106] Next, the focus turns to important insights from the ECtHR's judgement in the Centrum för Rättvisa v. Sweden case.[107] Both discussions reveal incompatibilities of the amended BND Act with the criteria and requirements put forward by the Luxembourg and Strasbourg Courts. With regard to the CJEU's Privacy International v. Secretary of State case, the Court did not pronounce on foreign intelligence legislation specifically but it did clarify that "a legislative measure [...] on the basis of which the competent national authority may require providers of electronic communications services to disclose traffic data and location data to the security and intelligence agencies by means of general and indiscriminate transmission [...] exceeds the limits of what is strictly necessary and cannot be considered to be justified, within a democratic society."[108]

This ruling, then, casts severe doubt on the compatibility of § 24 (4) of the BND Act which – as part of the rule set on so-called "suitability tests" (see the discussion in section 2.2.1)–embodies such a "legislative measure" that allows for "general and indiscriminate transmission" of data. Suitability tests are an exception to the general rule that content data may only be collected in bulk on the basis of search terms (§ 19 (5) BND Act). If the BND wants to perform suitability tests in order to generate new search terms or to assess the relevance of existing search terms, there seems to be no requirement for a written order by the president of the BND nor does the requirement that these tests may only be performed if factual indications exist that the selected telecommunications networks bear appropriate data for the purposes of strategic foreign surveillance seem to apply. What is more, there is no requirement, as is the case in some other democracies,[109] for the ex-ante authorization involving independent oversight bodies nor is the duration and the volume of the data collection in pursuit of suitability tests subject to clear limitations or ex post reviews.[110]

Against this backdrop, it is highly questionable whether the obligation under § 24 (4) BND Act which compels service providers to assist in suitability tests when their assistance is deemed necessary, can be considered within the limits of what is strictly necessary and thus justified, within a democratic society. Rather, the authors see therein an unduly broad obligation on the part of service providers to transmit "data to the security and intelligence agencies by means of general and indiscriminate transmission."[111] Taking into account the fact that the BND may transmit data from suitability tests automatically in bulk to the German Armed Forces and given that data collected in pursuit of a suitability test may, under certain exceptions, also be processed for purposes other than testing, for instance if factual indications suggest a grave threat, casts further doubt on the compatibility with EU case law. Furthermore, consider the CJEU's finding that "since general access to all retained data, regardless of whether there is any link, at least indirect, with the aim pursued, cannot be regarded as being limited to what is strictly necessary, national legislation governing access to traffic data and location data must rely on objective criteria in order to define the circumstances and conditions under which the competent national authorities are to be granted access to the data at issue."

With this in mind, and recalling the CJEU's logical conclusion that "those requirements [then] apply, a fortiori, to a legislative measure [...] on the basis of which the competent national authority may require providers of electronic communications services to disclose traffic data and location data to the security and intelligence agencies by means of general and indiscriminate transmission," the question arises whether the requirements that the CJEU formulated with respect to data retention in the QDN case, should equally apply to all legislative measures that compel service providers to transmit data in bulk to the security and intelligence services. If the same reasoning were to be applied to the provisions in the BND Act by which service providers can be compelled to cooperate with the BND, they would very likely be viewed as obligations to transmit personal data in a general and indiscriminate manner not limited to what is strictly necessary in a democracy. Moreover, in the LQDN case, the CJEU stipulated that the following categories of decisions by security and intelligence services ought to be subject to an independent court's or administrative body's jurisdiction:

- a decision giving an instruction to providers of electronic communication services to carry out general and indiscriminate retention of data (paragraph 139);

- decisions on national security grounds requiring providers of electronic communication services to retain general and indiscriminate traffic and location data (paragraph 168)

- decisions authorising automated analysis (paragraph 179);

- the sharing of real time traffic and location data (paragraph 189);

- national rules which authorise automated analysis (paragraph 192).

And, as argued by the Court in the PI case, safeguards governing the interaction between service providers and security and intelligence service that apply to data retention should, a fortiori, also apply to the interaction between intelligence agencies when it comes to data transfers between them.[112] By analogy this would require that orders according to § 25 BND Act would also have to be added to the explicit competence catalogue of the judicial oversight body. At present, it seems that such decisions "giving an instruction to providers of electronic communications services to carry out such [transmissions are not] subject to effective review, [n]either by a court [n]or by an independent administrative body."[113] Whether or not some of the other enumerated decisions are sufficiently subject to the jurisdiction of the ICC and whether the CJEU requirements should at all apply to the BND Act is a matter that requires further consultation.[114] At present, the ICC does not seem to have jurisdiction over decisions by the

Federal Government that compel service providers to retain data. The BND Act provides evaluation intervals for the general retention of the personal data the BND stores, however (see e.g. mandatory evaluation after seven years for bulk interception, § 27 BND Act). As argued above, the BND Act also allows for the automated transfer of data from suitability tests to the German Armed Forces without granting the ICC an explicit review mandate in this regard.

## Gaps in comparison to ECtHR standards

While the ECtHR has in principle accepted the compatibility of the Swedish foreign intelligence framework with the European Convention on Human Rights, it nonetheless alluded to a range of relevant criteria in its Centrum för Rättvisa decision which the BND Act might also be tested on in the future. For instance, the judgement noted that "relevant safeguards against arbitrariness" should be included in the independent ex ante authorization procedure. To achieve this, the Swedish bulk interception law "provides for the mandatory presence of a privacy protection representative at that court's sessions, except in urgent cases. The representative, who is a judge, a former judge or an attorney, acts independently and in the public interest but not in the interest of any affected private individual. He or she has access to all the case documents and may make statements."[115] The BND Act does not foresee a similar "safeguard against arbitrariness"[116] when it comes to the approval processes of the ICC. That is, it does not include systematic "points of friction"[117]– such as a privacy protection representative, some kind of adversarial council, advisory body or similar outside perspectives that serve to harden the authorization mechanism against regulatory capture.

Thus far, the judicial control body only hears the perspective of the BND when reviewing the lawfulness of bulk warrants. But a judicial review procedure is meant to weigh contrasting interests before coming to a conclusion. In order to establish a more "courtlike" (gerichtsähnlich) review when deciding on surveillance operations in practice, the perspective of those affected by surveillance needs to be strengthened procedurally. In light of the special protections for certain professional groups, for example, it might be a profitable approach to involve adversarial representatives that argue in the interests of affected groups, such as protected professions or other vulnerable demographics.[118] In addition, the ECtHR also emphasized that any independent authorization process "implies necessity and proportionality analysis"[119] and goes on to underscore that it might be difficult for the judicial approval body "to appreciate the proportionality

194

aspect where only categories of selectors are specified"[120] in applications for bulk interception. Against this backdrop, the fact that no individual search terms or descriptions of categories of selectors must be listed in the bulk warrants (§ 23 (6) sentence 2 BND Act), calls into question whether the ECtHR would be satisfied with the judicial approval process pursuant to the new BND Act.

In practice, the several hundred thousand search terms used by the BND are exempt from ex ante approval of legality, which substantially weakens the required assessment of necessity and proportionality. Moreover, the ECtHR's Rättvisa judgement also examined whether the Swedish ex post oversight body, the Foreign Intelligence Inspectorate (SIUN),[121] is adequately equipped to assess aspects of the proportionality of the interference with the rights of individuals in SIGINT activities. It considers that SIUN conducts "numerous detailed examinations of, in particular, the selectors used" and that "it is tasked with granting the FRA access to communications bearers after verifying that the requested access corresponds to the permit issued by the Foreign Intelligence Court."[122] The BND Act does not provide for direct access to bearers of communications for the ICC, nor does it foresee a similar double verification of approved warrants. The ability to unblock particular bearers and to grant access to specific cables or facilities after checking a warrant is a powerful control competence that would significantly shift the power dynamic between the BND and the ICC compared to what is currently foreseen in the law. If it identifies undue SIGINT conduct, the Swedish Foreign Intelligence Inspectorate can also decide – with binding effect – "that the collection must cease or that recordings or notes of collected data must be destroyed."[123] By contrast, whether and to what extent the complaint mechanism available to the administrative control body of the ICC (§ 52 BND Act) may have binding consequences for the BND is not specified in the BND Act. In addition, the Swedish oversight body itself is subject to audits by the Swedish National Audit Office that evaluates whether the oversight activities made a difference and how it could be improved.[124] The evaluation of the effectiveness of the ICC's oversight, in turn, is conducted mostly inward looking by the ICC itself (§ 61 BND Act). Overall, neither the judicial, nor the administrative control body of the ICC seem to fully match the oversight competences and level of access to data that the Swedish SIGINT law provides and that the ECtHR deemed relevant to allow for an effective independent assessment.

## Data purchases remain insufficiently regulated

While the BND Act covers foreign intelligence collection mainly, there certainly can be instances where it receives larger datasets from individuals, such as informants or company owners who have voluntarily handed this to them. What is more, the BND may purchase datasets on the open market or in less open corners of the web. The rules that should govern the access and subsequent use of data resulting from these kinds of purchases or gifts, and whether and how to involve independent oversight in the process, are not yet settled in the legal framework. Put differently, the current BND Act does not seem to include a provision on the governance and oversight of the service's purchase of commercially available data. By contrast, the UK's intelligence oversight body IPCO seems to be following this lead more attentively, when it states that it has conducted "an extensive review of bulk datasets held by third parties to which UK intel community had access", so as "to provide assurance that BPD (bulk personal dataset) warrants were being obtained where applicable."[125] Germany has not established bulk personal dataset warrants. As with bulk interception of foreign-foreign telecommunications, where the Federal Government has long tried to argue that no specific provisions were necessary because of the BND's general mandate (§ 1 (2) BND Act), it can be said that unspecified regulation for such bulk data purchases exist. Yet, even the general provision in paragraph 1 section 2 of the BND Act covers only the collection and analysis of information, and one should argue that purchases cannot be sufficiently subsumed under this norm in the absence of further, more detailed provisions on the process, safeguards and oversight.

## Ineffective data volume limitation

Other intelligence laws, such as the Article 10 Act include volume limitation based on transmission capacities within individual telecommunication networks. For the BND Act, lawmakers decided to adopt a more abstract limit based on entire telecommunication networks. They argued that the BND might want to collect all data from a specific telecommunications network in its entirety, in some cases. For example, if a foreign state uses its own network for communication between public bodies.[126] The amended BND Act limits the amount of data that the service may collect to no more than 30 percent of the transmission capacity of all globally existing telecommunications networks (§ 19 (8) BND Act). Whether this rule implies an actual limit to bulk interception has been subject to debate during the policy making process. Eco, a business association of internet service providers, argued that 30 percent of all global telecommunications networks does not constitute a verifiable limit in their official commentary on the draft law. They explained that about 70.000 communications networks participate in international data traffic, which would mean that targeting roughly 20.000 networks would be permissible under the BND Act. In Germany alone about 1.250 carriers are linked to the internet. The legal volume limitation would consequently permit data collection up to a volume of 16 times the entire data traffic in Germany. Since a small number of larger telecommunication networks have a dominant share in overall data traffic, the ten largest providers typically carry about 95 percent of all data transmissions, the 25 largest networks transmit roughly 99 percent.[127] Thus, whether the volume limitation rule pursuant to paragraph 19 section 8 qualifies as a sufficient limit of bulk interception is questionable. Taking into account that the BND's technical and financial capacities will hardly suffice to get close to such an abstract data collection cap, the defined legal maximum will most likely remain a rather hypothetical construct with little practical value.

## Fundamental rights protection

### No redress mechanism for foreigners

It is a fundamental deficiency of the German foreign intelligence framework that the BND Act excludes effective ex post redress mechanisms against foreign surveillance by the BND.

International case law has repeatedly emphasized the significance of individual remedies: Both the British and the Swedish bulk interception regimes, which were recently assessed by the ECtHR, feature concrete, codified mechanisms for "ex post facto review" of bulk interception.[128] The CJEU has demanded more effective remedy options for EU citizens regarding data processing by US intelligence agencies in its Schrems II ruling,[129] while – on the European side of the Atlantic – the BND Act does not provide effective redress options for foreigners against its bulk collection programs, either. There is no legally defined path for foreign individuals, such as journalists abroad, who want to find out if their communications have been collected in SIGINT operations and, if so, to verify whether the collection and processing of their data was lawful. What is more, the legislators opted to explicitly waive notification rights for foreigners regarding the bulk collection of their personal data (§ 59 (1) BND Act). While an obligation to notify foreign individuals about past SIGINT activities was not required by the German constitutional judgement,

German citizens, organizations and residents, however, in principle enjoy a right to be informed if the BND has collected their communications.

While the collection of domestic communications is prohibited in principle under the BND Act, the BND may nonetheless retain domestic data to prevent considerable dangers. In such cases, the G10-Commission must be informed and needs to decide whether the affected domestic person or organization shall be notified, or whether the notification shall be deferred.[130] That the BND Act denies foreigners the right of notification, naturally, raises the question how they may seek redress and complaint against alleged surveillance of their communications. In the Rättvisa judgement, the ECtHR's Grand Chamber pronounced that "the absence of a functioning notification mechanism should be counterbalanced by the effectiveness of the remedies that must be available to individuals who suspect that their communications may have been intercepted and analysed."[131] Similarly, the Straßbourg court highlighted in its Big Brother Watch case that the British Investigatory Powers Tribunal (IPT), which has comprehensive jurisdiction over British intelligence activities, can examine any complaints about illegal interceptions regardless of notifications to the data subject.[132]

It uses, for example, specific methods to handle cases that involve classified material, such as closed procedures, considerations of assumed facts and a duty to inquire about additional material from the services in order to substantiate a complaint. Such a remedy – which is independent of any notification requirement and the authorization and oversight process – might even allow for more effective redress if a proper procedure is in place. Neither the legal framework regarding the Independent Control Council, nor that for the G-10 Commission feature provisions regulating how non-nationals can turn to them similar to the remedy processes available in the UK and Sweden. Plus, internet service providers and other carriers that the BND can compel to provide data have no complaint options either, for example to request a re-evaluation of the lawfulness of a bulk warrant.

### Legal protections are restricted to personal data

Another critical gap in the new BND Act is the exclusion of metadata from most safeguards. The collection and processing of metadata, such as traffic data or related communications data, is, due to the large volumes of data processed, the cornerstone of SIGINT. Digital communications produce much more metadata than content, because every piece of content is embedded in a variety of related pieces of metadata. In its Rättvisa decision, the ECtHR has also underscored and explained the tremendous significance of metadata:

"While the content might be encrypted and, in any event, may not reveal anything of note about the sender or recipient, the related communications data could reveal a great deal of personal information, such as the identities and geographic location of the sender and recipient and the equipment through which the communication was transmitted. Furthermore, any intrusion occasioned by the acquisition of related communications data will be magnified when they are obtained in bulk, since they are now capable of being analysed and interrogated so as to paint an intimate picture of a person through the mapping of social networks, location tracking, Internet browsing tracking, mapping of communication patterns, and insight into who a person interacted with."[133]

The court was clearly unconvinced that the collection of metadata is in any way less intrusive than the collection of content data. Consequently, it required that the same standards and safeguards should apply for metadata and content and used the eight step test that it developed to assess the Swedish SIGINT law consistently for both types of data.[134] Given that the BND Act excludes foreign traffic data and other foreign metadata from its requirements for bulk interception (§ 19) and CNE (§ 34), it is hard to imagine how it could successfully substantiate its compatibility with the standards of the European convention of Human Rights. Instead of abandoning the metadata vs. content distinction – as did the Netherlands and Sweden – the Federal Government of Germany reinforced the data differentiations in the BND Act. Consider the protection of confidential communications of journalists and lawyers abroad, as another example, which is strictly limited to personal data relating to an identified or identifiable individual or organization. Again, it is hard to conceive hypothetical cases in which the collection of traffic data of an attorney who communicates with a number of clients or a journalist who corresponds with a source would be less worthy of protection than the content. The BND Act, though, allows for the unrestricted collection of supposedly "non-personal" traffic data, which undermines trust in the confidentiality and integrity of communication channels and thus may have chilling effects on the exercise of fundamental freedoms, such as press freedom, around the globe.[135]

*Authorization process and oversight*

Laws can only go so far. Professional intelligence oversight requires much more than a solid legal basis and given that the ICC will only begin its important work in 2022, it may seem premature to point to weaknesses or poor practice at the outset. A few important things, however, can already be observed, which point to a continued need for further optimization.

## Obfuscation by fragmentation

This section already alluded to the different legal bases for very similar investigatory powers in Germany. Consider bulk collection: Depending on whether the BND intercepts domestic foreign traffic or foreign-foreign traffic, a BND analyst has to abide by two separate laws (the Article 10 Act and the BND Act, respectively) and two separate oversight bodies provide (quasi-) judicial oversight (the G10-Commission and the ICC, respectively). Service providers currently receive separate technical capability notices for very similar requests and the level of granularity in warrants and oversight obligations depending on whether a measure is based on the BND Act or the Article 10 Act are also notably different. Add to this the various different reporting obligations for different oversight bodies, and the call for a more consolidated investigatory powers framework and a less crowded oversight landscape becomes even more persuasive. At a minimum, future reforms should extend the remit of the ICC to other intelligence activities of the BND and abandon the underwhelming idea to provide professional quasi-judicial oversight through honorary members of an understaffed G10-Commission. Yet, frankly, the task for future legislators is far more daunting than this. Like in many other democracies, it becomes increasingly more difficult to defend the notion that the same investigatory powers and modes of government access and data processing can be governed and overseen radically differently across the security sector.

More specifically, the bulk collection practices by the various departments of the Federal Armed Forces embody the same risks to the enjoyment of the fundamental rights of Art. 10 and Art. 5 of the German Constitution. Yet, oversight over their access and use of such data is nowhere near as comprehensive and resourceful. As indicated previously, given the privileged partnership between the BND and the German Armed Forces, a comprehensive legal framework would go a long way to mitigate the inherent risk of collusive delegation or, to put it more mildly, creative non-compliance.[136] In addition, a more comprehensive framework with reduced but strengthened oversight bodies would limit the risk to oversight effectiveness that stems from duplication. For example, next to the oversight bodies of the Armed Forces that may look into bulk data processing, one also has the G10-Commission, the ICC and the Federal Data Protection Commissioner looking into this–each from different vantage points but in sum, it may amount to an inefficient investment of control resources, not just burdensome to the BND but also not in keeping with the objective of end-to-end oversight.

## Not enough value for compliance and transparency

Given the amount of resources that the Federal Government projected for the redesign of intelligence oversight in Germany and recalling the importance of trust in Germany's role as arbiter of privacy rights,[137] oversight needs to be effective and its processes – despite the necessary secrecy requirements – ought to be documented in a way that allows the public to (re-)build trust. They need to be confident that the oversight bodies are not merely consultants – or worse: mushrooms that like to live in the dark growing on manure[138] –but an independent force for positive change. The following discussion puts two question marks behind Germany's ability to meet this objective. The first one is tied to the aspect of oversight effectiveness, the other one to public trust. As regards the former, it is good that the BND Act now includes a more elaborate catalogue of purpose restrictions and data use limitations for both manual and automated contexts. For example, the BND is obliged to log data sharing: The recipients, the legal basis for the data transfer and the date of the transfer must be recorded.[139] This is good because complete and meaningful audit trails are necessary for internal controls and executive oversight by the Federal Chancellery.

Yet, they are also a basic prerequisite for effective datadriven intelligence oversight. As increasingly practiced in many European democracies, independent controls of data processing require, in particular, comprehensive, direct access to the log data that accumulates along the various stages of the intelligence cycle, for example, automated, standardized logs of filter errors, logs of purpose changes, data transfers and timely data destruction. These records must be available to judicial and administrative control in a machine-readable form in order to enable efficient data-driven oversight.[140] The audit logs that are currently required by the BND Act, however, are insufficient in this regard. Many of the logging requirements are narrow and cover only very specific operations, such as the deletion of personal data (e.g., § 27 (1) BND Act). Most importantly, the law does not clarify whether, and if so, how the ICC may access and use the logs. The respective provisions state that logs are exclusively available for carrying out controls of data processing, including data protection controls, which applies, according to our reading, solely to internal reviews conducted by BND staff. If this is the case, then the unfettered oversight access to all relevant data in paragraph 56 of the BND Act would be severely undermined.

Not only the BND but also the administrative control body would benefit enormously from the automated provision of logs. Already before the reform, it was most likely common practice for the BND to record and use log files for its internal purposes. Making the logs available to the administrative control body would allow for data-driven audits and boost oversight effectiveness. The Swedish oversight body SIUN, for example, runs statistical pattern analyses based on deletion audit trails.[141] This could be enabled, too, by a legal audit trail obligation that requires that comprehensive logs must be kept and maintained by the BND in such a way that it meets the needs of the ICC. While the BND is currently spending large sums of taxpayers' money on redesigning its operational systems to make them compliant with the amended BND Act, the needs of the independent overseers within the judicial and administrative branch of the ICC should equally be taken into account. As regards public trust and confidence in the lawfulness and legitimacy of foreign intelligence collection, the reporting obligation of the ICC to the standing parliamentary intelligence oversight body (Parlamentarisches Kontrollgremium, PKGr, § 55 BND Act) appears to be insufficient.

At present, it has to file a secret report about its activities to the PKGr at least every six months and it may report openly to the PKGr about complaints (see section 3.2.2) allowing the PKGr to then inform the Bundestag – and by extension the public. Yet, the public needs to know more about the processes and decisions of the ICC. And here, the secret activity reports to the PKGr and the limitation on complaints when it comes to public information keeps too much information away from the public eye. Granted, the government needs a core area of exclusive executive responsibility and its commitment to the Third Party Rule must be credible in the eyes of its international intelligence partners. Thus, it is understandable that according to paragraph 55, section 2 of the BND Act the secret activity reports of the ICC to the PKGr are limited to areas where the BND has executive control rights (Verfügungsberechtigung). Yet, in addition to complaints, the ICC could report on its general decisions and its experiences with audits, for example. It may seek inspiration here from the Dutch oversight body TIB. Not only does this body which is responsible for authorizations regularly publish reports not just in Dutch but also in English. It also provides insightful statistics on the thematic nature and totality of its authorization decisions, including the reasons for dismissals and rejections.[142]

What is more, the ICC should be encouraged through legislation but also through its interaction with other oversight bodies, to embrace public reporting as part of its mission so as to help cement public trust in its work – and by extension in the work of the BND. This is all the more important as the BND's mandate to interfere with fundamental rights through its collection and processing of personal data by means of bulk collection and computer network exploitation is now firmly established in German intelligence legislation. Having more substantive reports from the PKGr and ICC would help to assess the value added of certain intelligence powers over time and to trace how oversight instruments need to adjust in order to keep pace with the ongoing evolution of modern surveillance technology. What follows from this discussion, is that the current catalogue of the ICC's control competences, especially with regard to its administrative oversight body, and its general reporting obligations should be strengthened and enlarged. A future mandate for the ICC should also comprise the authority to:

- examine the lawfulness of the entire practice of the suitability tests (incl. those meant to generate search terms)

- examine and report on the recording and maintenance of log files (to which it must have full access)

- examine the processing of metadata, also including technical data that is not personal data in a narrow sense (Sachdaten ohne Personenbezug)

- engage in closer and more structured forms of cooperation with its domestic and international oversight partners[143]

- sanction malfeasance and abuse of investigatory powers by the BND or its political masters in the Federal Chancellery.

## Conclusion

In March 2021, the German Bundestag amended yet again the legal framework for one of Europe's most powerful intelligence agencies, the Bundesnachrichtendienst. This report highlighted key legislative changes regarding the provisions on strategic bulk interception, computer network exploitation and transnational data sharing. It also reviewed the institutional set-up and competences of Germany's new judicial and administrative oversight institution, the Independent Control Council. Analysing the quality of the legal framework, the degree of fundamental rights protection and the authorization and oversight process, the authors draw a sober conclusion: Despite noticeable improvements, the reform fails to address a number of known deficits and creates new accountability gaps. By international comparison, the BND Act now features an important high water mark: It no longer restricts the German Constitution's guarantee of the privacy of telecommunications and the right to press freedom to citizens and residents of Germany. Instead, these fundamental rights against state interference "also protect foreigners in other countries."[144]

At least de jure. In practice, however, non-nationals might not benefit much from their rights when confronted with surveillance by German intelligence. This is because the BND Act also does not incorporate the standard for effective remedy that the European Court of Justice recently found missing in U.S. intelligence legislation. At long last, the reform established genuine independent judicial oversight for some of the BND's key collection and processing practices. Still, the legal framework remains replete with too many ambiguities and omissions. The report highlighted the ICC's vague mandate for administrative oversight and the law's ineffective data volume limitation. It also deplored broad exemptions from the warrant requirement and cautioned against accountability gaps tied to suitability testing and data transfers between the BND and the German Armed Forces. Addressing and overcoming these legislative deficits will require more than quick fixes and gestural compliance. The new Bundestag should seize the opportunity to establish a comprehensive legal framework for investigatory powers across the intelligence and security sector. In so doing, it must also extend the remit of the ICC to other forms of intelligence collection and allow for more enhanced transparency reporting.

## Unofficial translation of § 19 BND Act § 19 Strategic Foreign Telecommunications Collection

(1) In order to fulfil its tasks, the Federal Intelligence Service may use technical means to process personal content data of foreigners abroad on the basis of previously ordered strategic collection measures (strategic foreign telecommunications collection), insofar as this is necessary for the purposes of

1. political information of the Federal Government or

2.    the early detection of threats of international significance emanating from abroad.

(2) A strategic collection measure shall limit the respective objective of the strategic foreign telecommunications surveillance by providing information on

1.    collection purpose,

2.    collection theme/priority,

3.    geographical focus and

4.    duration.

(3) Strategic collection measures pursuant to subsection 1, number 1, shall only be permissible if they serve to obtain information on foreign countries which is of foreign and security policy significance for the Federal Republic of Germany and for the surveillance of which the Federal Chancellery has commissioned the Federal Intelligence Service.

(4) Strategic collection measures pursuant to subsection 1, number 2, shall only be permissible if they serve to obtain information on foreign countries which is of foreign and security policy significance for the Federal Republic of Germany and which the Federal Chancellery has commissioned the Federal Intelligence Service to investigate, and if there are factual indications that knowledge may be gained through them

1.    with reference to the following areas of danger:

a)    national or allied defence as well as missions of the Federal Armed Forces or of allied armed forces abroad,

b)    crisis developments abroad and their effects,

c)    on terrorism or extremism which is prepared to use violence or which is aimed at the planned covert implementation of political, religious or ideological views, or the support thereof,

d)    international criminal, terrorist or state-sponsored attacks by malicious software malware on the confidentiality, integrity or availability of information technology systems,

e)    to organised crime,

f)    on the international proliferation of weapons of war within the meaning of the Act on the Control of Weapons of War as well as illicit foreign trade in goods and technical support services in cases of major significance,

g) threats to critical infrastructures; or h) hybrid threats

2. for the protection of the following legal interests:

a) Life, limb or freedom of a person,

b) the existence or security of the Federation or of a Land,

c) the existence or security of institutions of the European Union, the European Free Trade Association or the North Atlantic Treaty or the existence or security of a member state of the European Union, the European Free Trade Association or the North Atlantic Treaty,

d) the Federal Republic of Germany's ability to act in foreign policy matters,

e) important legal interests of the general public, the foundations of which affect the existence of human beings.

(5) The Federal Intelligence Service may only collect personal content data within the framework of strategic foreign telecommunications collection on the basis of search terms. These must be intended, suitable and necessary for the strategic collection measures in accordance with paragraph 1 and their use must be consistent with the foreign and security policy interests of the Federal Republic of Germany.

(6) Insofar as this is necessary to carry out strategic collection measures in accordance with paragraph 1, the Federal Intelligence Service may use technical means to gain access to the information technology systems of a foreign telecommunications or telemedia service provider abroad, even without the latter's knowledge, and collect personal data from the ongoing communication which the provider processes in the course of providing its service. In doing so, the Federal Intelligence Service may also collect personal data which the foreign telecommunications or telemedia service provider stores in its information technology systems during the processing of ongoing communications, provided that this data is collected within the time frame of the strategic reconnaissance measure in accordance with paragraph 1 and is not older than 48 hours before it is collected by the Federal Intelligence Service. If the Federal Intelligence Service gains access to an information technology system of a foreign telecommunications or telemedia service provider abroad in accordance with sentence 1, it may

also process inventory data of the foreign telecommunications or telemedia service provider which the latter processes on the occasion of the provision of its service, insofar as these are collected on the basis of search terms or relate to the counterpart of the data collected on the basis of the search term.

(7) The collection of personal data of the following persons from telecommunication traffic is not permitted:

1. German nationals,

2. domestic legal persons as well as

3. persons residing in the territory of the Federal Republic of Germany.

As far as technically possible, the use of automated filters shall ensure that such data are filtered out. The filtered data shall be deleted automatically without delay. The filtering methods shall be continuously developed and shall be kept up to date with the current state of the art. If, despite this filtering, data is collected contrary to sentence 1, this data shall be deleted immediately. This shall not apply if there are factual indications that the further processing of the data may avert a significant danger to the life, limb or freedom of a person, the security of the Federation or of a country or the security of other Member States of the European Union, the European Free Trade Association or the North Atlantic Treaty.

(8) Unrestricted strategic foreign telecommunications collection is not permitted. The volume of strategic foreign telecommunications collection shall be limited to no more than 30 per cent of the existing telecommunications networks.

(9) Strategic foreign telecommunications collection for the purpose of gaining competitive advantages (industrial espionage) is inadmissible.

(10) Personal data shall be identified immediately after data collection as follows: 1. Indication of the purpose of the data collection pursuant to paragraph

1; and

2. indication of the means of data collection. The tagging shall be omitted in the case of data transfers.

*Caught in the Act? An analysis of Germany's new SIGINT reform Research Report by Kilian Vieth-Ditlmann and Thorsten Wetzling 25 November 2021. Kilian Vieth-Ditlmann researches surveillance and democratic governance at the think tank Stiftung Neue Verantwortung (SNV). He is a member of the GUARD//INT research consortium, as well as project manager for the European Intelligence Oversight Network (EION) and part-time editor at aboutintel.eu. His work examines the potentials and limits of overseeing surveillance and reform approaches for human rights-based and more efficient intelligence and surveillance policy in Germany and Europe. Dr. Thorsten Wetzling heads the SNV's research unit on basic rights, surveillance and democracy. He currently directs the European Intelligence Oversight Network (EION), a collaborative research project to support and challenge intelligence oversight bodies across Europe. He is also a Principal Investigator for the international research consortium GUARD//INT which aims to build empirical and conceptual tools to better understand the limits and potential of intelligence oversight mechanisms. Thorsten is also founder and editor-inchief of aboutintel.eu – a European discussion forum on surveillance, technology and democracy. About the Stiftung Neue Verantwortung. The Stiftung Neue Verantwortung (SNV) is an independent, non-profit think tank working at the intersection of technology and society. Stiftung Neue Verantwortung (SNV) is a non-profit think tank working on current political and societal challenges posed by new technologies. We do not only invite government officials but everyone seeking information to engage with our work whether through giving us feedback on publications, participating in our events or seeking direct advice. Our experts work independently from partisan interests or political affiliations. SNV's core method is collaborative policy development, involving experts from government, tech companies, civil society and academia to test and develop analyses with the aim of generating ideas on how governments can positively shape the technological transformation. Many excellent research institutes and think tanks already contribute to the fields of foreign policy, economic policy or environmental policy in Germany. Issues related to new technologies however lack comparable expert organisations that focus on current politics and social debates. The Stiftung Neue Verantwortung (SNV) wants to fill this gap in the landscape of German institutes and think tanks. This think tank seeks to provide a focal point for all people whose work covers current political and social questions of the cross-sectional issue of digitalization. We compile and publish analyses, develop recommendations for action for policymakers, conduct expert workshops, invite experts to engage in publicly accessible policy debates, and explain contexts and backgrounds in the media. Our activities are affected by social developments and are constantly changing. Currently, we are dealing with the following questions, among others: Data Economy: The introduction of big data architectures in companies and the associated methods of artificial intelligence (including machine learning) are changing traditional value chains, competitive dynamics and consumer behavior in markets. How can economic policy react? Digital Rights, Surveillance and Democracy: How can government monitoring in a networked society be effectively controlled, reasonably limited, and sufficiently documented? Technology and Geopolitics: What is Europe's position within global semiconductor supply chains and what relevance and potential impact does this have on industrial competitiveness, technological dependency on foreign countries and national security? International Cybersecurity Policy: Cybersecurity and cyber defense are new areas for German policy. What can we learn from the global developments and strategies of other states? Artificial Intelligence: Developments in the field of artificial intelligence are forcing new dependencies in the global economy and changing the military power relations between states. What does this mean for German foreign policy? Strengthening the Digital Public Sphere: Strengthening the digital public sphere: Digital platforms open up new communication spaces for individuals and societies, but they also entail risks. What measures and reforms are appropriate to address not only symptoms, but structural challenges of digital platforms and information spaces? Data Science Unit: With the SNV Data Science Unit, we are expanding our think tank work to include quantitative, data-driven methods. SNV's Working Method: Many technology-intensive issues of politics are cross-sectional issues that change at a rapid pace. The combination of different knowledge, of continuous testing of ideas and of speed thus forms the core of the organisation. That is why Stiftung Neue Verantwortung works differently than conventional research institutes and think tanks. To guarantee the independence of its work, the organization has adopted a concept of mixed funding sources that include foundations, public funds and corporate donation. Creative Commons Contributions marked CC BY-SA are subject to a Creative Commons license (CC BY-SA – the "CC License"). This permits the use of the publication and website content of Stiftung Neue responsibility e. The duplication, distribution and publication, modification or translation of the content of the New Responsibility Foundation, as well as the creation of products derived from it, are permitted under the following conditions: attribution. The content must be clearly attributed to the author and the New Responsibility Foundation and the link www.stiftung-nv.de must be given as the source. Reuse under the same license. If the content is edited or used in any other way as a recognizable basis for your own creations, the newly created works or content may only be distributed using license conditions that are identical or comparable to those of this license. exceptions. The New Responsibility Foundation reserves the right to exclude content from the CC license. These are marked separately. The detailed license terms can be found here: www.creativecommons.org . If you have any questions about citing or using our content, please contact us at info@stiftung-nv.de . The Responsibility Movement; a dream of Dr. Viktor E. Frankl, Holocaust survivor and world-renowned clinical psychiatrist. It's a catalyst for a unifying global project to enshrine and share this fundamental value, Responsibility. Together, for our kids, grandkids, friends, family, and generations to come, we will build responsibility, both literally and figuratively. It's a movement to educate, elevate, and engage people from around the world empowering millions to make life better. Combined with an educational outreach program to teach the principles of responsibility, the worldwide Responsibility movement is the solution which solves many of the world's biggest problems. Responsibility + Liberty = Freedom. The Foundation Board of Directors oversees and holds the executive staff accountable. They also serve as advisors and help with the big picture of the Foundation. The executive staff runs and manages the day to day operations, strategy, and implementation of Foundation programs. The advisory council is a team of dedicated professionals and supporters with special skills that act as advisors and resources to help accomplish the goals of the Foundation.*

# Noted to Chapters

**Notes – Executive Summary**

1.  Commission on Race and Ethnic Disparities Report (March 2021

2.  Ibid

3.  Professor Daniel W. B. Lomas (ForgetJamesBond: diversity, inclusion and the UK's intelligence agencies, 02 July 2021

4.  Intelligence and Security Committee of Parliament Report on Diversity and Inclusion in the Intelligence Community-Presented to Parliament by the Prime Minister by Command of Her Majesty-September 2018

5.  Deputy Director of GCHQ, Nikesh Mehta in response to the Intelligence and Security Committee report (GCHQ website) on inclusiveness

6.  Baroness D'Souza in her parliamentary comment on Regulation of Investigatory Powers (Criminal Conduct Authorisations-Amendment) Order 2021 (SI 2021/601)

7.  Ibid

8.  The Covert Human Intelligence Sources (Criminal Conduct) Bill 2019–21 was introduced in the House of Commons on 24 September 2020-House of Common Library

9.  BBC-20 April 2021

10. The Intel Today 10 April 2022

11. Tom Van Rentergem, 07 April 2022

12. Ibid

13. Director of the Analysis Department at the Belgian State Security Service VSSE, Peter Lanssens lecture: "The Belgian civil intelligence service VSSE - general overview and current trends and threats, by Peter LANSSENS, director of the analysis department".

14. European Union Agency for Fundamental Rights, (2017

**Chapter 1: Challenges of European Union's Intelligence Cooperation, Institutional Reforms, Management of Law and Order, Foreign Espionage and Intelligence Failure**

1.  Beyond Global Britain: A realistic foreign policy for the UK. The European Council on Foreign Relations (ECFR).Policy Brief-15 December 2021

2   The rising fear of terrorism and the emergence of a European security governance space: citizen perceptions and EU counterterrorism cooperation, Journal of Contemporary European Studies, DOI: 10.1080/14782804.2021.1958202

3.  Secretary General of the Council of Europe, Marija Pejčinović Burić

4.  Christine Andreeva (Border security became priority for member states in the aftermath of the migrant crisis

5.  Global Britain in a Competitive Age, the Integrated Review of Security, Defence, Development and Foreign Policy, presented to Parliament by the Prime Minister by Command of Her Majesty-March 2021

6.  Beyond Global Britain: A realistic foreign policy for the UK. The European Council on Foreign Relations (ECFR).Policy Brief-15 December 2021

7.  Jeremy Shapiro and Nick Witney in their paper (Beyond Global Britain: A realistic foreign policy for the UK. The European Council on Foreign Relations (ECFR).Policy Brief-15 December 2021.

8.  The Kerslake Report: An independent review into the preparedness for, and emergency response to, the Manchester Arena attack on 22 May 2017

9.  A non-partisan, and international policy organization, Counter Extremism Project Report

10. The UK Parliament website comment (Police reform in England and Wales

11. Silvia D'Amato and Andrea Terlizzi in their paper (Strategic European counterterrorism? An empirical analysis-01 February 2022

12. Wim Klinkert in his paper (Intelligence and Espionage the Netherlands

13. Matthias Deneckere, Ashley Neat and Volker Hauck. The future of EU security sector assistance: learning from experience-May 2020

14. Javier Argomaniz, Oldrich Bures and Christian Kaunert (A Decade of EU Counter-Terrorism and Intelligence: A Critical Assessment-23 Dec 2014

15. Glenn Hastedt (The Politics of Intelligence and the Politicization of Intelligence: The American Experience, Intelligence and National Security, 28:1, 5-31, DOI: 10.1080/02684527.2012.749062. https://doi.org/10.1080/02684527.2012.749062-2013

16. Program Coordinator at the Intelligence Project at the Harvard Kennedy School's Belfer Centre, Maria A. Robson Morrow (Private sector intelligence: on the long path of professionalization-20 Mar 2022.

17. Review report about the use of cable interception by the AIVD and the MIVD- CTIVD, No. 75. Of Review Committee on the Intelligence and Security Services 15, March 2022

**Chapter 2: Intelligence Failure, the Achilles heel of Interoperability, Foreign Espionage, and Security Sector Reforms within European Union and the United Kingdom**

1. John Hollister Hedley (John Hollister Hedley (2005) Learning from Intelligence Failures, International. Journal of Intelligence and Counterintelligence, 18:3, 435-450, DOI: 10.1080/08850600590945416

2. Janani Krishnaswamy in her research paper. Why Intelligence Fails, The Hindu Centre-2013

3. Ibid

4. Assistant Professor Department of Political Science Towson University and Senior Research Scholar Centre for International and Security Studies at Maryland University, William J. Lahneman. National Intelligence Agencies and Transnational Threats: The Need for a New Intelligence Paradigm-27 January 2008

5. John Hollister Hedley (John Hollister Hedley (2005) Learning from Intelligence Failures, International Journal of Intelligence and Counterintelligence, 18:3, 435-450, DOI: 10.1080/08850600590945416.

6. Assistant Professor Department of Political Science Towson University & Senior Research Scholar Center for International and Security Studies at Maryland University, William J. Lahneman in his paper (National Intelligence Agencies and Transnational Threats: The Need for a New Intelligence Paradigm-27 January 2008.

7. Bruce Crumley, in his Al Jazeera article, Were the Paris attacks a French intelligence failure? Al Jazeera (November 17, 2015

8. Dr. Emmanuel Karagiannis in his article (Were the Attacks in Paris and Brussels an Intelligence Failure? Defence-in-Depth, the research blog of the Defence Studies Department, King's College London.

9. Robin Andersson Malmros in his paper (Prevention of terrorism, extremism and radicalisation in Sweden: A sociological institutional perspective on development and change, 07 Sep 2021.

10. Manne Gerell, Joakim Sturup, Mia-Maria Magnusson, Kim Nilvall, Ardavan Khoshnood and Amir Rostami in their research paper (Open drug markets, vulnerable neighbourhoods and gun violence in two Swedish cities-19 March 20212.

11. Robin Forsberg and Jason C. Moyer in their paper (Sisters but Not Twins: Prospects of Finland and Sweden's NATO Accession-02 February 2022.

12. Rune Ellefsen and Sveinung Sandberg in their paper (Everyday Prevention of Radicalization: The Impacts of Family, Peer, and Police Intervention, Studies in Conflict & Terrorism, DOI: 10.1080/1057610X.2022.2037185, 2022.

13. David Rising and Philipp Jenne have reported to Associated Press (Austria plans intelligence agency reforms after attack: Austrian leaders are calling for more legal options to fight extremism and for an overhaul of the country's domestic intelligence agency in the wake of this week's deadly attack blamed on an Islamic State sympathizer-5 November 2020.

14. Epicentre.Work in its recent report (12 benchmarks for the reform and oversight of intelligence services in Austria. February 10, 2021.

15. Neil Dooley (2022). Frustrating Brexit? Ireland and the UK's conflicting approaches to Brexit negotiations, Journal of European Public Policy.

16. David Ehl 's DW analysis (Northern Ireland's peace faces new Brexit threats: The 1972 Bloody Sunday massacre was a turning point in Northern Ireland's conflict. Peace has prevailed for a quarter of a century. That is a success that must now be defended against new threats-30 January 2022

17. Dr Hager Ben Jaffel and Dr Jeremy Pearson have reviewed the relationship between the UK and European Union in their article (Intelligence, law enforcement and Brexit, UK in a Changing Europe. 26 Feb 2021.

18. Dr Stefania Paladini has noted in her comment (Intelligence and National Security. Birmingham City Business School.

19. Mark Galeotti in his analysis (The secret battlefield: How the EU can help Georgia, Moldova, and Ukraine protect against Russian subversion. Policy Brief 15 December 2021, European council on foreign relations 15 December 2021.

**Chapter 3: The UK Big-3, Foreign Espionage, Intelligence and Cooperation with European Union Secret Agencies.**

1. Christiaan Menkveld. Understanding the complexity of intelligence problems

2. The debate MPs "ashamed" of aspects of the UK. Withdrawal from Afghanistan and concerned about parallels emerging in the UK's response to Ukraine on 4, March, 2022

3. Bowman H. Miller in his research analysis (U.S. Intelligence Credibility in the Crosshairs: On the Post-War Defensive

4. Xinhua News Agency (British security tactics proved ineffective, outdated. March 1, 2015

5. Robert Jervis (Reports, Politics, and Intelligence Failures: The Case of Iraq. ISSN 0140-2390 Print/ISSN 1743-937X Online/06/010003-50 2006 Taylor & Francis DOI: 10.1080/01402390600566282.

6. Anisa Heritage and Pak K. Lee, (Global Britain': The UK in the Indo-Pacific: While its involvement is broadly welcomed in the region, the U.K. must first clarify what its Indo-Pacific presence will entail. The Diplomat--January 08, 2021.

7. Abigail Julia Blyth in his thesis (The British Intelligence Services in the public domain: Thesis submitted in partial fulfilment of the requirements for the degree of PhD. Department of International Politics Aberystwyth University 2019.

8. Ibid

9. Ibid

10. Intelligence and Security Committee of Parliament. Diversity and Inclusion in the UK Intelligence Community. Presented to Parliament pursuant to section 3 of the Justice and Security Act 2013. 18 July 2018.

11. Professor, Daniel W. B. Lomas has highlighted this in his paper (Daniel W. B. Lomas. July 2021 ForgetJamesBond: diversity, inclusion and the UK's intelligence agencies, Intelligence and National Security, 36:7, 995-1017, DOI :10.1080/02684527.2021.1938370

12. OpenDemocracy. The Belhaj case shows British intelligence agencies are out of control: Tony Blair's non-apology to the victim of 'extraordinary rendition'–and Jack Straw and Theresa May's attempts to draw a line under the issue–raise more questions than they answer.. Open democracy-22 May 2018), Richard Norton-Taylor.

13. Adam Brown, Secret affairs with radical Islam: why Britain's covert foreign policy needs to change. November 8th, 2010

14. 16 December 2020, the Investigatory Powers Tribunal revealed that the UK intelligence unilaterally assumed the power to authorise agents to commit crimes in the UK–potentially without any legal basis or limits on the crimes they can commit. Reprieve, the Pat Finucane Centre, Privacy International, and CAJ were challenging a secret policy under which MI5 authorised covert agents, known as covert human intelligence sources or CHIS, to commit crimes in the UK.

15. British foreign intelligence was forced by the Tribunal to apologise when its officers wrongly sought to stop independent judges from scrutinising the agency's activities: "These revelations come only a day after the Investigatory Powers Commissioner severely criticised MI6 for "several weaknesses" in its agent-running within the UK, leading to "several errors". It found that MI6 needed to "better recognise" and "authorise activity in compliance with" the law in the UK. The Johnson Government sought to put these practices into legislation with the Covert Human Intelligence Sources (Criminal Conduct) Bill, which at present contains no expressed limits on the crimes covert agents may be permitted to commit, even against torture, murder, or sexual violence.

**Chapter 4: Chapter 4: Terrorist Attacks, Radicalization and Security Sector Reforms in the UK and European Union**

1. Dr Hager Ben Jaffel. Dr Jeremy Pearson, Intelligence, law enforcement and Brexit-26 Feb 2021

2. Oldrich Bureš. Intelligence sharing and the fight against terrorism in the EU: lessons learned from Europol, European View (2016) 15:57–66. DOI 10.1007/s12290-016-0393-7. Published online: 03 May 2016

3. Senior associate fellow, Institute for Statecraft-London, Fatima Lahnait in her paper (Combating radicalisation in France: from experimentation to professionalization. (Lahnait, Fatima. "La lucha contra la radicalización en Francia: de la experimentación a la profesionalización". Revista CIDOB d'Afers Internacionals, issue 128 (September 2021), pp. 105-125. DOI: doi.org/10.24241/rcai.2021.128.2.105/en

4. Dick Zandee, Adája Stoetman and Bob Deen in their research paper, (The EU's Strategic Compass for security and defence squaring ambition with reality. Clingendael Report, May 2021. Netherlands Institute of International Relations 'Clingendael'.

5. Danny Pronk and Claire Korteweg (Sharing the Burden, Sharing the Secrets: The future of European intelligence cooperation. Clingendael Report-September 2021. The Clingendael Institute, the Netherlands.

6. Peter R. Chai, Bryan D. Hayes, Timothy B. Erickson & Edward W. Boyer in their research paper (Novichok agents: a historical, current, and toxicological perspective. Peter R. Chai,Bryan D. Hayes, Timothy B. Erickson & Edward W. Boyer (2018) Novichok agents: a historical, current, and toxicological perspective, Toxicology.DOI: 10.1080/24734306.2018.1475151

7. Al Jazeera news on 05 September 2018 reported Russians charged with Skripal nerve-agent poisoning: Prosecutors name two Russians as suspects in attempted assassination of ex-spy.

8. Research scholar at the Centre for Security Studies, Metropolitan University, Prague, Oldrich Bureš in his paper (Intelligence sharing and the fight against terrorism in the EU: lessons learned from Europol, European View (2016) 15:57–66. DOI 10.1007/s12290-016-0393-7. Published online: 03 May 2016

9. Danny Pronk and Claire Korteweg (Sharing the Burden, Sharing the Secrets: The future of European intelligence cooperation. Clingendael Report-September 2021. The Clingendael Institute, the Netherlands.

10. Christine Andreeva highlighted lack of confidence between partners that affect cross border and cross agency lack of cooperation. Christine Andreeva (2021 The evolution of information-sharing in EU counter-terrorism post-2015: a paradigm shift? Global Affairs, 7:5, 751-776, DOI: 10.1080/23340460.2021.1983728

11. Theodore Christakis, Kenneth Propp in their paper. How Europe's Intelligence Services Aim to Avoid the EU's Highest Court—and What It Means for the United States-March 8, 2021

12. Kilian Vieth-Ditlmann and Thorsten Wetzling, (Caught in the Act? An analysis of Germany's new SIGINT reform. Research Report-25 November 2021. The Stiftung Neue Verantwortung.

## Chapter 5: Surveillance Blankets, in Estonia, Bulgaria and Sweden, Challenges of Intelligence Cooperation and Human Rights

1. Christiaan Menkveld, Understanding the complexity of intelligence problems, in his research paper noted that effective intelligence and security services need to take the complexity of an intelligence problem into account when determining the aims of their investigation, the strategy of intelligence collection and its analytic approach.

2. 11 March, 2021, BBC

3. Privacy International, December, 2021

4. Statewatch, monitoring the state and civil liberties in Europe (11 March 2021) in its report noted the covert human intelligence sources (Criminal Conduct Act). Covert Human Intelligence agents might be secret police officers, informers and state agents.

5. The Guardian Newspaper, In February 2021, three Chinese spies were expelled who were potentially associated with China's Ministry of State Security.

6. Sophia Hoffmann, Circulation, not cooperation: towards a new understanding of intelligence agencies as transnationally constituted knowledge providers-2021.

7. The ISC member, Stewart Hosie, said: "the government took its eye off the ball, because of its focus on counterterrorism, adding that the government had badly underestimated the response required to the Russian threat". The report criticised British intelligence agencies for failing to effectively respond to the espionage activities of Russian intelligence. The committee noted: "Had the relevant parts of the intelligence community conducted a similar threat assessment prior to the [EU] referendum, it is inconceivable that they would not have reached the same conclusion as to Russian intent, which might then have led them to take action to protect the process."

8. Rob Mudge (From Russia with love: How damaging is the 'Russia Report' for the UK?-DW, July 21, 2020

9. Financial Times, (George Parker and Helen Warrell in London and Henry Foy in Moscow-21 July 2020

10. Foreign, Commonwealth & Development Office and Elizabeth Truss warned that the UK, together with the US and other allies, exposed historic malign cyber activity of Russia's Federal Security Service (FSB). In its commentary

on 24 March 2022, FCO noted: "KGB's successor agency, the Federal Security Service (FSB) was behind a historic global campaign targeting critical national infrastructure, and long list of cyber operations included UK energy sector, US aviation and a Russian dissident in the UK targeted using sophisticated hacking and spear-phishing.

11. Precious Chatterje-Doody (The Evolution of Russian Hybrid Warfare: United Kingdom-29 January 2021

12. A British Pakistan national Gauhar Khan was tasked to kill another Pakistani dissident wanted by the Inter-Services Intelligence (ISI) in the Netherlands. A London Court heard Muhammad Gohar Khan was offered £100,000 (about $134,000) by the ISI to kill Waqas Goraya in Rotterdam, but he failed to track his target down, and was arrested by Scotland Yard police on his return to the UK. The jury given unanimous guilty verdict of conspiracy to murder. Mr. Waqass Goraya, told BBC that "Pakistani intelligence services (ISI) were ultimately behind the plot and that it forms part of a wider crackdown on dissenting voices both inside and outside Pakistan.

13. 26 May 2021, Eanna Kelly reported to Science business News

14. Ibid

15. Ibid

**Chapter 6: The Crisis of Danish Intelligence, Iran and China's Espionage Networks in Denmark, The PET Report, State Surveillance and Human Rights**

1. The PET report also warned: "threat from foreign state intelligence activities targeting Denmark and Danish interests abroad presents our society with a number of significant political, security-related and economic challenges.

2. 12 January 2022, analyst Charles Szumski (Danish military intelligence chief jailed for espionage-EURACTIV.com

3. Nikita Belukhin (The Scandal in Denmark's Military Intelligence: Too Much Transparency? Modern Diplomacy, 25 March 2022

4. Christiaan Menkveld (Understanding the complexity of intelligence problems

5. 11 March, 2021, BBC

6. Statewatch, monitoring the state and civil liberties in Europe (11 March 2021

7. In February 2021, three Chinese spies were expelled who were potentially associated with China's Ministry of State Security

8. Sophia Hoffmann in her paper. Circulation, not cooperation: towards a new understanding of intelligence agencies as transnationally constituted knowledge providers-2021

9. 21 July 2020, Intelligence and Security Committee Russian report

10. Ibid

11. Rob Mudge (From Russia with love: How damaging is the 'Russia Report' for the UK?-DW, July 21, 2020

12. Financial Times, (George Parker and Helen Warrell in London and Henry Foy in Moscow-21 July 2020

13. 24 March 2022, FCO statement

14. Precious Chatterje-Doody (The Evolution of Russian Hybrid Warfare: United Kingdom-29 January 2021

15. British Pakistan national was tasked to kill another Pakistani dissident wanted by the Inter-Services Intelligence (ISI) in the Netherlands. A London Court heard Muhammad Gaohar Khan was offered £100,000 (about $134,000) by the ISI to kill Waqas Goraya in Rotterdam, but he failed to track his target down, and was arrested by Scotland Yard police on his return to the UK.

16. 26 May 2021, Eanna Kelly report to Science business News

**Chapter 7: The Home Office Web-Spying Powers, the French and German Intelligence Reforms, Intelligence Diversity-Reforms and Foreign Intelligence Networks in the United Kingdom.**

1. 11 March, 2021, BBC

2. Intelligence and Security Committee of Parliament in its report (2018) emphasized the need of security sector reforms. I had already published several articles on this issue in different newspapers, in which I pointed to the fact that without security sector reforms, the UK law enforcement would not be able to address national security threats. In February 2021, the Times of London reported that Britain's foreign intelligence agency, the Secret Intelligence Service (SIS or MI6), was relaxing rules to allow applicants with dual UK nationality. Chief of the SIS Richard Moore apologised for the historical treatment of LGBT (Lesbian, Gay, Bisexual and Transgender) officials and the bar to gay men and women serving in SIS.

3. Duncan Bartlett in his recent article (UK Intelligence Agency Targets China's United Front: Spymasters in the U.K. and other countries are going public in their push against CCP influence. The Diplomat January 22, 2022.

4. BBC correspondent, Frank Gardner (BBC-30 November 2021) reported Mr. Moore's public speech envisaged adaptation of artificial intelligence quantum computing and digital technology to completely transform the way human intelligence gathered by spies, presenting MI6 with major challenges in the digital age.

5. 14 January, 2022, BBC reported MI5 accusations against a lawyer of trying to influence politicians on behalf of China. Home Secretary Priti Patel said it was "deeply concerning" that someone "who has knowingly engaged in political interference activities on behalf of the Chinese Communist Party has targeted parliamentarians.

6. 31 March 2022, Director General of GCHQ, Sir Jeremy Fleming in his public speech warned: "Believe it or not, it's only 36 days since Vladimir Putin launched an unprovoked and premeditated attack on Ukraine. It's been shocking in every sense of the word. But it wasn't surprising. We've seen this strategy before. We saw the intelligence picture building. And we're now seeing Putin trying to follow through on his plan. But it is failing. And his Plan B has been more barbarity against civilians and cities.

7. Kyle S. Cunliffe (Hard target espionage in the information era: new challenges for the second oldest profession

8. Tobias Bunde and Sophie Eisentraut, (Munich Security Brief, July 2020

9. The DW New report (15 May 2020) noted a revised bill on reform of the German domestic intelligence agency to boost liaison with regional authorities. In Germany, both the BND Act and its sibling, the G10 Act, as well as their technological underpinnings, are both openly discussed making it easier to confront their legality

10. Poland and Balkan's States are facing the same challenges where the process of security sector reforms is in danger due to the intransigence of former stakeholders and networks. The National Security Strategy of the Republic of Poland was approved on 12 May 2020 by the President of the Republic, which spotlights and asserts adoption of different restructuring strategies.

11. The CBS News in September 2019 reported clandestine human smuggling networks in Athens. The networks were transporting jihadists to Greece, and then to other European states. However, the EU inspection team of Greek sea and land borders (CNN, Telegraph, and Greek Reporter PBS Frontline, and CTC Sentinel) noted: "Serious deficiencies in the carrying out of external border control by Greece, in particular due to the lack of appropriate identification and registration of irregular migrants at the islands, of sufficient staff, and of sufficient equipment for verifying identity documents.

12. Human Rights Watch on 01 March 2020

13. Ibid

## Chapter 8: Democratization of Intelligence in Romania: War of Strength between Democratic and Communist Intelligence Stakeholders.

1. Intelligence: History and Role in American Society, Compiled by Janet L. Seymour, Air University Library, Maxwell AFB, Alabama

2. The Romanian Secret Services, Politics and the Media: a Structural Overview, Dragomir, Elena, 2011. Balkanalysis.com, 20 April, http://www.balkanalysis.com/ romania/2011/04/20/the-romanian-secret-services-politics-and-the-media-a-structural overview

3. Deputy Head of Romanian intelligence service resigns amid political scandal, Ernst, Julian, 18 January (2017), http://www.intellinews.com/deputy-head-of-romanian-intelligence-service-resigns-amid-political-scandal.

4. The Romanian Intelligence Service during the Cold War, thesis submitted to the Faculty of the Graduate School of Arts and Sciences of Georgetown University, Gheorghe, Eliza Rodica, Washington, DC, April 16, 2010. https://repository.library.georgetown.edu/bitstream/handle/10822/553496/gheorgheRodica

5. Reforming Afghan intelligence agencies, Musa Khan Jalalzai in Daily Times, 23 December 2014.

6. The Afghan Intel Crisis, Algora Publishing, Musa Khan Jalalzai 2017 New York.

7. Romania's Intelligence Community: From an Instrument of Dictatorship to Serving Democracy, Matei, Florina Cristiana, 2007,"International Journal of Intelligence and CounterIntelligence 20", No. 4.

8. The Secret Policeman's Fall: In Post-Communist Romania, the Government is Making Real Progress towards Transparency and Openness, Monica Macovei," Guardian Unlimited, October 26, 2006

9. Secret Police Row Grips Romania, BBC News, August 17, 2006.

**Chapter 9: The Key to Intelligence Reform in Germany: Strengthening the G10-Commission's Role to Authorise Strategic Surveillance. Dr. Thorsten Wetzling**

Bäcker, M. (2015): Der BND baut sich einen rechtsfreien Raum: Erkenntnisse aus dem NSA-Untersuchungsausschuss. Available at: http://www.verfassungsblog.de/ der-bnd-baut-sich-einen-rechtsfreien-raum-erkenntnisse-aus-dem-nsa-untersuchungsausschuss.

Bäcker, M. (2014a): Erhebung, Bevorratung und Übermittlung von Telekommunika- tionsdaten durch die Nachrichtendienste des Bundes. Stellungnahme zur Anhörung des NSA-Untersuchungsausschusses am 22.Mai 2014, p. 1-23.

Bäcker, M. (2014b): Der Fall des Geheimen – Ein blick unter den eigenen Teppich. In FlfF-Kommunikation FlfF e.V. (Ed..), p. 35-40.

Çaliskan, S. (2015): Rechtsverletzungen statt Kampf gegen die NSA. Gastbeitrag in der Frankfurter Rundschau vom 21.07.2015. Available at: http://www.fr-on-line.de/ gastbeitraege/nsa-skandal-rechtsverletzungen-statt-kampf-gegen-die- nsa,2997630 8,31266000,view,asFirstTeaser.html

Deutscher Bundestag (2015): Schaar: Sicherheitsdienste effektiver beaufsichtigen. Textarchiv des Bundestages. Available at: http://www.bundestag.de/dokumente/textarchiv/2015/kw03_pa_1ua/352812

Epping, V. (2012): Grundrechte – 5. Auflage. (Berlin: Springer Verlag). Große Strafrechtskommission des Deutschen Richterbundes (2008): Das Verhältnis von Gericht, Staatsanwaltschaft und Polizei im Ermittlungsverfahren, Strafprozessuale Regeln und faktische (Fehl-?) Entwicklungen, Gutachten im Auftrag des Bundesministerium der Justiz.

Heumann, S. (2015): Bundesnachrichtendienst unter Beobachtung: Erste Erkenntnisse aus eineinhalb Jahren Überwachungsdebatte. Impulspapier der stiftung neue verantwortung. Available at: http://www.stiftung-nv.de/publikation/bundesnachrichtendienst-unter-beobachtung-erste-erkenntnisse-aus-einein-halb-jahren

Heumann, S. & Wetzling, T. (2014): Policy Brief. Strategische Auslandsüberwachung: Technische Möglichkeiten, rechtlicher Rahmen und parlamentarische Kont-rolle. Stiftung neue Verantwortung, p.1-27. Available at: http://www. stiftung-nv. de/ sites/default/files/052014_snv_policy_brief_strategische_ auslandsuberwa- chung. Pdf

Huber, B. (2013): Die strategische Rasterfahndung des Bundesnachrichtendienstes – Eingriffsbefugnisse und Regelungsdefizite. Neue Juristische Wochenschrift, Heft 35/2013, p. 2572-2577.

Huber, B. (2014): Die Fernmeldeaufklärung des Bundesnachrichtendienstes: Rechtsgrundlagen und bestehende Regelungsdefizite. Vorgänge nr. 206/207. Also Available at: https://netzpolitik.org/2015/die-fernmeldeaufklaerung-des-bun- desnachrichtendienstes-rechtsgrundlagen-und-bestehende-regelungsdefizite.

Huber, B. (im Erscheinen): Selektorenlisten und Sonderermittler. Neue Zeitung für Verwaltungsrecht. Ausgabe 19/2015.

Krempl, S. (2015). NSA-Ausschuss: Peter Schaar sieht große Lücken bei BND-Kontrol- le. Available at: www.heise.de

Löffelmann, M. (2015): Regelung der „Routineaufklärung", recht + politik, Ausgabe 6/2015, Available at: http://www.recht-politik.de/wp-content/ uploads/2015/06/Ausgabe-vom-22.-Juni-2015-Regelung-der-Routineaufklärung-PDFDownload.pdf

Privacy and Civil Liberties Oversight Board (2014): Report on the Surveillance Program Operated Pursuant to Section 702 of the Foreign Intelligence Surveil- lance Act. Available at: https://www.pclob.gov/library/702-Report.pdf

Regierungskommission (2013): Bericht der Regierungskommission zur Überprüfung der Sicherheitsgesetzgebung in Deutschland. Available at: http:// www.bmi. bund. de/SharedDocs/Downloads/DE/Broschueren/2013/regierungskommissi- on-sicherheitsgesetzgebung.pdf?__blob=publicationFile

Roggan, F. (2006): Verdeckte Ermittler in Polizei- und Strafprozessrecht", in: Roggan, F. and Kutscha, M. (Ed.), Handbuch zum Recht der Inneren Sicherheit – 2. Edition, (Berlin: Berliner Wissenschaftsverlag).

Schantz, P. (2015): Rechtsschutz gegen die strategische Fernmeldeüberwachung: Ein blinder Fleck im Rechtsstaat. Neue Zeitung für Verwaltungsrecht, Ausgabe 13/2015, Seiten 873-877.

Scott, B. (2015): Expert Statement for the Committee of Inquiry of the German Parliament. stiftung neue verantwortung, July 2015.

SPD-Bundestagsfraktion. (2015): Eckpunkte der SPD-Bundestagsfraktion für eine grundlegende Reform der strategischen Fernmeldeaufklärung des BND mit in- ternationaler Vorbildwirklung. Available at: http://www.spd-bundestags-frakti- on.de/ sites/default/files/2015-06-16-spd-eckpunkte_reform_straf-ma-r-endfas- sung.pdf Strozyk, J. L. (2015): Überwachung des Internetknotens: DE-CIX verklagt BND. Available at https://www.tagesschau.de/inland/decix-klage-bnd-101.html

Venice Commission of the Council of Europe. (2015): "Update of the 2007 Report on the Democratic Oversight of the Security Services and Report on the Democrat- ic Oversight of Signals Intelligence Agencies." Available at http://www.venice.coe.int/ webforms/documents/default.aspx?pdffile=CDL-AD(2015)006-e. Vereinte Nationen (2015): Das Recht auf Privatheit im digitalen Zeitalter. Resolution der Generalversammlung A/Res/69/166.

Vladeck, S. (2015): The case for a FISA Special Advocate, in: Texas A&M University Law Review (forthcoming). Available at: http://papers.ssrn.com/sol3/papers. cfm?abstract_id=2546388

Werkmeister, C. (2011): Probleme bei der Grundrechtsberechtigung von Ausländern. Availabe at: http://www.juraexamen.info/probleme-bei-der-grundrechtsberechtigung-von-auslandern/

Wetzling, T. (2015): Großbaustelle Geheimdienstkontrolle. Gastbeitrag für die Frank- furter Allgemeine Zeitung. Available at: http://www.faz.net/aktuell/politik/ inland/bnd-nsa-affaere-reform-der-geheimdienstkontrolle-noe-tig-13565482. html

Wetzling, T. (2015a): Expert Statement for the European Parliaments' Committee on Civil Liberties, Justice and Home Affairs (LIBE). Available at: http://www.europarl.europa.eu/committees/en/libe/events-nationalparl. html?id=20150528CHE00195United Nations High Commissioner for Human Rights (OHCHR). (2014): Das Recht auf Privatheit im digitalen Zeitalter. Bericht A/HRC/27/37.

Bundestag Drucksachen

Drucksache 17/8247. Unterrichtung durch das Parlamentarische Kontrollgremium. Bericht über die Kontrolltätigkeit gemäß §13 PkGrG (Berichtszeitraum September 2009 – Oktober 2011).

Drucksache 17/8639. Unterrichtung durch das Parlamentarische Kontrollgremium. Bericht über die Kontrolltätigkeit gemäß §13 PkGrG (Berichtszeitraum 1. Januar bis 31. Dezember 2010).

Drucksache 18/5453. Entwurf eines Gesetzes zur Aufhebung des Artikel-10-Gesetzes und weiterer Gesetze mit Befugnis für die Nachrichtendienste des Bundes zu Beschränkungen von Art. 10 des Grundgesetzes. des Bundestages.

Drucksache 18/59. Unterrichtung durch den Bundesbeauftragten für den Datenschutz und die Informationsfreiheit gemäß §26 Abs. 2 des Bundesdatenschutzgesetzes.

Drucksache 18/843. Antrag der Fraktionen CDU/CSU, SPD, DIE LINKE, und Bündnis90/Die GRÜNEN: Einsetzung eines Untersuchungsausschusses.

Expert interviews

The author conducted interviews in summer 2015 with members of the G 10-Commission and experts connected to the intelligence services and the Bundestag. To respect the wishes of some of the interviewees, the author anonymised their personal information.

**Endnotes**

1   A so-called „routine surveillance" includes no collection of „communications of German citizens or individuals who are located on the German territory" (Löffelmann 2015:2). The work of the NSA Inquiry Committee of the Bundestag made it however clear that no clean separation of the data can be entirely guaranteed. In its report, the US-American Privacy and Civil Liberties Oversight Board (PCLOB) also pointed to the enormous costs and the difficulty linked to identifying and taking out the data of the country's own citizens in the very large collection of data (PCLOB 2014:100).

2   If the legislator has made use of this option, the question of the „substitute to the legal recourse" is open. According to the Federal Constitutional Court, this should include a "re-examination" equivalent to court control in material terms and as regards the procedure" (2 BvF 1/69).

3   See for instance the following comment of the Parliamentary Intelligence Oversight Body: "During the reporting period, several visits of foreign delegations took place. One important aspect that explains the interest of the delegations for the work of the Body is the good reputation of control in this country. The structure of control and the competence regulated primarily in the PKGrG and the Article 10 Law are indeed exemplary for the design of parliamentary control in other states, especially those in Eastern Europe." (Drucksache 17/8247: 9)

4   At the federal level, this includes the Act on the Protection of the Constitution (BVerfSchG), the Act on the Federal Intelligence Services (BND-G), the MAD Act (MADG), the Article 10 Law (G10-G), the Act on the Parliamentary Intelligence Oversight Body (PKGrG), the Telecommunications Act (TKG) and the regulation on technical and organisational measures for the surveillance of telecommunications (TKÜG), the BSI-Act (BSIG), the Federal Data Protection Act (BDSG), the AZR Act (AZRG), the Customs Investigation

Services Act (ZFdG), the Anti-Terror Database Act (ATDG) as well as the Act for the Establishment of a Standardised Central Database of Police Offices and Intelligence Services at Federal and State (Länder) Level for Combatting Violent Right-Wing Extremism (RED-G).

5   The general guidelines by the social-democrat (SPD) parliamentary group additionally deplores the fact that "the application of German data protection right has been eluded for years in this area (Key word "Space theory")".

6   According to §6 of the Article 10 Law, the BND must assess immediately and then every six months whether the collected personal data is necessary to fulfil its task. If the data is neither necessary nor required for transmission to another office, then it must be immediately deleted under the supervision of an official who is qualified to hold the position of a judge.

7   "Balancing of privacy and other human rights concerns against other interests comes in at several points in the process, but two crucial points are when a decision is made to use particular selectors, and when human analysts decide whether or not to keep the information in question. [...] The second type of decision is of a „data protection" character, which can be overseen afterwards by an expert administrative body. Such a body must be independent and have appropriate powers." (Venice Commission 2015: para. 121).

8   After all, the BMI can „in case of danger, instruct the execution of surveillance measures even before the Commission has been informed" (§15 para. 6 Article 10 Law).

9   According to §13 Article 10 Law, the legal recourse "against the instruction of surveillance measures according to §§ 3 and 5 para. 1 sentence 3 No. 1 and their execution" is not permitted before the targeted persons are notified. Since however, this does not apply to all risks listed under § 5 Para. 1, it is impossible to say whether the judicial control is excluded from the outset for all G 10 measures.

10  The große Strafrechtskommission (criminal law committee) of the German Association of Judges (Deutscher Richterbund) comes to the unanimous conclusion that "The commission sees deficits in the effective judicial control of state intervention powers (Richtervorbehalte) due to insufficient resources available to the court and prosecuting authorities." (Große Strafrechtskommission 2008: 224).

11  See on this matter e.g. the comments of the Venice Commission: "There is empirical evidence that such privacy advocates in law enforcement and internal security surveillance can have some significance in helping ensure that the parameters of investigations really are drawn as narrowly as possible. See the Swedish official inquiry into secret surveillance (SOU 2012: 44). Privacy advocates (nominated by the Bar Council and appointed by the government) represent the interests of targeted persons and organizations in the authorization process before the Swedish Defence Intelligence Court."

(Venice Commission 2015: para. 104). The idea of a civil liberty advocate has also been the subject of many discussions in the USA over the past year. Senator Blumenthal's legislative proposal (https://www.congress. gov/ bill/113th- congress/senate-bill/1467/text) showed a particular depth of detail. The Presidential Review Group on Intelligence and Communications Technologies also took up this idea in its 28th recommendation. Stephen Vladeck's study on this topic is also recommended reading (Vladeck 2015).

12  The corresponding wording of the Presidential Policy Directive – Signals Intelligence Activities (PPD-28) under Section 4 reads: "To the maximum extent feasible consistent with the national security, these policies and procedures are to be applied equally to the personal information of all persons, regardless of nationality".

13  See for instance the following argumentation of the Federal Constitutional Court: "Should the exercise of fundamental rights automatically affect the legal order in other states and should the conflicting interests of the bearers of fundamental rights be settled in a jurisdiction where the German legal order does not have sole claim to validity, then the power of the legislature are greater than when legal relations of mainly domestic nature are settled. In particular, the legislature is not precluded from considering specific circumstances that characterise the matter in need of elaboration but escape its power. The German legislator thus has the choice between protecting German fundamental rights standards in an undiminished form, [...] or maintaining a field of application, thus accepting a reduction of fundamental rights standards. Under these circumstances, and with regards to the constitution, the legislator is not precluded from choosing the second option." (BVerfGE 92, 26: para. 62)

14  These recommendations for a practical design of the G 10 justifications are based on the ideas formulated in Senator Blumenthal's legislative proposal towards the end of the sixth section.

15  An example can be found on the following page: http://www.dni.gov/files/do-cuments/0315/FISC%20Opinion%20and%20Order%20May%2018%202012. pdf

16  Thus, when one is working on improving democratic control over telecommunication surveillance, one should consider the question of whether this practice, the legal reform of which requires numerous legal and institutional changes, actually draws in sufficient information gain. As regards the related question of the necessity of data preservation, neither the Max-Plank-Institute nor the research service of the Bundestag was able to "find evidence that the types of massive communication surveillance resulted in the promised increase in security" (Çaliskan 2015)

17  The operator of the internet node DE-CIX is presently considering whether to file an action before the Federal Administrative Court. The actions of

the organisation Reporters without Borders and that of Prof. Härting are already pending before the Federal Administrative Court. Additionally, the G 10-Commission is considering whether to file a lawsuit against the government before the Federal Constitutional Court for inspecting the list of selectors. Considering the large number of open legal questions, further lawsuits are likely to be filed. In Autria, the deputy Peter Pilz filed a lawsuit against the Deutsche Telekom and two members of the German government.

**Chapter 10: Caught in the Act? An Analysis of Germany's New SIGINT Reform. Kilian Vieth-Ditlmann and Thorsten Wetzling**

1    This research was funded by the Deutsche Forschungsgemeinschaft (DFG, German Research Foundation - Project Number 396819157) and by the UK Economic and Social Research Council project 'Human Rights, Big data and Technology' [ES/M010236/1].

2    For an analysis of the 2016 reform of the BND's legal framework for foreign intelligence collection see: Wetzling, Thorsten, "New Rules for SIGINT Collection in Germany: A Look at the Recent Reform," 23.07.2017, Lawfare, https://www.lawfareblog.com/new-rules-sigint-collection-germany-lookrecent-reform

3    BND Act judgement and original media summary of the Federal Constitutional Court available at: https://www.bundesverfassungsgericht.de/SharedDocs/Pressemitteilungen/EN/2020/bvg20-037.html

4    With a reported budget of € 1.079 billion in 2021 and roughly 6.500 official employees, the BND is a sizable foreign intelligence service, wielding significant technical resources to conduct bulk collection and computer network operations among other methods such as human intelligence collection.

5    The Bundestag passed the reform on 25.03.2021, it will enter into force on 1.01.2022, but a range of transitional provisions and transitional periods apply (§ 69 BND Act).

6    References to all the cases cited can be found in the annex.

7    European Court of Human Rights, Centrum for Rattvisa v. Sweden, 19.06.2018, recital    131,https://data.guardint.org/en/entity/wdwrxl9tv6f?page=40.    The Court also observed that "if Norway's draft law is enacted, it will also authorise bulk interception" (recital 132).

8    Pierucci, Alessandra and Jean-Philippe Walter. (2020). Better protecting individuals in the context of international data flows: the need for democratic and effective oversight of intelligence services, Joint Statement by the Council of Europe's Chair of Convention 108 and the Council of Europe's DataProtection Commissioner. Available at: https://rm.coe.int/statement-schrems-ii-final-002-/16809f79cb

9   OECD Committee on Digital Economy Policy. 2020. Statement: Government Access to Personal Data Held by the Private Sector. See: https://www.oecd.org/digital/trusted-government-accesspersonal-data-private-sector.htm.

10  At the outset, it should be noted that other intelligence disciplines, such as human intelligence gathered by agents abroad, are not part of the report's focus. Neither does this paper provide an analysis of other intelligence reforms that the Bundestag adopted in 2021. On the reform of the law governing domestic intelligence agency (Bundesverfassungsschutzgesetz) and the law on domestic surveillance measures (Article 10 Act) see, for example: Vieth, Kilian and Dietrich, Charlotte, "New hacking powers for German intelligence agencies", https://aboutintel.eu/germany-hacking-reform/.

11  For example, the internet exchange point DE CIX in Frankfurt is one of the largest in the world, with an average overall traffic of more than 6.5 terabits per second at this hub. For more detailed traffic statistics see: https://de-cix.net/en/locations/frankfurt/statistics

12  Note: In this paper, we use the terms "bulk interception" and "bulk collection" to refer to this statutory power, because these concepts are more frequently used in the English language.

13  A separate law, the Article 10 Act, regulates the interception of domestic communications. The article 10 Act, however, also goes beyond "interception of domestic communications" in that foreign domestic traffic, i.e., communication that involves both foreign and domestic participants, is regulated in § 5 of the Article 10 Act. For more information on the Article 10 Act and recent reform attempts, see e.g. Wetzling, Thorsten, 2016, https://www.stiftung-nv.de/sites/default/files/snv_g10.pdf; Vieth, Kilian and Dietrich, Charlotte, 2020, https://aboutintel.eu/germany-hacking-reform/

14  Federal Constitutional Court, BND Act Judgement, 19.05.2020, recital 59, https://data.guardint.org/en/entity/neb3eo8hl9h?page=43

15  For some forms of intelligence collection, the government will continue to refer to the very broadly formulated general authority to collect information provided in paragraph 2 of the BND Act, directly available (in German) at: https://data.guardint.org/en/entity/dwo3l04euwc?page=5

16  Explanatory Statement of the draft BND Act, 25.11.2020, p. 57

17  There is a lack of legal definitions that allow to clearly distinguish between metadata and "traffic data" as well as "personal traffic data" (§ 26 BND Act), see: Federal Data Protection Commissioner, Official Statement on the draft BND Act, 18.12.2020, p. 6f, https://www.bundestag.de/resource/blob/822374/aab1552370d14e223a56bf66ef23f041/A-Drs-19-4-682-data.pdf

18  According to "Part 4 Authorisations - Subpart 3 - Practice Warrants - Section 91 - Application for issue of Practice Warrant" New Zealand's Intelligence and Security Act 2017 establishes a detailed authorization procedure for testing

and training warrants that involves the Chief Commissioner of Intelligence Warrants und des Inspector General. See:https://www.legislation.govt.nz/act/public/2017/0010/latest/whole.html#DLM7118938

19 While there is no limitation rewarding the volume of traffic that may be collected by means of so-called suitability tests for either purpose, only the suitability test according to purpose 1 is subject to a six months' time limit, which may also be renewed for an unspecified number of times for further six months (§ 24 (2) sentence 2 and 3 BND Act).

20 Federal Constitutional Court, BND Act Judgement, 19.05.2020, recital 168,https://data.guardint.org/en/entity/neb3eo8hl9h?page=46

21 Whether this volume limitation of 30 percent applies to suitability tests that the BND can conduct according to paragraph 24 of the BND Act is not specified.

22 Federal Constitutional Court, BND Act Judgement, 19.05.2020, recital 273,https://data.guardint.org/en/entity/neb3eo8hl9h?page=7123    Ibid.

24 Federal Constitutional Court, BND Act Judgement, 19.05.2020, recital 194,https://data.guardint.org/en/entity/neb3eo8hl9h?page=52

25 § 53 (1) German code of criminal procedure (Strafprozessordnung)

26 § 53 (1) sentence 1, number 3, 3a, 3b, 4 of the German code of criminal procedure

27 The Federal Association of Tax Consultants, for example, submitted a statement in the legislative process which requested that tax counselling should be protected under § 21 BND Act, too. Tax advisors process sensitive personal data on a long-term basis, they argued, which permits comprehensive insights into the economic and personal circumstances of their clients. Similar arguments could probably be made for other professions that work under increased confidentiality requirements. Full statement in German:Bundesst euerberaterkammer, 3.12.2020, https://www.bundesregierung.de/resource/blob/976020/1826352/4f5c9136681    ee130b65e4906141072.d0/2020-12-09-bnd-gesetzentwurf-stellungnahme-bundessteuerberaterkammer-1--data.pdf?download=1

28 § 29 (3) BND Act refers to the relevant criminal offenses listed in § 100b (2) of the German code of criminal procedure, https://www.gesetze-im-internet.de/stpo/__100b.html as well as to the foreign trade act, §§ 17 and 18, https://www.gesetze-im-internet.de/awg_2013/__17.html

29 Explanatory Statement of the draft BND Act, 25.11.2020, p. 68

30 Explanatory Statement of the draft BND Act, 25.11.2020, p. 69

31 Federal Constitutional Court, BND Act Judgement, 19.05.2020, recital 25,https://data.guardint.org/en/entity/neb3eo8hl9h?page=19

32 See the International repository of legal safeguards and oversight innovation for an analysis of good practices in governing intelligence data handling throughout the entire signals intelligence cycle:https://www.intelligence-oversight.org/; and: Wetzling, Thorsten and Vieth, Kilian 2018

33 Federal Constitutional Court, BND Act Judgement, 19.05.2020, recital 173,https://data.guardint.org/en/entity/neb3eo8hl9h?page=47

34 Search terms can be connection IDs, geographical areas, but also the identifiers of an entire telecommunications network of a closed user group. Search terms may also be actual words or phrases, as well as search patterns. In practice, though, the search terms are more often formal communication identifiers such as IP address ranges or email addresses. Content-related search terms, for example names of specific chemical compounds used for the weapon production, are used less frequently. See: Explanatory Statement of the draft BND Act, 25.11.2020, p. 64

35 Explanatory Statement of the draft BND Act, 25.11.2020, p. 71

36 Federal Constitutional Court, BND Act Judgement, 19.05.2020, recital 24,https://data.guardint.org/en/entity/neb3eo8hl9h?page=37

37 §§ 19 (5), 20, 21, 22, 23 (5) of the BND Act

38 See table 1 for definitions

39 For example, the Federal Constitutional Court decided in a different ruling that the collection of metadata produced by mobile phones with the help of IMSI catchers (sometimes called stingrays) does not violate the right to confidential communications in Article 10. Federal Constitutional Court, Mobile Phone Tracking Judgement, 22.08.2006, press release in German available at:https://www.bundesverfassungsgericht.de/pressemitteilungen/bvg06-093.html

40 Explanatory Statement of the draft BND Act, 25.11.2020, p. 78

41 eco, Official Statement on the draft BND Act, 18.02.2021, p. 4,https://www.bundestag.de/resource/blob/823354/a8060be2f61786ee68a7baec7be153e9/A-Drs-19-4-731-E-data.pdf

42 Amnesty International Germany criticized these exceptions, arguing that it does not comply with the prohibition to process domestic metadata. Even if one regards hashing traffic data as a form of immediate deletion, there is a risk to re-identify individuals in combination with other data. See:Amnesty International Germany, Official Statement on the draft BND Act, 17.02.2021, p. 7,https://www.bundestag.de/resource/blob/823300/941d473299f4e353f088a4f7bf6eb1c1/A-Drs-19-4-735-data.pdf

43 While the use of hacking operations has been common practice before, the legislators now established a legal norm that explicitly permits the hacking of foreign IT systems by the BND. The creation of a legal basis for the BND's

hacking operations is acknowledged as an attempt to establish legal clarity for this intrusive surveillance power. See: Explanatory Statement of the draft BND Act,25.11.2020, p. 94.

44 Explanatory Statement of the draft BND Act, 25.11.2020, p. 94

45 Explanatory Statement of the draft BND Act, 25.11.2020, p. 96

46 Cf. § 34 (1) number 2 BND Act, in connection with § 19 (4)) BND Act

47 However, under the amended Article 10 Act of 5.07.2021, the BND, as well as all other German intelligence agencies are allowed to use means of CNE against domestic communications. There are constitutional complaints pending against this domestic hacking mandate (see Vieth and Dietrich 2020 for an English commentary on the draft law).

48 For example, the collection of protected professional communications of an individual, such as the communication of a foreign journalist with a source, is allowed if the journalist might be participating in certain criminal offenses or if the infiltration of her device is necessary, for instance, to prevent serious threats to vital goods of the general public (§ 35 (2) number 2, littera b) BND Act); see also discussion in section 3.1.2 above.

49 Cf. § 34 (7) sentence 1 BND Act: "The Federal Intelligence Service [BND] shall immediately check whether the personal data collected as part of an CNE measure in accordance with section 1 are required alone or together with data already available for the purposes pursuant to section 1" (own translation).

50 Listed in § 37 (2) BND Act

51 Most recently, the public debates about the proliferation and abuse of hacking tools such as "Pegasus" by the NSO Group have triggered renewed calls to regulate the trade in such spy weapons, see e.g. "Joint open letter by civil society organizations and independent experts calling on states to implement an immediate moratorium on the sale, transfer and use of surveillance technology" https://www.apc.org/en/pubs/joint-open-letter-civil-society-organisations-andindependent-experts-calling-states-implement; "German Chancellor Angela Merkel Calls For MoreRestrictions On Spyware" https://www.ndtv.com/world-news/german-chancellor-angela-merkel-callsfor-more-restrictions-on-spyware-2492352

52 For a vulnerabilities assessment and management model see: Herpig, Sven, "Governmental Vulnerability Assessment and Management: Weighing Temporary Retention versus Immediate Disclosure of 0-Day Vulnerabilities," August 2018, https://www.stiftungnv. de/sites/default/files/vulnerability_management.pdf

53 See BND website on cooperation (in German):https://www.bnd.bund.de/DE/Die_Arbeit/Kooperationen/kooperationen_node.html

54 Federal Constitutional Court, BND Act Judgement, 19.05.2020, recital 27, https://data.guardint.org/en/entity/neb3eo8hl9h?file=15978344731474zg14a 5ky0w.pdf&page=38

55 NSA Inquiry Committee Report, 28.06.2017, p. 516 ff, https://data.guardint. org/en/entity/xaoryados7?page=516; for an overview of all reports related to the NSA Inquiry Committee (in German), such as the special report on the use of selectors and the special votes of the parliamentary opposition, see: https://data.guardint.org/en/entity/jpspzqpia5

56 Federal Constitutional Court, BND Act Judgement, 19.05.2020, recital 233, https://data.guardint.org/en/entity/neb3eo8hl9h?page=61

57 Court of Justice of the European Union, Schrems II Judgement, 26.07.2020, recital 171,https://data.guardint.org/en/entity/k4ae1290jz?page=38

58 Own translation of § 30 (6) sentence 1 BND Act.

59 Federal Constitutional Court, BND Act Judgement, 19.05.2020, recital 239, https://data.guardint.org/en/entity/neb3eo8hl9h?page=62

60 It must be recognizable (erkennbar), which does not indicate a proactive obligation of verification.

61 For example, the Military Intelligence Command of the Armed Forces (Kommando Strategische Aufklärung), that also includes several battalions for electronic warfare and reconnaissance, see:https://www.bundeswehr.de/ de/organisation/cyber-und-informationsraum/kommando-ndorganisation-cir/kommando-strategische-aufklaerung

62 The legal basis for bulk interception is § 29 (5) BND Act, for automated data sharing of hacking data § 38 (5) BND Act applies.

63 § 29 (13) BND Act in connection with § 30 (9) BND Act

64 See discussion in section 2.2.2 above on filtering of domestic data and other safeguards.

65 Federal Constitutional Court, BND Act Judgement, 19.05.2020, recital 258,https://data.guardint.org/en/entity/neb3eo8hl9h?page=68

66 Federal Constitutional Court, BND Act Judgement, 19.05.2020, recital 27, https://data.guardint.org/en/entity/neb3eo8hl9h?file=15978344731474zg14a 5ky0w.pdf&page=38

67 Federal Constitutional Court, BND Act Judgement, 19.05.2020, recital 263,https://data.guardint.org/en/entity/neb3eo8hl9h?&page=68

68 Cf. § 19 section 1 number 2 BND Act; section 2.2.2 of this report

69 The court noted: "To the extent that the shared data includes data of journalists, lawyers or other professions meriting confidentiality protection, [...] it must generally be subject to ex ante oversight resembling judicial review," see: Federal Constitutional Court, BND Act Judgement, 19.05.2020,recital 240,

https://data.guardint.org/en/entity/neb3eo8hl9h?page=63; cf. United Nations Office of theHigh Commissioner for Human Rights, Letter of the Special Rapporteurs of 29 August 2016, OL DEU2/2016, p. 7, https://www.ohchr.org/ Documents/Issues/Opinion/Legislation/OL_DEU_2.2016.pdf

70   §§ 29 (8) and 30 (9) BND Act in connection with § 42 (1) number 5 BND Act

71   § 29 (8) in connection with § 30 (9) BND Act

72   § 30 (5) BND Act in connection with § 42 (2) number 2 BND Act

73   Federal Constitutional Court, BND Act Judgement, 19.05.2020, recital 177, https://data.guardint.org/en/entity/neb3eo8hl9h?page=48

74   Federal Constitutional Court, BND Act Judgement, 19.05.2020, recital 274f, https://data.guardint.org/en/entity/neb3eo8hl9h?page=72

75   The composition and mandate of this new oversight body are codified in paragraphs 40 to 58 of the BND Act.

76   Explanatory Statement of the draft BND Act, 25.11.2020, p. 101

77   The central legal norm is § 5 of the Article 10 Act on strategic foreign-domestic communications surveillance. These bulk interception measures continue to be subject to the, by now far less rigorous,quasi-judicial control of the G10-Commission.

78   See answer to question 21 provided by the Federal Chancellery to a parliamentary inquiry:"Befugnisse und Kontrolle des Bundesnachrichtendienstes nach dem Urteil desBundesverfassungsgerichts zur Auslands-Auslands-Fernmeldeaufklarung," 26.01.2021, no.19/26120, https://dserver.bundestag. de/btd/19/261/1926120.pdf

79   The first president of the ICC is Josef Hoch, who had already presided over the precursor oversight body, the Independent Committee. Vice president is Till Oliver Rothfus, a former federal administrative judge. The other four elected members are: Johanna Schmidt-Rantsch, Elisabeth Steiner, Christian Tombrink und Dietlind Weinland. See: Deutscher Bundestag, press statement, 23.06.2021, https://www.bundestag.de/dokumente/textarchiv/2021/kw25-pa-pkgr-849378; Federal Government, press statement, 8.06.2021, https:// www.bundesregierung.de/bregde/aktuelles/bundesrichter-josef-hoch-zum-praesidenten-des-unabhaengigen-kontrollrates-ernannt-1925366

80   The explanatory statement of the law outlines the projected costs for setting up and running the new oversight structure. It projects costs for 62 staff positions, including 27 senior staff members (höherer Dienst) for the Independent Control Council as a whole. With this, the amended law aims to address the stipulation in § 57 of the BND Act that the ICC should be endowed with adequate human resources and equipment.

81   Figures retrieved from public federal budget:https://www.bundeshaushalt. de/#/2021/soll/ausgaben/einzelplan/0414.html

82 Expected one-time and annual costs are only projections included in the draft law; see: Explanatory Statement of the draft BND Act, 25.11.2020, p. 4

83 For the rules concerning judicial independence, see the German Judges Act (Richtergesetz) paragraphs 25 and following: https://www.gesetze-iminternet.de/drig/BJNR016650961.html#BJNR016650961BJNG000500666

84 Furthermore, the Federal Commissioner for Data Protection must be consulted before the BND creates new shared databases with foreign public bodies. See: §15 (1) sentence 4 and 5 BND Act.

85 Federal Constitutional Court, BND Act Judgement, 19.05.2020, recital 292,https://data.guardint.org/en/entity/neb3eo8hl9h?page=75

86 The Swedish intelligence oversight body, for example, has a duty to issue public reports that include review activities related to SIGINT. See, e.g. European Court of Human Rights, Centrum for Rattvisa v. Sweden, 25.05.2021, recital 352, https://data.guardint.org/en/entity/wdwrxl9tv6f?page=79

87 "Carter of the Intelligence Oversight Working Group" https://english.ctivd.nl/documents/publications/2019/12/12/index; "Strengthening oversight of international data exchange between intelligence and security services"https://www.comiteri.be/images/pdf/publicaties/Common_Statement_EN.pdf

88 United Kingdom Investigatory Powers Act, section 158, regarding bulk acquisition warrants authorizes both the collection of communications data in bulk from a telecommunications operator and the selection for examination of the data obtained under the warrant (see: https://data.guardint.org/en/entity/jqw6xmbdk4b?page=142); more examples for warrant types and bulk warrant criteria: https://www.intelligence-oversight.org/phases/application-process/

89 New Zealand Intelligence and Security Act 2017, Subpart 3, practice warrants, https://www.legislation.govt.nz/act/public/2017/0010/latest/whole.html#DLM7118938

90 § 33 (1) BND Act in connection with § 31 BND Act

91 Federal Constitutional Court, BND Act Judgement, 19.05.2020, recital 263,https://data.guardint.org/en/entity/neb3eo8hl9h?page=68

92 European Court of Human Rights, Centrum for Rattvisa v. Sweden, 19.06.2018, recital 139,https://data.guardint.org/en/entity/tivrjsdq1ei?page=43

93 Federal Constitutional Court, BND Act Judgement, 19.05.2020, recital 194, last sentence,https://data.guardint.org/en/entity/neb3eo8hl9h?searchTerm=157&page=53

94 § 42 (1) number 2 in connection with § 23 (5) number 3 BND Act

95 Federal Constitutional Court, BND Act Judgement, 19.05.2020, recital 272, https://data.guardint.org/en/entity/neb3eo8hl9h?page=71

96   See, for example, the online repository of good legal provisions and oversight practice regarding bulk collection: www.intelligence-oversight.org. As regards Germany's post-Snowden intelligence reform trajectory, see, for example, Wetzling, Thorsten, 2020.

97   For a rare public statement on the general availability of legal protections against government surveillance and oversight frameworks, see the 2018 report of the UN Special Rapporteur of the right to privacy to the UN Human Rights Council, notably page 27. "More than 80 percent of the United Nations Member States do not have any law which protects privacy by adequately and comprehensively overseeing and regulating the use of domestic surveillance [...]. The situation relating to foreign intelligence is much more fluid, elastic. What actually constitutes a necessary and proportionate measure in a democratic society [...] is still very much work-in-progress all across Europe [...]. Even where legislation exists regarding the oversight of intelligence it is often largely silent on what happens when personal data is shared across borders and what further safeguards should be put in place in such cases" (UN Human Rights Council, 2018).

98   Federal Constitutional Court, BND Act Judgement, 19.05.2020, recital 174, https://data.guardint.org/en/entity/neb3eo8hl9h?page=48

99   Interested readers are invited to contact the German Parliament to obtain a copy of the (by now outdated) "Gesetzessammlung: Rechtsgrundlagen fur die Tatigkeit und die Kontrolle der achrichtendienste des Bundes (September 2018)." It features 31 separate pieces of legislation.

100  Source: TIB and CTIVD memo on Convention 108, https://english.ctivd. nl/documents/publications/2021/02/17/memo-en. For a more detailed discussion on the relevance of Article 11 of this modernised Convention for democratic intelligence in Europe, see: Wetzling, Thorsten and Dietrich, Charlotte, 2021, "Report on the need for a guidance note on Article 11 of the modernised Convention," https://rm.coe.int/t-pd-2021-6-draft-guidance-note-onexceptions- under-article-11-of-the-/1680a2d512

101  Answer of the Federal Government to the minor interpellation 19/2583, p.5 https://dserver.bundestag.de/btd/19/261/1926120.pdf

102  National Security and Intelligence Review Agency, 2020, p. 16, our emphasis.

103  Court of Justice of the European Union, Privacy International v Secretary of State, 06.10.2020, https://data.guardint.org/en/entity/35ernv51jnp

104  Court of Justice of the European Union, La Quadrature du Net and Others v Premier Ministre and Others, 06.10.2020, https://data.guardint.org/en/entity/20gb4kvky39j

106  European Court of Human Rights, Centrum for Rattvisa v. Sweden, 25.05.2021, https://data.guardint.org/en/entity/wdwrxl9tv6f

107 Court of Justice of the European Union, Privacy International v Secretary of State, 06.10.2020, recitals 78-81, https://data.guardint.org/en/entity/35ernv51jnp

109 According to "Part 4 Authorisations - Subpart 3 - Practice Warrants - Section 91 - Application for issue of Practice Warrant" New Zealand's Intelligence and Security Act 2017 establishes a detailed authorization procedure for testing and training warrants that involves the Chief Commissioner of Intelligence Warrants und des Inspector General. Available at: https://www.legislation.govt.nz/act/public/2017/0010/latest/whole.html#DLM7118938

110 While there is no limitation rewarding the volume of traffic that may be collected by means of socalled suitability tests for either purpose, only the suitability test according to purpose 1 is subject to a six months time limit, which may also be renewed for an unspecified number of times for further six months (§ 24 (2) sentence 2 and 3 BND Act).

111 Even more so, since, more generally, the new rules on the remit of the new judicial oversight body do not specify whether it has jurisdiction over decisions by the Federal Government to issue technical capability notices (as they are called in the Investigatory Powers Act) to service providers in accordance with § 25 BND Act.

112 Court of Justice of the European Union, Privacy International v Secretary of State, 06.10.2020, recital 79, https://data.guardint.org/en/entity/35ernv51jnp?page=19

113 Court of Justice of the European Union, La Quadrature du Net and Others v Premier Ministre and Others, 06.10.2020, https://data.guardint.org/en/entity/20gb4kvky39j?page=40

114 See, for example, the discussion in German by Muller and Schwabenbauer (2021).

115 European Court of Human Rights, Centrum for Rattvisa v. Sweden, 25.05.2021, recital 297, https://data.guardint.org/en/entity/wdwrxl9tv6f?page=79

116 Ibid.

117 Murray et al., 24.05.2021, p. 12

118 Also consider this statement on the merit of adversarial voices: "to avoid being a rubber stamp, the process needed an adversary [...] to challenge and take the other side of anything that is presented to the FISA Court [...] anybody who has been a judge will tell you that a judge needs to hear both sides of a case before deciding" (Bradford Franklin, Sharon, 29.05.2020).

119 European Court of Human Rights, Centrum for Rattvisa v. Sweden, 25.05.2021, recital 299, https://data.guardint.org/en/entity/wdwrxl9tv6f?page=79

120 European Court of Human Rights, Centrum for Rattvisa v. Sweden, 25.05.2021, recital 301, https://data.guardint.org/en/entity/wdwrxl9tv6f?page=80

121  Statens inspektion for forsvarsunderrattelseverksamheten (SIUN), http://
www.siun.se/index.html

122  European Court of Human Rights, Centrum for Rattvisa v. Sweden,
25.05.2021, recital 347-348, https://data.guardint.org/en/entity/
wdwrxl9tv6f?page=89

123  European Court of Human Rights, Centrum for Rattvisa v. Sweden, 25.05.2021,
recital 350, https://data.guardint.org/en/entity/wdwrxl9tv6f?page=90

124  European Court of Human Rights, Centrum for Rattvisa v. Sweden, 25.05.2021,
recital 54, https://data.guardint.org/en/entity/wdwrxl9tv6f?page=16

125  IPCO/OCDA, 2020, para 2.29, p. 13, https://data.guardint.org/en/entity/
v6vk5dcc88?page=14

126  Explanatory Statement of the draft BND Act, 25.11.2020, p. 66

127  eco, Official Statement on the draft BND Act, 18.02.2021, p. 3,https://www.
bundestag.de/resource/blob/823354/a8060be2f61786ee68a7baec7be153e9/
A-Drs-19-4- 731-E-data.pdf

128  European Court of Human Rights, Big Brother Watch v. UK, 25.05.2021,
recital 413ff,https://data.guardint.org/en/entity/8bxe5z9q3ar?page=125
; Centrum for Rattvisa v. Sweden,25.05.2021, recital 354ff, https://data.
guardint.org/en/entity/wdwrxl9tv6f?page=91

129  Court of Justice of the European Union, Schrems II Judgement, 26.07.2020,
recital 191,https://data.guardint.org/en/entity/k4ae1290jz?page=40

130  If the BND processes domestic personal data collected in hacking operations,
the BND Act also requires a notification of the affected German individuals
or organizations (§ 34 (6) in connection with § 59 (2) BND Act).

131  European Court of Human Rights, Centrum for Rattvisa v. Sweden,
25.05.2021, recital 355, also 272, https://data.guardint.org/en/entity/
wdwrxl9tv6f?page=91; information about the complaint mechanism
provided by the Swedish oversight body SIUN available at: http://www.siun.
se/begaran.html

132  European Court of Human Rights, Big Brother Watch v. UK, 25.05.2021,
recital 414, https://data.guardint.org/en/entity/8bxe5z9q3ar?page=126;
information about the complaint mechanism provided by the British IPT
available at: https://www.ipt-uk.com/content.asp?id=27

133  European Court of Human Rights, Centrum for Rattvisa v. Sweden, 25.05.2021,
recital 256, https://data.guardint.org/en/entity/wdwrxl9tv6f?page=68

134  European Court of Human Rights, Centrum for Rattvisa v. Sweden, 25.05.2021,
recital 277, https://data.guardint.org/en/entity/wdwrxl9tv6f?page=74

135  Dittmer, Lisa, 15.12.2020, p. 6f

136 At the moment, the Federal Government may have an undue incentive to delegate more tasks to intelligence units of the Armed Forces due to the fact that processing of data from bulk collection is less rigidly overseen there. Of course, this is unlikely to be a sole criteria for such decisions but good legislative practice ought to be more mindful of such factors, too.

137 At the international level, the credibility of Germany's efforts to table a new resolution for better privacy protections at the UN level in the wake of the Snowden revelations was challenged in light of the various spying practices and oversight deficits that emerged from the Bundestag's NSA inquiry committee.

138 A metaphor used by the former senior member of the U.S. House of Representatives Intelligence Committee Norman Mineta, quoted in: Glennon, Michael, 2016.

139 Audit trail obligation for data sharing pursuant to § 29 (16) in connection with § 30 (9) BND Act

140 Vieth, Kilian and Wetzling, Thorsten. 2019, p. 22ff

141 SIUN, 22 February 2018, Section 4.1, http://www.siun.se/dokument/Arsredovisning_2017.pdf

142 For instance, the TIB reports that it examined and decided upon 2.159 orders for surveillance measures between May 2018 and April 2019. It also accounts for the number of rejections and the types of reasons for it (TIB, 2019).

143 For an elaboration of new forms of cooperation between different intelligence oversight bodies, see Wetzling, Thorsten and Vieth, Kilian, 2020.

144 German Federal Constitutional Court, BND Act Judgement, 19.05.2020, Headnote 1, https://data.guardint.org/en/entity/neb3eo8hl9h?page=1.

## References

Amnesty International Germany. 2021. Official Statement on the draft BND Act. https://www.bundestag.de/resource/blob/823300/941d473299f4e353f088a4f7bf6eb1c1/A-Drs-19-4-735-data.pdf.

Bradford Franklin, Sharon. 2020. "A Key Part of Surveillance Reform Is Now in

Jeopardy." Slate Magazine. May 29, 2020. https://slate.com/technology/2020/05/usa-freedom-reauthorization-act-fisa-reformsurveillance-    amicus-curiae.html.

Brown, Ian, and Douwe Korff. 2021. "Exchanges of Personal Data After the Schrems II Judgment." Study requested by the LIBE committee. European Union: European Parliament. https://www.europarl.europa.eu/RegData/etudes/STUD/2021/694678/IPOL_STU(2 021)694678_EN.pdf.

Council of Europe. 2018. Convention 108+.https://data.guardint.org/en/entity/o2r9zbeii5n.

Court of Justice of the European Union. 2020a. "La Quadrature Du Net and Others Judgement." C-511/18; C-512/18 and C-520/18. https://data.guardint. org/en/entity/20gb4kvky39j.

———. 2020b. "Privacy International Judgement." C-623/17. https://data.guardint. org/en/entity/35ernv51jnp.

———. 2020c. "Schrems II Judgement." Case C 311/18. https://data.guardint.org/ en/entity/k4ae1290jz.

Dittmer, Lisa. 2020. "The Unwanted Reader: BND Draft Bill Would Continue the Surveillance of Journalists and Their Sources." About:Intel. December 15, 2020. https://aboutintel.eu/bnd-failure-journalistic-safeguards/.

Eco. 2021. Official Statement on the draft BND Act. https://www.bundestag.de/ resource/blob/823354/a8060be2f61786ee68a7baec7be1    53e9/A-Drs-19-4- 731-E-data.pdf.

EOS Committee. 2019. "Annual Report 2018." https://eos-utvalget.no/wpcontent/ uploads/2019/05/eos_annual_report_2018.pdf.

European Court of Human Rights. 2021a. "Big Brother Watch and Others v. the United Kingdom." Applications nos. 58170/13, 62322/14 and 24960/15. https://data.guardint.org/en/entity/8bxe5z9q3ar.

———. 2021b. "Centrum for Rattvisa v. Sweden." Application no. 35252/08. https://data.guardint.org/en/entity/wdwrxl9tv6f.

Federal Constitutional Court, 1. Senat. 2020. "BND Act Judgement." https://www. bundesverfassungsgericht.de/SharedDocs/Entscheidungen/EN/2020/05/ rs20200519_1bvr283517en.html.

Federal Government. 2020. Explanatory Statement of the BND Act. https://dserv- er.bundestag.de/btd/19/261/1926103.pdf.

Glennon, Michael J. 2016. National Security and Double Government. Reprint Edition. London: Oxford University Press.

IPCO/OCDA. 2020. "Annual Report of the Investigatory Powers Commissioner 2019." London. https://ipco-wpmedia-prod-s3.s3.eu-west-2.amazonaws. com/IPC-Annual-Report-2019_Web-Accessible-version_final.pdf.

Miller, Russell. 2020. "The German Constitutional Court Nixes Foreign Surveil- lance." Lawfare. May 27, 2020. https://www.lawfareblog.com/german-consti- tutional-courtnixes-foreign-surveillance.

Muller, Michael, and Thomas Schwabenbauer. 2021. "Unionsgrundrechte und Datenverarbeitung durch nationale Sicherheitsbehorden." NJW 29: 2065– 2144.

Murray, Daragh, Pete Fussey, Lorna McGregor, and Maurice Sunkin. 2021. "Effec- tive Oversight of Large-Scale Surveillance Activities: A Human Rights Per- spective." Journal of National Security Law and Policy 11 (3). https://jnslp.

com/2021/05/24/effective-oversight-of-large-scale-surveillanceactivities-a-human-rights-perspective/.

National Security and Intelligence Review Agency. 2020. "NSIRA Annual Report 2019." https://www.nsira-ossnr.gc.ca/wp-content/uploads/2020/12/AR-NSI-RA-Eng-Final.pdf.

Rojszczak, Marcin. 2021. "Extraterritorial Bulk Surveillance after the German BND Act Judgment." European Constitutional Law Review 17 (1): 53–77. https://doi.org/10.1017/S1574019621000055.

TIB. 2019. "Annual Report 2018/2019." https://www.tibivd. nl/binaries/tib/documenten/jaarverslagen/2019/04/25/annual-report-2018-2019/TIB+Annual+Report+2018-2019.pdf.

UN Human Rights Council. 2018. "Report of the Special Rapporteur on the Right to Privacy." A/HRC/37/62. https://undocs.org/A/HRC/37/62.

Vieth, Kilian, and Charlotte Dietrich. 2020. "New Hacking Powers for German Intelligence Agencies." About:Intel. October 27, 2020. https://aboutintel.eu/germany-hacking-reform/.

Vieth, Kilian, and Thorsten Wetzling. 2019. "Data-Driven Intelligence Oversight. Recommendations for a System Update." Stiftung Neue Verantwortung. https://www.stiftung-nv.de/sites/default/files/data_driven_oversight.pdf.

Wetzling, Thorsten. 2017. "New Rules for SIGINT Collection in Germany: A Look at the Recent Reform." Lawfare. June 23, 2017. https://www.lawfareblog.com/new-rulessigint-collection-germany-look-recent-reform.

———. 2020. "Germany's Troubled Trajectory with Mass Surveillance and the European Search for Adequate Safeguards." German - Israeli Tech Policy Dialog.IPPI and Heinrich Boll Foundation. https://doi.org/10.13140/RG.2.2.29938.32965.

Wetzling, Thorsten, and Charlotte Dietrich. 2021. "Report on the Need for a Guidance Note on Article 11 of the Modernised Convention." Council of Europe. https://rm.coe.int/t-pd-2021-6-draft-guidance-note-on-exceptions-under-article-11-of-the-/1680a2d512.

Wetzling, Thorsten, and Kilian Vieth. 2018. Upping the Ante on Bulk Surveillance. An International Compendium of Good Legal Safeguards and Oversight Innovations.Schriften Zur Demokratie 50. Berlin: Heinrich-Boll-Stiftung. https://www.stiftungnv. de/en/publication/upping-ante-bulk-surveillance-international-compendium-goodlegal-safeguards-and.

———. 2020. "Stellungnahme im Rahmen der Verbandebeteiligung zum Entwurf eines Gesetzes zur Anderung des BND-Gesetzes zur Umsetzung der Vorgaben des Bundesverfassungsgerichts und des Bundesverwaltungsgerichts." Berlin, Germany: Stiftung Neue Verantwortung. https://www.stiftungnv.de/sites/default/files/stellungnahme_refe_bndg_wetzling_vieth.pdf.

# Index

## A

Al Jazeera  34, 70, 104, 202, 205

All Party Parliament Group  105

al-Qaeda  15, 17

Area of Freedom, Security and Justice  21

## B

BND Act  75, 109, 146, 148, 149, 150,
151, 152, 153, 154, 155, 156,
157, 158, 159, 160, 161, 162,
163, 164, 165, 166, 167, 168,
169, 170, 171, 172, 173, 174,
175, 176, 177, 178, 179, 180,
181, 182, 183, 184, 185, 186,
187, 188, 189, 190, 191, 192,
194, 209, 216, 217, 218, 219,
220, 221, 222, 223, 224, 225,
226, 227, 228, 229

Boko Haram  23, 66

Brexit  3, 7, 8, 10, 11, 12, 13, 36, 42, 43,
44, 45, 46, 53, 63, 64, 67, 72, 97,
203, 205

British Intelligence Services  54, 55,
57, 204

Bulgarian Code of Criminal Procedure  79

## C

Centre for Protection of National
Infrastructure  57

Clingendael Institute  67, 72, 205, 206

Cold War period  1

Common Security and Defence Policy
(CSDP)  20, 66, 72

Crown Prosecution Service  61, 70

## D

Data Protection Commissioner  125,
129, 130, 191, 218

## E

EU-27  3, 8, 26, 53

EU Court of Human Rights  77

EU fundamental rights  78

EU intelligence  1, 3, 8, 20, 26, 64, 71,
72, 73, 109, 111

European Arrest Warrant  45, 63

European Convention on Human
Rights  5, 79, 124, 184

European Council on Foreign Relations  3, 11, 13, 14, 201

European Counter Terrorism Centre
12

European Court of Human Rights 5, 79, 103, 145, 147, 170, 181, 217, 223, 224, 225, 226, 227, 228

Europol 12, 13, 36, 45, 47, 64, 65, 68, 71, 73, 205, 206

**F**

Federal Intelligence Service (BND) 9, 71

Federal Security Service 52, 98, 207

Five Eyes Intelligence Oversight and Review Council (FIORC) 81

Foreign Espionage i, iii, v, 10, 26, 49, 201, 202, 203

**H**

High National Security College 116

Human intelligence (HUMINT) 31, 85, 86

**I**

Indo-China war 27

Indo-Pacific 7, 8, 53, 204

Instrument contributing to Stability and Peace 20

International Crime Coordination Centre 45, 64

Inter-Services Intelligence 100, 207, 208

Islamic State 10, 16, 34, 40, 41, 52, 73, 102, 203

**K**

Kargil war 27

Kerslake Report 15, 201

**L**

La Quadrature du Net 79, 181, 225

Lashkar-e-Taiba 15, 66

**M**

MI5 20, 51, 56, 57, 58, 60, 61, 62, 81, 82, 95, 100, 104, 105, 107, 108, 112, 204, 209

MI6 20, 51, 56, 58, 59, 60, 61, 62, 95, 99, 100, 104, 105, 108, 205, 208, 209

Mukti Bahani 27

**N**

National Cyber Security Centre 57, 86

National Salvation Front 113, 115

National Technical Assistance Centre 57

NATO Intelligence Warning System 68

**O**

Organisation for Economic Co-operation and Development 147

Organisation for the Prohibition of Chemical Weapons 69, 70

**P**

Parliamentary Intelligence Oversight Body 125, 129, 132, 138, 213, 214

# R

Romanian National Intelligence
      Agency 116

# S

Schengen Information System 45, 63

Security Service of Ukraine 47

Signals intelligence (SIGINT) vi, 24,
      31, 75, 122, 123, 124, 125, 126,
      130, 132, 133, 141, 142, 145,
      149, 152, 153, 155, 156, 157,
      162, 163, 164, 165, 166, 167,
      168, 169, 172, 173, 175, 177,
      178, 185, 187, 188, 189, 198,
      206, 216, 219, 223, 229

Snowden case 51

# T

Taliban 15, 49, 50, 51, 65, 66

# U

UK Big 3  3, 26

# W

Wafa Media Foundation 17

Weapons of mass destruction 7, 49,
      51, 52, 60, 111

# About the Author

Musa Khan Jalalzai is a journalist and research scholar. He has written extensively on Afghanistan, terrorism, nuclear and biological terrorism, human trafficking, drug trafficking, and intelligence research and analysis. He was an Executive Editor of the Daily Outlook Afghanistan from 2005-2011, and a permanent contributor in Pakistan's daily *The Post, Daily Times*, and *The Nation, Weekly the Nation*, (London). However, in 2004, US Library of Congress in its report for South Asia mentioned him as the biggest and prolific writer. He received Masters in English literature, Diploma in Geospatial Intelligence, University of Maryland, Washington DC, certificate in Surveillance Law from the University of Stanford, USA, and diploma in Counter terrorism from Pennsylvania State University, California, the United States.

CPSIA information can be obtained
at www.ICGtesting.com
Printed in the USA
LVHW100551070622
720605LV00003B/69

9 789393 49976